The Man Who Would Marry Susan Sontag

LIVING OUT
Gay and Lesbian Autobiographies

Joan Larkin and David Bergman
SERIES EDITORS

Raphael Kadushin
SERIES ACQUISITION EDITOR

The Man
Who Would Marry
Susan Sontag

And Other Intimate Literary Portraits
of the Bohemian Era

Edward Field

THE UNIVERSITY OF WISCONSIN PRESS

The University of Wisconsin Press
1930 Monroe Street
Madison, Wisconsin 53711

www.wisc.edu/wisconsinpress/

3 Henrietta Street
London WC2E 8LU, England

3   5   4   2

Printed in the United States of America

Library of Congress Cataloging-in-Publication Data
Field, Edward, 1924–
The man who would marry Susan Sontag and other
intimate literary portraits of the Bohemian Era / Edward Field.
p.   cm. — (Living out)
Includes index
ISBN 0-299-21320-x (cloth: alk. paper)
1. Field, Edward, 1924–
2. New York (N.Y.) — Intellectual life — 20th century.
3. Field, Edward, 1924 — Friends and associates.
4. Authors, American — 20th century — Biography.
5. Bohemianism — United States — Biography.
6. Gay men — United States — Biography.
7. New York (N.Y.) — Biography.
I. Title.   II. Series.
PS3556.I37Z47   2005
811′.54 — dc22   2005005440

ISBN 0-299-21324-2 (pbk.: alk. paper)

TO NEIL DERRICK

Contents

Preface

Once, at a family wedding, a cousin of mine said to the young people we were sitting with, "Before there were hippies, there were beatniks, and before there were beatniks, there were bohemians, and that's what she *was." Pointing at me.*

Theodora ("Teddie") Blum McKee

The bohemian era of the literary world I knew has vanished, and it may be necessary to define it for the current generation, which is very different from mine and which seems to see the arts as a power struggle as well as a pathway to celebrity and money. We called that "selling out," but nowadays who can afford not to sell out—you have to do anything that allows you to pay the rent and, if possible, go on with your creative work.

Looking back, it seems a quirk of my generation, so different from today's, that we believed a true artist should flee the blandishments of the world in order to create his work. If you became famous it must only happen in spite of your rejecting fame, and preferably after death, when you could no longer "sell out." Nobody I knew ever admitted he wanted to be famous. If we secretly wanted popular success, we weren't prepared to compromise in any way for it.

It should be stressed from the beginning that bohemian life was not about celebrities. There were a few big successes, of course, like Edna St. Vincent Millay and Allen Ginsberg, and scandalous figures like the now-forgotten poet Maxwell Bodenheim, whose sexual exploits and tawdry death were headline events, but mostly we were all sharing the adventure of the arts and sexual freedom together. If fame came, it was usually a by-product of personal exploration and development, though it's true that Ginsberg was a natural promoter of himself and his circle of friends. That was really beside the point, or maybe was the point, for bohemian life was about unconventionality and ideals, and the Beats famously combined both. And if you just wanted to enjoy living in the Village, you could always say you were a poet. In fact, "poet" was the generic term for any bohemian without talent or ambition.

When I arrived in Greenwich Village in 1946 after World War II as an NYU student on the GI Bill, I was immediately captivated by what seemed to me the glamour of the bohemian world with its legends of artists and writers, and even more, by its acceptance of homosexuals. From then on, I had no interest in an academic career, as almost any neophyte writer might today, or any conventional path, even if this meant abandoning the possibility of a secure income—poetry would certainly never bring me one. Being gay, of course, I was not going to have the responsibility of supporting a family. Not that Villagers worried about that much—women were considered able to take care of themselves. A symbol of the bohemian disdain for money was Joe Gould, the scion of the wealthy clan, who had rejected everything his family stood for and slept in Village doorways clutching a paper shopping bag, supposedly with his great poetic opus in it. That was what my commercial artist father worried about when he saw me drawn into Village life—that I would become a homeless bum, standing in the snow in Washington Square without a coat.

But the Village was the first taste of relaxing and just being myself that I had ever known—the need to hide being gay unnecessary—and it was exhilarating. For the bohemian world's first principle was Sexual Freedom, which welcomed all the rejects and refugees from a Puritan America that never allowed much dissent in any area, especially out in the provinces. In the Village it was the opposite, and whatever you were was acceptable. If we were social outcasts, we were proudly, defiantly so. But back then, we were a pitifully small band in exile—homosexuals, blacks, sluts, psychotics, drag queens, radicals of all varieties, artists, ne'er-do-wells. Nowadays, when you can live your alternate lifestyle in almost any part of the country (even if the Matthew Shepherds are still murdered sometimes), it is probably hard to imagine how small a community we were.

The bohemian world was also in the vanguard of political thinking, in reaction to the racism and economic inequality of the country, with its hypocritical cant about democracy. And it was in the Village that the artists unanimously opposed our entry into World War I to the point of declaring, from the top of the Washington Square arch, the Village an independent republic. Greenwich Village, admittedly with limitations, was freer than the rest of the country about black-white socializing. Except behind the barn, which has always been integrated, even in the Deep South, Greenwich Village was the only place in segregated America where one could see mixed-race couples in the open. I had never known blacks before, but now I walked the Village streets, sometimes hand in hand, with black friends. But even here, there were thugs, and some restaurants and businesses didn't like serving mixed-groups. But in the arts/bohemian community integration was an established fact. To find a freer atmosphere than the Village, blacks had to go to Paris, which at the time was pretty much a haven from prejudice.

Oddly, along with left-wing politics and rejection of religion, bohemians at the same time were equally devotees of mystical practices like ouija boards, astrology, and palm reading. Not to speak of the writings of Kahlil Gibran. And Gurdjieff. And Madame Blavatsky. Well before all the gurus set up shop in the sixties. Vegetarianism often went along with all that.

Modern art was our real religion, our Movement. The "moderns" were part of an arts generation that rejected popular culture and took pride in being difficult—obscurity was practically a requirement for avant-garde poetry. At the same time, modern poetry broke with the Victorian conventions of florid expression, though the struggle between a literary language and colloquial usage continues. Looked at another way, modern art was always about demonstrating its superiority over the common herd, setting oneself apart from the "philistines" out in the provinces of America who demanded simplicities and banalities, who stifled creativity and your sexuality. In short, we were out to sound different from the daily papers, from advertising culture, from anything conventional. What's more, the goal was even to sound different from each other. For instance, each of the poets who are in the canon of modern poetry has a unique voice. There were always imitators to be sure, but it is telling that none of the poets in this book learned their craft in workshops, as almost all do today, which produces such a uniformity of style. In my youth, if you wanted to be a writer, you didn't take a course or enter an MFA program. Alma Routsong, Fritz Peters, Frank O'Hara, Robert Friend, May Swenson, Arthur Gregor, Richard Howard, and Ralph Pomeroy learned their craft by doing it, on their own. Robert Friend was the only academic among them, but he too never attended a "workshop." It distresses me that the universities as an establishment now have such a lock on poetry. It's a kind of pre-censorship that controls where poetry can go.

One of the main factors that ended the bohemian era, the necessity for a bohemian "movement," was the Supreme Court decision in the late 1950s to allow Grove Press to publish Henry Miller's previously banned *Tropic of Cancer* and the notorious *Lady Chatterley's Lover* by D. H. Lawrence. The censorship of books before then — with the sneaking in of forbidden books like James Joyce's *Ulysses* past Customs and the U.S. Post Office — which resulted from a government that functioned as a moral arbiter over literature, has largely disappeared, though censorship in the mass media is increasing. Those publishing barriers falling resulted in the whole country loosening up, and spread many of the ideas of bohemianism around the country. So the freedom to read was one of the main forces that has liberalized the United States, led it to grow up, and in some sense made the Village and its little band of bohemians outmoded.

It was Andy Warhol who declared the end of bohemianism with his camp emphasis on celebrity. Suddenly, becoming successful and famous became the goal of creative artists, and the bohemian ideal was finished. Among my "portraits," Susan Sontag is a good case in point. She came out of the academic world, was an academic, but in her desire to be a writer, initially took the arch-bohemian Alfred Chester as her role model. However her ambitions were entirely different from his starving-artist-in-a-garret mentality, for she was unwavering in her quest for fame. She only belonged to the bohemian world because she was a lesbian, but she networked relentlessly. Frank O'Hara bridged the old world and the new. He cared little for personal fame, but didn't sneer at the rich, and, indeed, cultivated them as intimates and art patrons—he saw the future. James Baldwin also became famous, but it was never his goal. Historical necessity, which he could not refuse, chose him as a spokesman for his people at a moment when his voice could make a difference. Thus, each of my subjects could be defined in a different historical relationship to bohemianism.

Acknowledgments

Some of these chapters have appeared in different versions in *The Gay and Lesbian Review, Raritan, New York Stories, Worcester Review, Exquisite Corpse, Contemporary Authors (Autobiography Series)*, and *Looking for Genet: Literary Essays and Reviews* by Alfred Chester.

I would like to thank David Bergman for his enormously perceptive suggestions that helped to shape this book in its current form.

The Man Who Would Marry Susan Sontag

1

I discovered poetry as a soldier during World War II. In 1943, my unit, having finished Basic Training in Miami Beach, was boarding a troop train for a slow journey of several days across the country to an unknown destination, when a Red Cross worker handed each of us a bag of necessities for the trip, toothbrush, comb, candy bar— and a paperback. My book was, fatefully, a Louis Untermeyer anthology of great poems of the English language, which I devoured on the train. Three days later when I got off that train I knew what I wanted to be—a poet—in spite of, at the age of eighteen, never having written a line.

That anthology was essentially my total knowledge of poetry until two years later, when, as a newly minted navigator, I guided a B-17, one of the famous Flying Fortresses, across the North Atlantic to an airbase in England. My best buddy in another plane in the convoy was a prematurely bald fellow navigator, whom I was secretly in love with. Dave had gone to Cornell and was cynical about everything. When I confessed to him that Rupert Brooke was my favorite poet, he laughed scornfully and said that the greatest modern poet was T. S. Eliot. I'd never heard of him. He showed me "Prufrock" and "The Waste Land" and I was mystified. I didn't have a clue what they were about!

My real introduction to modern poetry came on an airbase in the Midlands, two hours north of London, from which I was flying bombing missions over Germany. After an exhausting daylong flight I would go to the Officers' Club on the base and drink whiskey sours to unwind, and it was there that I met my first real poet ever. Coman Leavenworth, a gnomelike young man with a crooked, one might say dirty, smile and a beak of a nose that seemed to reflect his aristocratic Anglo-Saxon origins, had already published poems in literary magazines like *Poetry* (Chicago). As a ground officer with a less demanding job than us fly-boys, Coman got down to London regularly, and over drinks in the Officers' Club I would drink in his reports about the poets he met at the Gargoyle Club, a hangout for writers—among them, the English poets George Barker and Stephen Spender, and the Americans, now largely forgotten, Harry Brown and Dunstan Thompson—most of whom seemed to be gay, or if married, gay friendly. How the English poets stayed out of the services I don't know, but the Americans, in and out of uniform, were all working either for *Stars & Stripes,* the newspaper of the U.S. Army, or for the Office of War Information. After the war, Harry Brown's best-selling war novel *A Walk in the Sun* was made into a movie and he became a successful screenwriter.

Under Coman's influence I bought George Barker's *Noctambules,* a now-forgotten poem that began, thrillingly, with the unforgettable words, in that era of persecution of homosexuals and near-blackout of gay writing, "The gay paraders of the esplanade, the wanderers in time's shade . . ."—I already knew what he was talking about there, for most of my sexual experiences had been, necessarily, pickups in the dark—and a little book of Dylan Thomas with its bracing lines, "my wine you drink, my bread you snap." But it was Dunstan Thompson's poems that really knocked me for a loop. "The red-haired robber in the ravished bed. . . ." and "The boy who brought me beauty brought me death. . . ." and "Waiting for the telephone to ring / Watching for a letter in the box. . . ." I was hooked for life. I'm still dazzled.

In December 1945, a year after my arrival in England with the Army Air Corps, and with the war over, I returned to America on an aircraft carrier whose flight deck crumpled under battering North Atlantic gales. One of the first things I did after getting home was to contact Dunstan Thompson, whom I had heard so much about from Coman Leavenworth, and who, a civilian again, was also now back in the States. Still wearing my Air Force uniform with silver wings and battle ribbons on my Eisenhower jacket—a new addition to the uniform that hugged the body fetchingly and led Coman to say with his dirty grin that the top brass must have been horrified when they realized they'd allowed such a revealing innovation—I met Dunstan Thompson for drinks at the 1-2-3 Club on New York's Upper East Side, where a cocktail pianist tinkled away in the background to the subdued conversation at the tables. It was a new world for me, a world of sophistication. The perfect aesthete, Thompson had a wonderful dome of a head with bulging eyes and a minimal chin, and he waved his long delicate fingers expressively—a dead ringer for a drawing of Keats in the National Portrait Gallery in London. I was in awe. His poetry did nothing to disguise the fact that he was homosexual—in fact, his high aesthetic pose more than justified it. He used the word "gay" with abandon in his poems, though it was still not in general use—"like that" and "queer" were more common. Dunstan had been to Harvard and was at a stage of cultural development I could never hope to reach, though I would make lists in my notebook of all the subjects I needed to master, the books I should read. I had barely begun writing poetry myself, but I already knew I didn't belong in that elegant Upper East Side setting he fit into so easily—I'd never be Dunstan Thompson's kind of poet or intellectual.

I guess if I'd gone to bed with him, as he wanted, our relationship would have developed and I might have learned more about him. As it turned out, this was to be our only contact. But he continued to be my favorite poet for years, and I still read with pleasure those flagrantly open paeans and elegies to his affairs with doomed sailors and soldiers and airmen.

Shortly after our meeting Dunstan left the States to live in England and would never return. It was a great mystery when he disappeared from the literary world, and I was not to learn his extraordinary story for many years. Coman Leavenworth also dropped out of my life, though later on, when I sent him an announcement of my first book, he replied with a condescending note that, from a high aesthetic position, referred distastefully to the book as a commercial proposition. Protected by his family's money from the "commercial" world of poetry with its uglinesses, he seems to have kept his purity by retreating behind the protecting walls of his Park Avenue apartment.

That February 1946, I re-enrolled at New York University, which I had attended briefly before the war, and quickly discovered the literary set in the cafeteria. Learning about Existentialism and orgone boxes and socialism became far more exciting than anything in my classes, so my attendance was spotty. Though I proclaimed myself a poet, my efforts to write didn't amount to much, and what I did was either instinctive outpourings of a juvenile nature or textbook exercises in poetry forms I read about in Harvard scholar Robert Hillyer's poetry manual, recommended to me by Dunstan Thompson. At NYU, I think I was accepted by the undemanding cafeteria crowd more for my good looks than my knowledge.

At the cafeteria I also met a person who was later to figure significantly in my life, someone who lived his life as a complete bohemian.

2

Even before his death in 1971, Alfred Chester was almost completely forgotten. By the late sixties, his life had degenerated into madness, and with his irrational behavior he had alienated as many people as he could, even breaking off with his closest friends. During the years after he disappeared from the literary scene and attempted to silence with drugs and alcohol the voices in his head that were involved in his creative powers, his work went out of print, and it was too painful to think much about him. Yet, for years, he had been a brilliant presence in the literary world, his writing had been widely admired, he was an important influence on the literary development of such writers as Cynthia Ozick and Susan Sontag . . . and my best friend.

It seems strange to say about someone who would become such a rich presence in my life, but Alfred Chester was only this odd-looking guy in the NYU cafeteria where I hung out with the bohemian/literary crowd. I knew he wrote for the college literary magazines, but I arrogantly dismissed those as amateur publications, and had no idea that fledgling writers like Cynthia Ozick and Sol Yurick, who were also at NYU then, saw Alfred as their main competition. I had no reason to feel superior, since I was merely scratching away clumsily at my poetry and wasn't getting published anywhere. But Alfred was a few years younger than me and had come straight to college from high school, whereas I had already been out in the world fighting a war, so I looked on him as not only a weirdo, but a kid. When he was teased, he wiggled all over like a dog, excited by the attention.

What made Alfred look so odd was that he wore a wig, because he was completely hairless. It was the first thing anyone noticed about him. Without natural sideburns to blend into and no eyebrows on his Fu Manchu face, the wig had to be obvious, but what made it all the more so was its orangey color, electric against his pasty-white skin, as if he was determined to rub in our faces the one thing that wrecked his life, his hairlessness. Through the years I remember that wig was in a terminally ratty state, and it just sat pasted on his humpty-dumpty head. But nobody who knew him ever dared mention it, no matter how close a friend you were, and even the word "hair," if it happened to slip out, hung in the air uncomfortably.

Wig aside, Alfred never looked like an ordinary person, with his lashless tartar eyes that turned into slits when he laughed, showing crooked, tobacco-stained teeth, and his head seemed to join his pudgy body, avoiding a neck entirely. Years of yoga exercises and dieting did nothing to alter his perennial softness, until after he went mad, when a powerful, squat peasant body emerged, as if his mind had to go before he could become his true physical self.

Except for that one detail, I think that Alfred, who was born in 1928 in the middle-class Flatbush section of Brooklyn, New York, would have had a conventional boyhood. It was X-ray treatments for a childhood disease that left him hairless. This was probably the reason that, instead of a public school, he was sent to an Orthodox Jewish yeshiva, where he had to wear a skullcap indoors, hiding his baldness—the baldness that made him feel and look like such a freak, and contributed to his madness and early death.

Compared to my own, his background was privileged, even if his immigrant parents never understood him any more than mine did me. But his furrier father was proud enough of him to name his business the Alfred Fur Company, after his youngest child with the mop of curly blond hair that was soon to disappear forever. After his hair fell out, his family took him to a "hair restorer" from Manchuria, brought to New York at great expense, and when that desperate measure failed, made the fateful decision to buy him the wig. The moment the wig was put on him, he wrote later, "it was like having an axe driven straight down the middle of my body. Beginning at the head."

Cynthia Ozick, who, somehow, I never met in the NYU cafeteria, movingly evoked him in 1946: "Here, one afternoon, is Alfred Chester, holding up a hair, a single strand, before a crowd. . . . 'What is that hair?' I innocently ask, having come late on the scene. 'A pubic hair,' he replies, and I feel as Virginia Woolf did when she declared human nature to have 'changed in or about December 1910'—soon after her sister Vanessa explained away a spot on her dress as 'semen.' . . . Chester at sixteen is a whole year younger than I; he has transparent eyes and a rosebud mouth, and is in love with a poet named Diana [pure fantasy, of course]. He has already found his way to the Village bars, and keeps in his wallet Truman Capote's secret telephone number. We tie our scarves tight against the cold and walk up and down 4th Avenue, winding in and out of the rows of second-hand bookshops crammed one against the other. . . . We are the sorrowful literary young."

I had been forced, by the rules of the GI Bill, to register in the School of Commerce again, where my father had enrolled me before the war and from which I escaped by enlisting in the Air Force. I was still escaping, and spent most of my time, even when I should have been in class, with the more congenial bohemian literary set in the cafeteria, where we disdained the nearby tables of Young Communists, splinter groups like Trotskyites and Schachtmanites, African American students, and the frat boys with their bimbos. Our table boasted the likes of the "fabulous" (the adjective of choice at the

9

time to describe him) Lloyd George W. Broadfield III, who posed as a writer, though he never wrote anything as far as anyone could see, spouted the ideas of two of our gods, Henry Miller and Wilhelm Reich, and always carried under his arm the latest book about Oscar Wilde. George Broadfield was a Negro, as we called it then, and though it was unlikely in that segregated time, claimed to come from a family of State Department diplomats. He made the equally dubious claim that he had a job with an oil company, an industry which at that time barred Jews, not to mention blacks. Later, he lived abroad for decades, working for governments in Africa, where according to his accounts he was able to behave grandly, traveling with an entourage in official limousines. Memoirs of the Paul Bowles circle in Tangier report him as a major sycophant and pest, besieging the Bowleses. I never minded his pretensions, though, for he was, if high-handed, good-hearted and fun-loving. Living in New York again in the seventies, he was finally murdered by a Haitian hustler, a fate he didn't deserve. The painting of the young George Broadfield by Beauford Delaney hangs in the Schomburg Collection.

Our cafeteria table was generally nonpolitical. None of us debated the incarceration of Ezra Pound in a mental hospital for broadcasting from Italy during the war, since to us he was clearly an anti-Semite and a traitor. Inconceivably, though, literary Trotskyites at the nearby table made the pilgrimage to Washington to sit at his feet and worship, an act of perversity, surely, when it was mostly reactionaries who stood up for Pound. One of the hangers-on at our table, an oily-looking youth with a sweaty round face, had testified against his own parents before the House Un-American Activities Committee, and was said to be working his way through college as a spy, reporting on communist activities among the students—with a foolish bravado I declared that I was a communist too and dared him to turn me in. He laughed at me.

After growing up in a white-only town in the suburbs and the still-segregated army, this was my first chance to get to know black people. The flamboyant George Broadfield knew everybody in the Village and Harlem, and brought me to the nearby loft of Beauford

Delaney, a black painter about whom Henry Miller had written a pamphlet. Delaney lived and painted in a factory loft in the industrial area adjacent to NYU and covered the grimy walls of his loft with long, pristine rolls of industrial paper, placed around the perimeter of the room, that he pulled up from the floor and tacked below the ceiling. While Beauford sketched me shortly after I met him, he gave me my first marijuana cigarette, and I promptly fell asleep, only to awaken hours later to find him beaming at me from his easel—Beauford always beamed in a particularly embracing way. Years later—this was before he left for Paris for good in the early fifties—I would see him seated in the darkened orchestra of Variety Photoplays, a jackoff movie house I frequented just north of the Bowery, where the clientele was a mixture of bums, day laborers, off-work taxi drivers, and immigrant family men escaping from their crowded slum tenements, all of whom found the odorous fraternity sexually liberating. On my way down the aisle to a seat, as I passed Beauford, sitting among his Greek and Italian *frotteurs,* he was again beaming at me with delight, and complicity.

George Broadfield also took me to meet the legendary scholar Dr. Alain Locke, one of the early theorists of black power, who had astonishing African tribal masks on the cool aquamarine walls of his elegant apartment. George led groups of fellow students as if on pilgrimage to the shabby apartment of Gertrude Stein—not the real Gertrude Stein, of course, who was then having a revival in Paris, after greeting the liberating GIs. This was a Stein cousin with the same name, without any observable literary talent but excellent bohemian credentials. George was thrilled by the relationship, if it in fact existed.

In Washington Square, I made the acquaintance of Anatole Broyard, a devastatingly handsome young writer from New Orleans, who was what we then called an octoroon and looked as white as me, though my credentials in that area seemed equally dubious, back then when Jews were Semites, not Caucasians—in my home town of Lynbrook, Long Island, where there were no Negroes, my immigrant family, dark and alien, were the Negroes, and were treated as such. A hugely fat painter named Dante was always flirting outrageously with Broyard in the Square, though Broyard was heterosexual—not that that was an insuperable barrier, and Dante knew it. With some people, flattery will get you everywhere. Broyard never succeeded in fulfilling his ambition of writing a novel, but later became a brilliant book reviewer for the *New York Times* and, passing for white, lived out his life in upscale ex-urbanite Connecticut.

I mostly hung out with Wilmer Lucas, a fellow student with a smooth café-au-lait complexion and writing ambitions, whom I had a crush on, though he too was straight. Or maybe I thought I should be in love with him because he was so handsome and we looked good together. We stayed out night after night, going to bars and jazz clubs like Small's Paradise in Harlem, and Carnegie Hall to see the ravaged, nearly voiceless Billie Holliday who had just been released from drug rehab in Lexington, Kentucky, disguising the damages with glittering diamond earrings. It was to be her last concert before her death.

Alfred Chester was merely one of our group, and still barely in my field of consciousness. We were all once invited to Alfred's house in Brooklyn, but were confined to the basement by an edict of his mother, and it was awkward to hear them arguing whenever he made trips up the stairs to get food and drink for us. I was told by his cousin Shirley who grew up close to him that his mother, ignorant but good-hearted, ridiculed him for his literary interests and railed at him for being "no good" and "lazy." Still, Alfred always preferred his mother's side of the family. They were emotional, but earthy and honest, and he liked to boast that an aunt had been the madam of a brothel in the Black Sea port of Odessa, famous for its colorful Jewish gangsters—whenever he spoke of her, he grinned with delight and his eyes became gleaming slits.

In his will, his father had set aside money for Alfred's education—to go to medical school. Even though he didn't go, Alfred still felt the money should be his, whatever he did with his life. Unfortunately, his family felt otherwise. Alfred also felt he was cheated out of his share of the Alfred Fur Company, which went to his older brother after his father's death. He was always trying to sue the family. For though he was willing to work hard at his writing, he never seriously considered the possibility of getting a job and throughout his life turned to his family for financial support, which they doled out grudgingly. It seemed to be more congenial to his nature, rather than keep begging for money, to try outrageous schemes to trick them, like announcing from abroad a fictitious marriage in order to receive wedding presents. In any case, it is likely that he would have found himself at odds with them simply because it was too much to expect perfectly ordinary people of limited education to understand the creativity of such a gifted child and the imperatives of his talent.

Being older than the cafeteria crowd and aware that I was gay, I sometimes hung out at a gay bar on Macdougal Street called Macdougal Tavern—the whole block is demolished now—where the young James Merrill would come in looking like the preppy-school boy that he was in a bowtie and horn-rimmed glasses where most of the rest of the clientele were in casual bohemian garb—I was in my regular costume of navy blue merchant marine sweater and left-over suntan pants from the war. After the bars closed, we'd all go to a Village cafeteria, where late one night I met another poet, Howard Moss, who invited me back to his apartment, claiming he had a Stromberg-Carlson that fried bacon and eggs—an unusual come-on that intrigued me, but not enough to go with him. Though Howard was a man who dressed and behaved formally, when the situation was appropriate he displayed his lustiness. It was several years after I turned him down in the cafeteria, when he had already become the poetry editor of the *New Yorker,* that I did visit his West 10th Street apartment. He lived in what I'd call an elegant style—he had a harpsichord in his apartment, and real furniture. I was supposedly invited for dinner, but, having just had a book accepted by a publisher, he celebrated by gulping down three martinis where one would have been lethal, and, wildly drunk, groped me and pronounced me adequate—I had nothing to say about it! Dancing about the room in his enthusiasm, he pulled my tie so tight around my neck it couldn't be unknotted. I was outraged, for it was my favorite tie, and fled. Perhaps it was my way of again getting out of going to bed with him. Over the years he repeatedly asked me to send him poems for the *New Yorker*—though I knew that, with my heartfelt and often-raunchy poems, I didn't belong in the *New Yorker*'s dandyish pages. I did see the phrase "glory hole" in a *New Yorker* poem once, but think it slipped by the editor's red pencil out of ignorance. In the seventies, Howard kept telling me they were loosening up, but by that time I was loosening up even further. Naturally, though, I thought it would be a better magazine if they published poets like me more often. But he was lovable to the end. On his deathbed, when a boyfriend visited him, Howard asked him to drop his pants and show him his ass. And died contented.

In my first few terms at NYU—I can't remember ever being assigned a faculty advisor—I took the courses I thought I needed, like French and Greek and art history, before I suddenly realized that to get my degree I would also have to take all the required courses, which I had no interest in at all. With the influx of huge numbers of veterans, these basic lecture courses were held in amphitheatres where you never got to know the teachers and they could not possibly notice individual students. I found these, and the required reading, insufferably boring. I was living on Long Island with my parents, commuting back and forth on the Long Island Railroad, and after staying out half the night with Wilmer, often in Harlem, it became impossible to wake up at seven to catch the train back to the city to make my nine o'clock classes. Besides, I hadn't done the reading. Often I slept on till noon, precluding any attendance at all, except for a late afternoon rendezvous at our table in the cafeteria.

The GI Bill had strict rules about regular attendance, so, in 1948, anticipating disaster due to my spotty attendance and neglected course work, I dropped out of college and went to France, determined to make the thousand dollars saved from my wartime flying pay last a year—this budgeting was not unrealistic in that era of a Europe on the edge of bankruptcy. My immigrant parents were horrified by my going back to a Europe from which "we fled for our lives," as they kept saying. They eventually settled the matter for themselves by telling people I was going to Paris to study. But drawn by the magnet of Paris, the cultural and Existentialist capital of the world, I had no doubt that I was going there to "become a poet."

On the ten-day sea voyage, I was lucky enough to meet a remarkable man, the poet Robert Friend.

3

When I read the poems of Robert Friend, the relationship to my own poetry is perfectly obvious. He was the father who passed on to me the key, and his own poetry is the mother ground I started from. It is true that Dunstan Thompson, W. H. Auden, and Constantine Cavafy were major influences on me almost from the beginning, but first there was Robert Friend.

His poem "Dancing with a Tiger" is a good metaphor for us:

> A crowded floor of couples at a dance
> and only I,
> his tail wrapped round us both,
> dancing with a tiger.
> . . . but suddenly
> —what had I said to him?—
> the strong grip loosened,
> . . . and he growled. . . .

In our relationship, he was the tiger, which made things complicated. If he was intellectually stimulating to be with, he could certainly be a royal pain in the ass, or to follow the metaphor of the poem, growl and swipe me with a paw.

I met him on the converted troop ship on which I was able to book passage to France in June 1948, for with the end of the war there weren't enough ships to accommodate the rush of people back to Europe, so the wartime "liberty ships" were adapted for civilian traffic—it was far from luxurious and there were still military double-decker bunks in the hold. By chance and the imperatives of the alphabet, Field and Friend were seated next to each other in the ship's dining room. I quickly learned that the distinguished, owl-eyed, professorial man next to me was a published poet, and though I had no grounds for claiming that I too was a poet, except that I wished to be, he accepted me at face value. Ten years older than me and a native of Brooklyn, he had been teaching in Puerto Rico and Panama for some years, and after getting his Masters at Harvard, had landed a job at Queens College, a lucky break that would bring him back to New York again. So he was celebrating by going to Paris for the summer. A mistake, for postwar Paris turned out to be even more seductive than New York.

During the ten-day sea voyage, he gathered, or rather, there gathered around him, a group of young would-be artists and writers who were taking the leap into the unknown of a Europe that had been closed to the outside world during the long years of the war and promised the intellectual thrill of a new movement, Existentialism, that had arisen out of the drama of the German occupation and was flourishing in the feverish atmosphere of postwar Paris in the ambience of Left Bank cafés and cellar clubs. Not only the founder of Existentialism, Jean-Paul Sartre, and his sometime lover and intellectual partner Simone de Beauvoir, but Albert Camus, Pablo Picasso, Cocteau's actor/lover Jean Marais, and chanteuse Juliette Greco were to be seen at the Café de Flore and the Deux Magots in St. Germain-des-Près, the red-hot center of the movement, where most of us were headed.

Robert Friend was a natural teacher, and it was with evident pleasure that he led the group's discussions throughout the voyage. It has been true through the ages and in all cultures that when there is sexual interest on the part of the teacher, the student blossoms in the particular glow of his attention, and learns. I myself thrive on being paid attention to, and one of the reasons for my failure in college, I think, was the hopeless anonymity of sitting in those postwar classes swollen by returning GIs, and trying to concentrate on the drone of the professor's voice. Face to face with Robert Friend, discussing literature and ideas, was not like studying and nothing like school. I didn't respond to him physically—indeed, I didn't see him that way, with his round shoulders and undeveloped body that seemed a mere appendage to his mind—I just loved the attention. On the ship he was having a more-rewarding flirtation with a teenage French boy from Toulouse. Robert was "just" a friend. And I blossomed.

We continued our discussions for several months on the Left Bank in Paris, where intellectual and sexual life among the expatriates and refugees from every country of the world flourished in spite of that spartan postwar period of *coupures*—electricity cuts—and rationing. Escaping our unheated rooms, Robert and I sat in warm cafés—mostly at the Café Pergola at the Mabillon metro stop—poring over the poetry in the Oscar Williams anthology of modern verse. It also had tiny pictures of the poets, and the beautiful ones, like Frederick Prokosch, certainly caused me to study their poems with special interest, since a friend had once declared that it was too bad I was so handsome or I might have been a good poet—the good-looking poets in this authoritative anthology indicated he was wrong about my chances.

From Robert I learned to probe the words like a talmudist to discover the often elusive meanings in this fiercely difficult poetry whose battle cry was "Obscurity," which only served as a keener goad to figuring it out. In those early decades of the twentieth century, when being openly gay was dangerous, obscurity was a useful device for poets like Hart Crane, whose elaborate syntax and layers of meaning masked the sexual content of his poems—and which made Dunstan Thompson's openness all the more daring. Further, Robert showed me the poems he was working on, and I was able to follow them draft after draft, as they emerged from their chrysalis in the various rewritings, and that way learned how poetry is made. Even in later years, when both of us began to write more easily, trusting our impulses more, his language always had the weight of consideration, rather than the throwaway language that is the mark of the most fashionable poetry of today. But in that era of the New Criticism, it was gospel that the more you rewrote the better your poetry was bound to become, especially if it became impenetrable in the process of building into it several layers of ambiguity. The method toned down emotional excess and produced a cool, mental poetry, which alienated ordinary literate readers. Though poets did develop from the discipline a formidable technique, it eventually became obvious to me that endless rewriting didn't necessarily produce masterpieces, just mostly indigestible chunks. But Robert's own poetry grew in clarity and precision in the rewriting, because he aimed for that and was the least pretentious of men. During his Communist years he wrote poems about the greed of capitalist society and the need to protest against it. But by now his influences reflected his studies in English literature. Besides moderns like W. H. Auden and Hart Crane, he particularly admired and studied seventeenth-century poets like Herrick and Donne, whose elegant versification was not particularly suited to the activist and theoretical subject matter that the Party demanded, but was quite appropriate to the ironies and paradoxes of life that were his major subjects.

He often dealt with gay and sexual issues as directly as possible, addressing his "lower self," or representing himself as the Outsider, in the guise of a cripple or a hunchback, not only because he felt unattractive but because of the homosexual's marginal position in society:

> I am glad to be as I am:
> too twisted
> for others' melting adoration. . . .
> The Cripple

In spite of our belief in sexual liberation, he often bemoaned the loss of sexual innocence, strange for a man so sexually free, so uncorrupt:

> Children, children, on the world's white shore,
> by the glitter of sea and the open gate,
> run before manhood leaps with a cry
> and seizes you by your little soft throat. . . .
>
> Warning

Reflecting a number of his failed relationships with men, he wrote clever, despairing poems about the impossibility of two people ever connecting:

> A little more of irresponsible love
> and a little less of responsible affection
> could have saved. Your code
> of honor breeds pestilence of stone. . . .
>
> The Irrational Source

Though it was not his main direction, he wrote some of his best poems about relationships with women. He often complained that women adored him, whereas men played hard to get. It's true that gay men, me included, were looking for an ideal that a beautiful, masculine body represented. Alfred Chester, more realistic, always said, that it was a delusion to imagine "that love was implicit in beauty."

In the postwar prosperity, the certainties of socialist thinking based on the failure of capitalism in the Depression were open to question. This affected Robert keenly, and when we met he was in a period of political rethinking. His thirties radicalism was evaporating in the changed climate and improved circumstances of his life and the world around him. For even if the free-wheeling postwar world offered possibilities he couldn't have imagined earlier—and the prewar anti-Semitism was rapidly fading—a poverty-stricken childhood was still ingrained in him, when "his father fled to the warmer darkness of woman after woman," many nights his mother had to send the children to bed hungry. And when the electricity was cut off for nonpayment of bills,

> . . . the boy of seventeen
> had to write his poems by candlelight. . . .
>
> History

He told me that he didn't realize it at the time, his head was so in the clouds with poetry, but when he started at Brooklyn College his clothes were ragged.

Brownsville, the neighborhood in Brooklyn he grew up in, was then a Jewish immigrant slum, rather than the African American one it later became, and typical of Eastern European Jews then, street corners were lively with political discussions—every faction represented. And after the isolation of Europe's Jewish ghettos and shtetls, there was a hunger for what was called "culture." When Robert formed a poetry group called the Houynyms, named after Swift's enlightened horses in *Gulliver's Travels,* the readings in his mother's kitchen became so popular, he told me, that people crowded onto the porch outside, in hopes of catching the magic syllables.

The years after his graduation from college, the height of the Depression, involved initiation into the activist world of the Communist Party, which was reflected in his poetry:

> . . . and the cash,
> went sliding down Park Avenue in the crash.
>
> Subway

It was the Depression that sent him to Puerto Rico on a teaching assignment, which was his opportunity to discover his sexuality that had been stunted by his deprived bringing up, the antagonism of the Communist Party to homosexuality, and the unreal romantic landscape of poetry he wandered in. Not just sexuality, but a sensuality that his aestheticism had blinded him to—an appreciation of his body. It was William Carlos Williams, poet and practicing obstetrician, who opened his eyes. Robert presents himself as:

> The perfect paradigm
> of the young poet—
> quivering, sensitive,
> painfully sincere . . .

21

Dr. Williams was waiting
in the San Juan hotel lobby,
and having listened

somewhat impatiently
soon diagnosed the case . . .
he led him to the terrace
that overlooked the sea,
and said:
Look,
pointing to the bathers
running along the beach
and sporting in the waves.

Ars Poetica

Just the right prescription from the good doctor! Robert went to "sport in the waves" himself with those boys, who, he quickly discovered, were ready for any erotic pleasure they could get. He learned to swim, play tennis, and take advantage of the decidedly un-puritan morality of the Caribbean. Thereafter and throughout his life he always made out with Latin Americans who liked his professorial looks. But by the evidence of the poems he remained the professor, even in bed:

That afternoon
he was wearing nothing but a crucifix
that dangled from his neck
I, not even that.

Between the fervor of our probings
that were somehow turning metaphysical,
I began to question God.

Startled out of our embrace,
he leapt onto the floor,
where kneeling by the bed
he made the sign of the Cross.

He must have been absolved,
for jumping back into our bed again,
he finished with the blasphemer.

The Catholic Lover

After our summer in France in 1948, he couldn't make himself return home, even to the long-desired teaching job in New York. Though his funds were dwindling, he stayed on in Paris and we continued to meet at the Café Pergola, where again, as on the ship, he attracted a group of French students, with whom he discussed philosophical and literary issues with a passion that overcame his clumsy French. When he finally ran out of money in the winter, he had no trouble, with his academic experience, getting a job in occupied Germany teaching American soldiers. I visited him in Munich where he was living in the luxury the military awarded itself as a prize of victory, had a handsome German lover, and was already translating German poets. Shortly after my visit, a sympathetic superior warned him that because of his membership in the Communist Party a decade earlier, he was a security risk and his passport was going to be taken away. This would force him to return to the States, where the country was in the grip of Cold War paranoia about a Communist conspiracy to take over the government.

One step ahead of the American authorities, he escaped to Israel. Even without the revelation of the horrors of the holocaust in Europe, American Jews of our generation were still so traumatized by the recent immigration of our parents to America, living in poverty and suffering from our own brand of anti-Semitism, that the creation of Israel was a miracle. Astonishing too to find that in Israel Jews cleaned the streets, delivered milk, taught school, even were streetwalkers! Robert lived first on a kibbutz where he studied the Hebrew language, but soon got a job on the faculty of Hebrew University in the English Department.

He was an atheist, as I was, but being a Jew is a complex issue, as much tribal as religious. Yet I didn't want to dismiss religion too easily—five thousand years of tradition, after all. But he settled that for me once and for all. "My way of being a Jew is to live in Jerusalem," he told me. A powerful statement that goes beyond politics and reaches into history. But while a supporter of Israel, which we both felt had changed our lives, he was also open to the culture of the Palestinians and studied Arabic.

"Ahel," Arabic for "family,"
cognate of "ohel," the Hebrew word for "tent" —
for desert dwellers a home:
grandfather, grandmother, father, mother, kids —
a family,
all under one roof —

their floor sand
covered by mats,
their roof and walls skin
flapping in the wind.

A Bedouin living in our kind of house
solid against the weather
complains,
"I can't sleep. The walls don't move."

Arabic Lesson

Here is revealed yet again the scholar, as well as an appreciation of the Moslem world, the essential ingredient that seems to be missing in most Israelis in their dealings with Palestinians. But Robert didn't start out that way in his early years in Israel — at that time, he made it clear to me that he considered the Palestinians backward and their religion regressive. He even pushed liquor on his Palestinian tricks, which shocked me when I heard of it, considering that it was forbidden to Muslims. Eventually, though, sexuality was the bridge to understanding — it was Palestinian lovers and, later when he needed assistance with everyday living, his Palestinian household help, that introduced him to their own world. He visited their families in the West Bank and learned about the unwarranted punishments being meted out by Israeli forces to ordinary Palestinian families. He had always lived alone until his last years when he was cared for by these devoted attendants whose mothers would send him fresh bread. One of the boys, whose brother had been killed by Israeli troops, was expected by his traditional family to marry the widow and raise her children, a fate that the gay Palestinian recoiled from. Robert arranged for a West Coast academic, who knew the boy, to sponsor him and get him into college in the States.

In spite of homosexuality being illegal in Israel during most of the half-century he lived there, Robert reported to me on his lively sex life, including afternoons at a hammam where groups of hassidic boys would come after school and make out. There was also a park nearby where gays congregated, though Robert himself never functioned in that kind of scene, nor in bars—his lovers came from his daily life, for instance taxi drivers who would stop in to see him after their night shifts ended. He was always open about his homosexuality, but now began writing explicitly gay poems. "The Teacher and the Indian" tells the story of his love affair with a student:

> Though the teacher had trained himself
> never to notice the looks of his students,
> he noticed this one . . . sitting in the last row,
> his good looks declared themselves at once.
> Brown-skinned, dark-eyed. . . .
>
> The Indian . . . kept coming up to his teacher's desk
> to express his gratitude. . . .
>
> The teacher . . . suddenly felt a tug at his sleeve
> and heard a voice saying, "Come on. Let's go."
> It was of course his Indian. . . . The teacher
> allowed himself, consenting even as he protested,
> to be pulled away by a firm arm meaning business.
>
> So, on an empty afternoon in an empty bar,
> the teacher found himself improbably
> drinking beer with his student . . .
> as they stared hungrily at each other.
>
> The game was won by both. That night
> they found themselves in a single bed. . . .

The plot continues, as the Indian tells about his first hot affair with a cowboy, riding out on the range together, and continues through the ensuing complications—truly a masterpiece of erotic narration.

Robert was the ultimate cat person, caring for innumerable stray cats in his neighborhood in defiance of Israeli law. He circumvented the prohibition against feeding them by opening his windows—he

25

lived on the ground floor—and laying the food out on plates around his large kitchen. His niece, Jean Cantu, reported to me that she "witnessed the 'swarms' firsthand when I visited him in Jerusalem in 1971. Robert used to throw chicken heads out of his kitchen window for them, which I still remember with repulsion. I started itching terribly after the first week in his apartment, which I thought might be mosquito bites, but wouldn't go away. I was also coming down with mono at the time, but didn't know it. Not ever having had cats, I didn't have a clue that I was having symptoms of flea bites!" I, myself, couldn't believe the scene when I saw it—cats of every description swarmed in, and in a minute the kitchen became filthy from their paws. He would take the sick ones to the vet, and sometimes fell in love with one and took it into the house to live with him. But out of these feline relationships charming poems emerged.

I, who was never comfortable in the educational establishment, on either side of the classroom, as teacher or student, found it remarkable that academe suited Robert so perfectly. Hebrew University was an ideal employer, giving him long leaves of absence in England and the United States. He finished his thesis on E. M. Forster, got his doctorate, and finally retired Professor Emeritus.

We continued our friendship over the years, though not without stresses. Robert had a difficult side, looking too closely (from my point of view) for slights and betrayals. As in his "Tiger" poem, he would suddenly growl and rake me with his claws. He analyzed my behavior as if it were the text of a poem. And perhaps I, with my own sensitivities, was an unreliable friend, retreating into unreachable corners when I should have been responsive. Once, when he was on sabbatical in New York City, I was preparing dinner for a couple of friends who were due at any moment, and he telephoned that he had just broken up with his Puerto Rican lover, and asked if he could come by. Thinking how he would sit there and pour out his tale of woe all evening, I told him, hard-heartedly, that with friends about to arrive and barely enough food for them it was impossible. He was devastated, and for months he brought this up to me, saying that all I had to do was "lay another plate," as well as the time in

France, thirty years before, when . . . but it's too tedious to repeat his accusations. He was simply like that—difficult. He made demands on me like a lover, which I wasn't, though I always honored him as my friend and teacher. He complained that I respected him more as a poet than as a friend, which was partly true. He never stopped listing my derelictions in friendship until I got fed up and told him I wasn't perfect, my faults were indeed many, and gave him an ultimatum: I'd rather we didn't communicate with each other any more if he didn't drop his litany of my betrayals. I was trying it on, of course, hoping to get him to lay off the nagging, but he was stubborn, and it actually led to a hiatus of several years in our correspondence. Finally, neither of us could keep it up, and broke down and resumed writing to each other. With the years, in spite of the strains and our differences, both of us evolved into a mutual admiration society. He continued to send me copies of his poems for suggestions, though he didn't always take them. For one thing, I tried to discourage him from using slang. He did it cleverly, but the slang was often embarrassingly out of date.

> What gave flat foot a hot foot
> was not the dollar burning in his pocket
> paid for by some doddering millionaire,
> to track down his soiled baby dove. . . .
>
> Detective Story

Ghastly!

His own loyalty was immeasurable. I will never forget that in 1971, after I had spent the summer bumming around Central Asia, more dead than alive with all kinds of intestinal bugs and a deep bronchial infection, I knew if I could just get to Israel, and Jerusalem where Robert lived, I would be saved. I barely made it to his door—and he took me in, got me medical treatment, cared for me, and restored me to health.

It is every poet's wish to write until the end. Robert Friend did it. His last poems, from 1998, the year of his death, were reduced to the simplicity of the circumstances of his dying, shed of all vanity, as well as the dregs of personality.

They tell me I am going to die.
Why don't I seem to care?
My cup is full. Let it spill.

4

Robert Friend in France was the basis of my education in modern poetry and in writing poetry. He somehow imparted to me the process, which I'd been unable to discover for myself in my previous attempts to write. Very soon, in 1949, I made my publishing debut in the glossy, multilingual quarterly Botteghe Oscure, which was published in Rome by the Princess Marguerite Caetani, an American heiress of the Philadelphia Chapin clan. Her nephew Paul Chapin, whom I had met in one of the Left Bank cafés, showed her my poems and she took a group for her second issue.

Paris was an education for me in many ways, as it has been for so many other Americans. It was the greatest bargain in the world after the war. I could live on two dollars a day, which included rent, eating all my meals in restaurants, sitting in cafés, and going to the theatre and opera, so my thousand dollars easily gave me a year. At St. Germain-des-Près I met the young Jimmy Baldwin, already a rising literary star, and the singer Anita Ellis, who picked me up in the mail line at American

Express, and though I told her I was gay, kept trying to make out with me. Her own brother Larry Kert, the Broadway musical star, was also gay, so it wasn't naiveté. The movie Gilda, *with Anita singing for Rita Hayworth especially the song "Put the Blame on Mame" had wowed everyone I knew. Anita treated me to luxuries like lunch in the Eiffel Tower and dinner at the opulent Hotel George V, where visiting Hollywood stars stayed.*

Many of the friends I made there have stayed with me throughout my life—Harry Goldgar, translator of Yeats into French and an early translator of Jean Genet into English, who spotted me at the Café Pergola where I wrote every day; Leslie Schenk, who, after a hiatus working for the UN around the world, settled in Paris and is devoting himself to writing again; the poet Arthur Gregor, who was returning to Europe for the first time since escaping the Nazis; and another poet, Ralph Pomeroy, and his best friend, Freddie Kuh.

A few weeks after arriving in Paris in June 1948, I was standing in line at American Express to pick up my mail, as everyone did in those days when it was free, when I noticed the two young Americans. They looked like charming schoolboys of fourteen and fifteen in their short pants, the younger with blond bangs and a face of angelic innocence, whom I got to know later as Ralph, and the other, a little darker and older, but not much, and equally innocent, even with his ironic, self-deprecating smile—this was Freddie. I wondered briefly what they were doing in Paris on their own, that year of 1948 when Americans began to return like the swallows after the long, hard winter—five winters, to be exact—of war.

Following my first sighting of the two boys in the American Express mail line, I began seeing them in the Left Bank cafés of the Quartier St. Germain I hung out in, the Café de Flore, the Deux Magots, the Royale, La Reine Blanche, even occasionally the august Brasserie Lipp with its dignified waiters and potted palms, and I soon learned that Ralph Pomeroy and Fred Kuh were older than they looked, in their early twenties, in fact. In the months ahead, we got to know each other well, since we lived through the following winter in Paris among a vastly diminished band of expatriates, after most of the others left at the end of summer. When I met a *grande dame* named Madame Khatchaturian—yes, a relative of the Soviet composer—she shivered on hearing that I planned to stay on in Paris through the winter, and said, in her heavy accent, "You are so brave. I go to New York, and central heating." And indeed the heat in our rooms only came on for a few hours occasionally during that bitter winter.

Under his blond bangs, Ralph Pomeroy had a painter's clear, gray-blue eyes, and a sulky, vulnerable mouth. He was often called *"le faux Truman"* for his startling resemblance to the author in the jacket photo, with similar bangs, reclining and holding a rose, on Capote's novel, *Other Voices, Other Rooms,* which made Capote famous. Actually, Ralph looked more like the photo than the real-life Truman Capote did. He was the idealized version.

But Ralph was already a published poet and artist in his own right, even if he had not had the electrifying success Capote, no older than he, was enjoying. Still, success seemed almost inevitable for someone as gifted and good-looking and as much of a hustler as Ralph Pomeroy. Though younger than me, he was far more experienced. Besides the allowance his father sent him, his rent was being paid by an older lover, a man who saw himself as Professor Higgins to Ralph's undeveloped Eliza Doolittle. Ralph's first poems had already appeared in *Poetry* (Chicago), quite a debut in the hermetic poetry world of that era. And he was a painter as well as a poet. Jean Cocteau, seeing his photo in the window of a shop, instantly wanted to use him in his film, *Orphée,* but unfortunately, Ralph had just left on a trip to Rome and couldn't be found. Perhaps this was a premonition of the bad luck that would shadow his career throughout the years. His timing was always terrible.

Out of the vast numbers of homosexuals in the armed forces, Ralph had been one of the unfortunate ones discharged in periodic roundups and wasn't eligible for veterans' benefits. Freddie Kuh wasn't on the GI Bill either and, like me, was living on savings—in his case, from working in his father's brokerage house in Chicago. I had found a spartan, but picturesque, furnished attic room, but Freddie and Ralph were living in a grander style. Freddie was in the tawdrily chic, modern little Hotel Montana, around the corner from the Café de Flore, where French movie people and artists crowded into the "American" bar, including celebrities like the thief/novelist Jean Genet. Sartre was more likely to be seen at his table in the up-stairs room of the Flore, where the tourists rarely went. Freddie's room at the top of the Montana, with its *vue panoramique,* had the incredible luxury of a private bath and hot water. The rest of us went to the public *Bains/Douches* once a week, and even bragged how long it had been since we'd bathed—I remember once going for a month without a bath. Ralph was in an even grander hotel room than Freddie's above the Brasserie Lipp, with two big windows overlook-ing the leafy Boulevard St. Germain with a view of the austere but elegant Eglise St. Germain across the intersection.

The two were high school friends from Chicago, where their artsy and gay interests had brought them together. But even if they were as passionate about the arts as anyone, Ralph and Freddie were not among those who did very much visibly in the way of work. If Ralph was clearly a painter and published poet, I wasn't sure whether Freddie had any real ambition to do anything himself, though I knew he was talented because at Raffy's restaurant on *rue du Dragon,* where we often ate dinner together, he used to draw such clever car-toons on the paper tablecloths. But that's as far as it went, and he was to make his name in a different way, unimaginable to any of us at the time. Ralph always seemed to wangle promises from someone to let him do covers for *Vogue* or show his paintings somewhere, so he must have been working, but never when I saw him. And when I went to call on Freddie at the Montana, he was usually lolling in his bath, entertaining friends who perched around the tub—I don't recall any evidence of a typewriter or art equipment. Unlike Ralph, Freddie never seemed to connect sexually with anyone, either, and was obsessed with an unresponsive Finnish-American painter named

Onni Saari, who did spend his days at his easel, though he, in turn, was enthralled by Ellsworth Kelly, also painting in Paris, but still unknown at the time.

Most habitués of the quartier were of the picturesque variety, like a good-looking youth, rumored to be Gore Vidal's lover, who rode around on a bicycle, and therefore was called "The Bicycle Boy." With her jet-black, straight hair, black fingernails, and waiflike appearance, Juliette Greco, who was singing in a *cave,* was the epitome of Left Bank bohemia. She didn't sleep in doorways anymore, as she had as a *gamine* during the Occupation but didn't look exactly clean and wholesome either. At the Café Royale across boulevard St. Germain from the Flore, Ralph introduced me to a pair of sunbaked Americans, newly returned from Tangier, typical drifters on the international arts scene. They were painter Buffie Johnson and novelist Gordon Sager, part of Jane and Paul Bowles's amoral, heavy drinking, hashish-smoking set. The stories about them were lurid—involving orgies and hustlers—but Buffie and Gordon, and even Ralph, himself, had a kind of innocence, a delight in their own decadence. Passionate in my idealism, their way of living seemed immoral to me in that postwar era with the DP camps still full of the flotsam from the war, though I also disapproved of those who chose the conventional path. The mystery to me was how this colorful pair, sprawled on the banquettes of the Royale in their flimsy Moroccan pajama pants and hooded tops, managed to support themselves.

Jimmy Baldwin, though a minor literary celebrity after publishing an essay in *Partisan Review* attacking Richard Wright, also supported himself God-knows-how. I was somewhat shy of him because he seemed to run with such a late night crowd, drinking the nights away, smoking grass, and squiring visiting Americans around the nightspots. I didn't know it at the time, but he was hanging out with those whiteys because they bought him meals and paid his hotel bill. Many of them were Southerners and, except for waiters and house servants, were having their first experience rubbing shoulders, and maybe more, with a black man. Paris, even more than the Village, was an equal-opportunity experience.

Like most Americans I knew, Freddie and Ralph could merely stammer a few words in French in shops and restaurants, but I was determined to learn the language, with its formalities of expression and structure. Still, I think what I learned most was from simply living there, absorbing French ways. The low prices from the war-shattered economy allowed someone like me to experience the richness of French life, from café life and the cuisine to the theater and the opera. Eating in little family restaurants where regular clients had their own napkins in rings and marked bottles of wine, was an education in itself. It was the last winter of rationing, but the food—nothing four-star, just the traditional cuisine—was a revelation.

You could call on famous arts figures in those days if you wanted to meet them, and they were happy to meet you, especially if you were young and attractive and talented. Ralph and Freddie, far more sophisticated than me, went to call on recently widowed Alice Toklas, who served them tea and her famous cookies in the painting-lined rooms of her flat that she had shared with Gertrude Stein. After Ralph showed her his own paintings, she advised him to stick to writing, much as Gertrude had advised Picasso to go back to painting when he showed her his poems. And on a visit to London, a smoke-blackened London still grim with shortages and rationing and with few of the amenities of France, I telephoned one of my idols, Stephen Spender. I loved his poetry, which I had first read during the war when I was stationed in England, and had heard how handsome he was from Coman Leavenworth at the Officers' Club. It was the confidence gained from the leap forward my writing had taken in the few months in Paris from knowing Robert Friend that emboldened me to do it. Spender did not hesitate to invite me to his house, and we had tea in his study. A tall rangy man with wild, gingery hair and a prominent nose, his hand was on my knee in no time. But even if I had been attracted to him, I could hear his wife, children, and the household staff just beyond the door! Later, he took me to a cocktail party given by the novelist Rose Macaulay at the Gargoyle Club (which I had longed to go to during the war, when Coman told me about it), where I met literary people I had only read about. T. S. Eliot came in—T. S. Eliot!—pushing his roommate, the editor John Hayward's wheelchair into the room, prompting a bright young novelist named Philip Toynbee to announce, "Let's introduce the two Americans!" I was not quite prepared for that, and luckily he didn't persist.

I attracted a lot of attention in those days with my curly black hair and ruddy complexion, and a beefy man rushed up to me and asked excitedly if I was Catalan. When I said, "No, Jewish," he looked horrified and fled. It was an affront to good manners to say you were a Jew in the genteel literary world back then, as proclaiming your homosexuality was. It was a subject about which it was better to be quiet—you were expected to be quietly ashamed—or perhaps just discreet. A number of the top poets felt free to make anti-Semitic remarks in, and outside of, their poems, and there was no way to protest. When I was at NYU, I had written to T. S. Eliot asking him about the ugly anti-Semitic passages in his poetry, and he answered me, claiming he was "no more anti-Semitic than anti-Lapp or anti-Eskimo." But of course the evidence is there in the poems. And the implication of his denial was that Jews were as remote from his position in life as Lapps and Eskimos. Unfortunately, needing money, I sold the letter along with a first edition of one of his books.

It was at the Café de Flore and Deux Magots that all visitors to Paris stopped that year. And sociable Ralph and Freddie managed to meet most of them. Running into Ralph on the rue de Rivoli, Capote was so intrigued by "the false Truman," that he whisked him off to lunch at the Ritz. When Orson Welles and Franchot Tone came to Paris to make a movie, Ralph and Freddie were there to guide them through the gay nightspots of Pigalle. Along with Ann Sheridan and Truman Capote, they all ended up one evening in a transvestite club called La Vie en Rose, where the floor show headlined a pair of Hungarian brothers in sequined drag, called "Les Sisters B." Capote, always outrageous, danced with one of the drag queens, Freddie told me, shocking Ann Sheridan.

At the end of the war I had been assigned to navigate a speedy courier plane, ferrying top brass around Europe, and during a stopover in Paris, I had stumbled onto Le Boeuf sur le Toit, off the Champs Elysées, my first gay bar. This was the famous surrealist club founded in the twenties by Jean Cocteau and his friends, which after the liberation was packed with gay servicemen from all the Allied armies. A Frenchman at the bar told me, with a knowing look, that General de Gaulle had appeared there one evening. Though I'd had plenty of sex, most of it the thrilling if furtive, sneaking-around variety, I had only just discovered the gay world, and this was my initiation. It was a thunderbolt! When I entered the club in my newly issued Eisenhower jacket with a white silk scarf around my neck and silver wings pinned to my chest, every head in the place turned. A young battle-scarred sergeant growled at me, bitterly, "You're not for any enlisted man like me." I would have been, if he hadn't moved away. But he turned out to be right, for I ended up with an American captain who took me to a hotel room upholstered whorishly in leopard-print drapes and bedspread.

Le Boeuf sur le Toit flourished after the war too, and one night there, Ralph and Freddie, who knew all about such nightspots, met Jean Cocteau's stocky, classically handsome little lover, Jean Marais, in full makeup. Later, when I was on the Greek island of Hydra, everyone was still talking of Marais's recent visit with a film crew, when he had openly made out with all the fishermen. This was not hard to do on Hydra if you didn't mind being known as a slut.

It was not just Freddie Kuh who couldn't concentrate on the page or canvas. I think neither Ralph nor I had the capacity to work hard enough, either. Like most poets, our energy came in spurts, and depended on regular encouragement. There is something about this on-again/off-again mentality uncongenial to the steady, hard work of writing any substantial creative work like a novel. Success in the arts demands a toughness we lacked. So the vision of ourselves as artists that was nurtured in Paris meant that, in the years ahead, we had quite a difficult row to hoe.

5

In the spring of 1949, unable to face returning home from Europe, I boldly cashed in my return boat ticket and went to Greece, which was still in the throes of civil war between the partisans who had liberated Greece from the German occupation and the royalist government the British had installed, which we were supporting with the Marshall Plan. I was at home in Greece as in no other place before, and started learning the mind-boggling, polysyllabic language immediately. Greece at that time was a country where, compared to the oppressive atmosphere in the States, being homosexual was no problem. Of course, women, like in most of the Middle East and the Moslem world, were possessions of men, even using for their married names the possessive form of their husband's name—if he was Mr. Constantinos, she was Mrs. Constantinou, meaning "of Constantinos" or "belonging to Constantinos." In movies like *Never on Sunday,* those loveable, happy prostitutes in the brothel in Piraeus were simple women who had made a single "mistake" and were shipped off by their families to be whores, the only thing a woman could be if not a wife. These restrictions never applied to the Greek upper classes, who were mostly educated in France and screwed around freely, but, except for them, in those days, if "good" women were kept indoors, men had complete freedom outdoors, where without women, they continued ancient traditions of homosexuality as an outlet.

Most of the poems in the first section of my first book *Stand Up, Friend, With Me,* were written there. I had begun to write in a less literary, more natural-sounding conversational style even before Greek friends introduced me to the homoerotic poetry of Cavafy, which combined the voice of the demotic language with the elegance of the literary tongue and evoked the spirit of classical Greek. In defiance of the prejudices of the poetry world, I stopped trying to be fancy and started using my parents' Yiddish inflections to soften the literary aspects in my writing—poetry, back then, sounded so goddamn artificial. I figured, that way, to get in the tenderness with which Cavafy always wrote and which Greeks used in speaking, as if addressing the child in each other, so under his influence my poems addressed the child in the reader. And I refused to obey the rules against what was called "sentimentality," which effectively inhibited poets from writing emotionally, a pernicious dogma that has been taught in all the writing workshops across the country and has resulted in sterility.

When my money ran out in Greece, I managed to find work as an artists' model to earn a few dollars a day to live on. Still, I could barely pay the rent for my room on an upper floor of a shabby hotel in Athens, whose lower floors housed prostitutes, and I could only afford apples and bread for dinner. What kept me alive was a famous Greek actress named Marika Kotopouli feeding me lunch every day—I would show up at her kitchen door and her maidservant would put a sumptuous meal on the table before me. After awhile, I began feeling a little spacey from living in a completely Greek world and hardly hearing or speaking English, and would go to the American library to read *Partisan Review.* After six months of spartan existence in Athens, with the help of the American consul I signed on as a deckhand on a freighter, destination Philadelphia.

When I came back to New York in 1950, I was flat broke, so I moved in with my family again on Long Island, a pattern I would repeat for many years. Alfred Chester was in graduate school at Columbia University, and I visited him in the furnished room in Manhattan, where he was living with his cocker spaniel—throughout his life, he seemed never to be without dogs, and often had cats as well. There I met the future writer Curtis Harnak, who was in graduate school with him, studying under scholars like Lionel Trilling and Jacques Barzun. Harnak had the sleek, handsome looks of an officer in the Austro-Hungarian army, with sly, amused eyes that took in everything. Later, when he was married to Hortense Calisher and became director of Yaddo, he told me that I was the first published writer he had ever met. I had only published a few poems at the time, but that was still impressive, even to me. The daunting task I faced was how could I live up to it.

It was not long before Alfred dropped out of the master's program and sailed for France where he lived for most of the fifties. In spite of having seen each other in the NYU cafeteria day after day, and even if we kept track of each other by mail throughout most of his decade in Europe and sent each other money in times of need (if we had any), we didn't know each other all that well. I was, I imagine, a glamorous older figure to him, and was able to recommend him to some of my literary connections in Paris. But truthfully, I didn't admire what I'd seen of his writing, influenced as it was by the Capote-esque Southern Gothic school, which I considered affected and decadent, even reactionary.

Once in the international world of Paris, however, Alfred turned out to be no shrinking violet and often behaved with swashbuckling boldness. With all his self-consciousness over his appearance, he was gregarious, with an irrepressible wit and energy that attracted people and convinced everybody who knew him that he was a budding genius. In Paris, he became a well-known figure, unkempt and shapeless, with his rumpled wig, "pharaonic nose," as he later described it, and lashless, pale, but quizzical eyes, as he hurried through the Left Bank streets and talked away the nights in cafés. If he was an immature schoolboy when I knew him in New York, in Paris he grew up fast.

He'd never had a real lover before—it was just crushes and fantasies. Sex, yes—in New York any place that's semi-private or murky becomes a place for quickies. He made out under the boardwalk in Coney Island, and on the long subway rides from Brooklyn into Manhattan had the tawdry adventures possible in the public johns of the stops along the way where the desperate might yearn for love but "settled for sex with unseemly haste," as Gore Vidal put it so memorably in his preface to Alfred's *Head of a Sad Angel, Stories 1953–1966.* At NYU he secretly yearned for a blond Tom Sawyer-type named Bob Diffenderfer, as he later labeled all the All-American Boys he could never be, but many of whom he got into his bed. Alfred must have preferred to keep the blond beauty unattainable, because Diffy never suspected Alfred was in love with him, he told me later. There was another boy from his Brooklyn high school Alfred talked about as a lover, though this sounded like a face-saving fantasy, much as the hero of his first novel *Jamie Is My Heart's Desire* longs after a wraithlike youth who may or may not exist. So, shortly after Alfred arrived in Paris, when Arthur D., a darkly handsome, young Israeli pianist, started pursuing him, it was a thunderbolt. Arthur didn't even consider himself gay. Nevertheless, they stayed together for about a decade, with plenty of ups and downs, as in all of Alfred's relationships throughout his life.

It was a decade also devoted to developing his craft, as well as in getting to know most of the literary figures of his generation. Alfred's letters from Paris are full of meetings with Carson McCullers, Eugene Walter, *Harper's Bazaar* literary editor Mary Louise Aswell, Mary Lee Settle, Jimmy Baldwin, Jean Garrigue, George Plimpton, film-maker/poet James Broughton, Eve Triem, and others soon to be established, such as Richard Seaver, then merely an editor of the literary magazine *Merlin,* and Robert Silvers, the future publisher of the *New York Review of Books.* He became a protégé of Marguerite Caetani of *Botteghe Oscure.* Famous for nurturing young talent, Caetani spotted Alfred immediately, and, in 1952, Alfred made his debut in the magazine with an essay, "Silence in Heaven," set in the suburb of Paris that he and Arthur had moved to. Caetani got her exotic name and title by marrying an Italian nobleman with plenty of property but no money—she had plenty of that. She established the glossy journal in memory of her son killed in the war, financing it with the income from a building she owned on Union Square in New York, and was famous for paying magnificently for material she published.

Besides the princess's generous payments for his work, which she continued to publish over the years, and the brief windfall of wedding *gelt* from his family for his fictitious marriage, he earned five hundred dollars for writing a pornographic novel, *Chariot of Flesh,* for Olympia Press's green Traveller's Companion series, under the pseudonym Malcolm Nesbit. He also edited Nabokov's *Lolita* for the series long before it could be published in the United States. Princess Caetani was eventually able to get him a Guggenheim Fellowship by pressuring Lionel Trilling and other well-known writers to sponsor his application. When she felt that Trilling's letter of recommendation was lukewarm, Alfred wrote me, Caetani returned it and demanded more enthusiastic sponsorship. His Guggenheim was a windfall for me, too, since I was at the MacDowell Colony and trying to raise money to pay for another couple of months there. Alfred sent me two hundred dollars.

In Paris, Alfred began a lifelong struggle with landlords, usually based on his inability, and sometimes on his reluctance, to pay the rent. Painter Nadia Gould, an NYU friend of ours who was then living in Paris, recalls, "The laws in France made it complicated for a landlord to evict a tenant. Alfred took advantage of this and would pay a month's rent in advance and then refuse to pay any more, living rent-free through the long period of legal proceedings. One tormented landlord—one of a series of landlords Alfred wiped the floor with—had the door to the apartment removed to get rid of him. Alfred took him to court, and we all had to go and testify, until the landlord was forced to restore the door."

His first book, *Here Be Dragons,* a collection of short stories very much in his Southern Gothic, mannered style, was published in

Paris in 1955 by Editions Finisterre, Robert Silvers's first but short-lived publishing venture, and shortly afterwards, was brought out in London by Andre Deutsch, beginning his long relationship with the editor Diana Athill. His novel *Jamie Is My Heart's Desire* had the unusual distinction of being published first in France in translation, followed by England, and subsequently in Germany, before it came out in the United States. A strange work also in his early mannered style, the protagonist is a mortician who has always felt more "at ease among the dead" than the living. This morbidity his friends took as cleverness, as well as his story "Cradle Song," where the mother gets rid of her newborn child by tossing it into a ravine.

Alfred was already suffering, though I didn't know it then, from the strange quandary that came to dominate his life—whether he had an "I." He suffered over not having an "I," his personality being "situational," by which he seemed to mean being someone else according to changing circumstance. When he mentioned this obsession to me, I thought he was being literary and dramatizing himself. But if his earliest work was influenced stylistically by Truman Capote, the plays of Pirandello, as in *Twelve Characters in Search of an Author,* had greater relevance to his major theme, which grew out of his inability to reconcile the different aspects of his nature, well-expressed in the title of his work-in-progress *I, Etc.* The Existentialists of the time didn't seem to help him, with their simplistic solution that only in action does one attain the authenticity of the Self. But his problems dovetailed exactly with the ideas of the mystic and teacher, G. I. Gurdjieff, who also believed that most of us do not have one "I," but many "I's," a different "I" according to the situation. To overcome this defect Gurdjieff offered his system of "The Work," but Alfred never actually joined a Gurdjieff study group.

This identity crisis was first referred to in his numerous letters from Paris in the mid-fifties and particularly in an interview with Hans de Vaal, a young Dutch writer he met in Paris. The interview, which appeared in a Dutch magazine, was an expression of the young Alfred Chester's ideas and has special significance in light of later developments: He already defines for De Vaal the Pirandellian ideas

42

about madness and identity that obsessed him throughout his life. And it is startling to see in it the beginning of his fascination with Paul Bowles, who led him to Morocco, and madness, ten years later. I don't think any of his friends took seriously how deep his anxiety was over this lack of an "I," which led a decade later to his final breakdown. We took it simply for fashionable angst.

6

Coming home from Europe in 1950 was a major shock, because I was faced with supporting myself for the first time. Until
then, I'd been a soldier, taken care of by the U.S. government, and in
civilian life was a student on the GI Bill, then lived in Europe on my
savings from the war—as a flying officer overseas I got extra pay
which I put aside. And here I was in my late twenties, never really
having worked and without any way of earning a living. Real-life
problems like getting a job and finding an apartment defeated me
from the start.

I was obsessed with poetry but couldn't see how to survive as a
poet. I made that survival more painful and difficult, since according
to my bohemian and leftist principles getting a steady job, especially
a white-collar job, would have meant "selling out." I didn't feel comfortable with teaching, but of course, I didn't have a degree, so I
couldn't have taught back then anyway. I kept leaving home whenever I found a cheap apartment in New York, but repeatedly ran into
trouble and ended up back in Lynbrook. My Old World parents
could understand a child moving out only for marriage, so there was

that guilt to contend with too. Once, when I was living in a coldwater basement flat on the Lower East Side, being very much the starving artist and terribly thin, Freddie Kuh, on a visit from San Francisco, where he had settled after Paris, arrived with a bag of groceries, and standing over me, made me drink down a glass of milk.

I found myself in an America that, compared to the pleasures of France and Greece, seemed unutterably grim. There was only a shabby little bohemian band that still hung out at the San Remo bar in the Village, and the whole block that included the gay MacDougal Tavern was being torn down by NYU to build a law school. The fifties was a period of national hysteria, those years of the witch-hunt of leftists and homosexuals, the Rosenberg executions, loyalty oaths, bomb shelters, and cold war hysteria, even the imprisonment and death of loony, nonconformist psychiatrist Wilhelm Reich for claiming that sitting in an orgone box to accumulate "orgone energy," removing "body armoring," and having good sex, aiming for the "cosmic orgasm," could cure cancer. The firing of "subversives" extended to homosexual men and women, for we were considered a security risk as being subject to blackmail. Espionage trials also had homosexual undertones, such as that of Whittaker Chambers vs. Alger Hiss with the rumor of an old affair between them. A number of citizens escaped to more hospitable countries abroad, if they were lucky enough to skip out before their passports were lifted. A few people, even more courageous, refused to cooperate by "naming names" or signing loyalty oaths, and either went to jail or became outcasts and were unemployable for years. But many artists and intellectuals, swept up in the panic that the United States was being taken over by "Stalinists," or perhaps just protecting their jobs, turned state's evidence and testified against each other. This divided the left, and all leftist thinking was generally devalued from then on. I don't think we have ever recovered from that trauma, for when I go to countries that never "outlawed" the far left and preserved the whole spectrum of political and intellectual thought, it feels freer and I breathe easier.

In light of the attack on ideas, dissent, and nonconformity, it was not surprising when painters retreated to the neutral ground of

45

abstract expressionism, poets got religion and concentrated on formal subjects like carousels and angels, and psychiatrists tried to make their queer patients straight by talk therapy, and when that failed, by shock treatments, even lobotomies. On the other hand, they couldn't stop sex, not in a crowded city like New York, with its body-to-body rush hour subways, standing room at the Metropolitan Opera, working class bathhouses on the Coney Island boardwalk with their crowded steam rooms, even the political speeches in Union Square, still attracting hard core remnants of the left, but also men on the loose who clustered around the speaker, rubbing against each other, combining eroticism and politics.

It was at the Chinese communist bookstore on lower Fifth Avenue, at that time the shabby end, that I discovered a collection of poems by the eighth-century Chinese poet Tu Fu and breathed in his free spirit. He was a complete human being and not only wrote about politics, but also was not afraid of being sentimental, both of which were discouraged in American poetry. He felt it was within his competence, indeed his duty as a poet, to advise rulers on how to deal with his country's problems, a country in turmoil, although they listened as little to poets in eighth-century China as they do today. I didn't see how to follow his lead, but inspired by my conviction that I should be part of the "working class," a "poet of the people," I haunted the hiring hall of District 65, a left-wing union. Yet, when I got jobs in factories and warehouses, I didn't stay long in any of them, I would work for a month or two, and, with a few dollars saved, quit to write for awhile—and was soon broke again. In 1951, I quite liked one job in a dress warehouse where I made up selections of ladies' garments on wheeled racks for different branches of a women's clothing chain—each store got dresses appropriate to its clientele. But that too I quit after a few months to take up a fellowship at the Yaddo artists' retreat in Saratoga Springs where one could bask in the luxury of a pseudo-manor house with a private studio. Blissful to be able to write for two months without worrying about money. And it was free!

Arriving at the back door of the Yaddo mansion, I was met by Clifford Wright, a large, fair-haired, Scandinavian American painter who served as the host, greeting new guests and making them comfortable, in return for which he got room and board plus a tiny stipend for his art supplies. He showed me to my room in the faux-baronial edifice, then walked me over to my studio, a simple cottage in the surrounding woods and quizzed me on my lunch box preferences—number of sandwiches? two fruits or three? thermos of soup? Already starving in the country air I ordered the maximum. I was soon to learn that this versatile young fellow saw his job as not only making guests comfortable and listening to their problems, but making love with everyone who seemed to need it, both men and women. He also claimed to masturbate four times a day, often on his paintings on paper, that lay scattered over the floor of his studio and which he would pick up from time to time and daub at, paint mixing in with semen.

That evening I joined the formidable Yaddo director Elizabeth Ames at the main table in the dining room where she presided, every inch a lady. Elderly and deaf, she put the receiver of her hearing aid on the table, and one knew to speak up. It was flattering to me, dark-eyed, half-savage youth that I was, that she liked me instantly. I didn't learn for some time that she had a long-time Jewish lover who was a Lower East Side painter and communist, so perhaps I was a type she was attracted to. Ramrod-erect, Elizabeth ruled Yaddo with a strict hand, for she was in a direct line of succession from the Spencer Trasks, who, loaded with loot from railroads and stock market, in the 1860s built Yaddo, filled it with "authentic" imitation furnishings brought back from their travels abroad, and became patrons of the arts. Luckily for me with my minimal, threadbare wardrobe, guests no longer had to wear evening clothes to the dining room, though slacks on the women among us were still not allowed. Elizabeth left little notes, written in her refined, spidery hand, on the mail table to chide loud drinkers on the lawn at night, or other abuses of the genteel atmosphere. Truman Capote and Leo Lerman, who had been there at the same time the season before, found the formality stultifying and tried to lighten it up by screaming and camping together at meals, which resulted in Elizabeth's most famous little note: "Less homosexual laughter at the breakfast table, please." Gentility was the order of the day, and a certain holy atmosphere ruled, reminiscent of the early days when the Trasks' artistic guests attested to the enlightenment of their hosts by putting on pageants in which they scattered rose petals before their benefactress Katrina Trask, proclaiming her Queen of Yaddo. A sign on the Yaddo circular road read: "Quiet! Artists At Work," and indeed, guests were discouraged from visiting other residents during working hours, which did not in the least keep them out of each other's rooms at night for riotous drinking parties and hanky panky.

When I arrived, I found the male guests divided into Rocks and Flits, categories, I believe, that came from private schools, where Flits were the sensitive boys who hung around the library and Rocks the athletes and studs. At Yaddo there was considerable antagonism between them. The Rocks were mostly writers who took macho James Jones as their model and wore lumberjack shirts and boots and stomped around scowling, especially at us sensitive types. But that made them all the more titillating for the women, especially in an era when every literate woman sought fulfillment with a man like the gamekeeper in *Lady Chatterley's Lover,* which was available in an expurgated edition, or the rough-hewn French movie star Jean Gabin or the homegrown stud Marlon Brando in *Streetcar Named Desire.* So women crossed the line, socializing with the Flits who were much more amusing and literate, but screwed with the Rocks.

But one could ignore the Rocks, and the atmosphere still allowed a good deal of leeway. Drinking was tolerated as a necessary safety valve, and the van from the liquor store in town delivered cases of booze every day to the mansion for cocktail parties in our rooms. At one of them I met painter Marie Mencken, a large, pear-shaped woman who was married to Willard Maas, a now-forgotten poet, who, Robert Friend had told me, held boy-parties in the Brooklyn Heights duplex he shared with Marie. That didn't bother his sophisticated wife in the least, for apparently it was his genius that kept them together—Marie told me coolly, as we sipped martinis, that if she didn't think Maas was a great poet she wouldn't stay with him. Willard Maas taught at Wagner College in Staten Island where his star poetry student was Gerard Malanga, who later joined the Andy Warhol Factory and performed at the Electric Circus in the East Village. When I left Yaddo Marie gave me one her art works, which involved sand and string glued to the canvas, a fragile combination, I learned to my dismay, when I went to take it out of a closet some months later to find that it had self-destructed.

After dinner, in the gothic wood-paneled music room, composer Ben Weber, a handkerchief in a pale, expressive hand, gave campy recitals, hilariously impersonating divas and lieder singers, with poet Hubert Creekmore accompanying. I remember Ben dramatizing all three characters in the "Erlkönig" by Schubert: the terrified child wailing to his father, driving their carriage through a winter landscape, that Death was chasing him, and beguiling Death cooing to the boy not to be afraid, until—with Hubert at the piano whipping it to a frenzy—the father finally understood and tried, hopelessly, to outrace Death. It was a hysterical, breathless performance that brought down the house, or at any rate the half dozen of us in the music room pews.

After hearing me sing some of my union songs, Ben and Hubert urged me to try Schubert's "Du bist die Ruh," and when I did, feeling ridiculous, they applauded, so I frequently performed in our musicales after dinner. Howard Swanson, the other composer in residence besides Ben Weber—there were only two composers' studios—taught me his song "The Negro Speaks of Rivers," based on a poem by Langston Hughes, which went into my slight but ambitious repertory.

In the privacy of their rooms Ben and Hubert held drag parties where Clifford joined them—he loved the theatrical fantasy of drag, which filled his paintings that featured gothic ladies and musclemen photos cut out of magazines set in operatic landscapes like stage sets. Hubert Creekmore worked in New York City for literary agent John

Schaffner who, in spite of being gay, was married to Perdita, the daughter of lesbian poet H. D. When I visited Schaffner at his office on 3rd Avenue, I couldn't fail to notice the back room with a big ramshackle sofa where his encounters with male hustlers took place.

Part of Elizabeth Ames's job was to maintain good relations with the politically conservative Saratoga Springs community. But the free-spirited Yaddo-ites sometimes made it difficult to present a bland image of the Yaddo goings-on. Occasionally, a horny guest, made desperate and incautious by the isolation at Yaddo, or preferring anonymous sex, was caught by police *in flagrante* with a pickup in the bushes of the downtown park, or in the public men's room in the basement of the police station, and Elizabeth Ames, herself completely tolerant but anxious to avoid a scandal, quietly arranged things with the town authorities. Then there were the drunks who made the rounds of the racetrack bars and ended up in the Saratoga jail. Once a year she buttered up the town fathers by giving a party for them in the rose garden. But she couldn't pacify townie vandals, resentful at the multiracial artists living in the lap of luxury, who kept overturning and daubing paint on the marble statues and the vine-covered pagodas.

Things had hardly settled down at the time of my arrival from a scandal that had erupted the year before. Poet Robert Lowell, who was subject to mental breakdowns, had telephoned the FBI that Yaddo was a nest of communist subversives, and in the paranoia of the time, the feds had swooped down in a raid, carting Clifford Wright off to jail and confiscating his address book, which left him terrified, since it was full of his gay friends, most of them in the closet in those dark days when being a homosexual was as risky as being a commie. Clifford's background check revealed, not that he was a communist, but that he had deserted the army—he explained to me later that he didn't see any reason to stay in the army once the war was over and just took off. It demanded all of Elizabeth Ames's considerable powers to get him out of jail.

Lowell was already unstable and coming out of his Catholic convert phase, but Lowell's eruption has never been properly explained in any of the biographies, afraid to explore Lowell's sexual conflicts. But in his diary, Clifford reports that the supposedly hetero poet had been seduced by Charles Sebree, a black composer/artist, and it tipped him over the edge. Clifford's diary entry for Dec. 27, 1948, reads, "Charles Sebree made a point of sleeping with him a couple of times and each time Cal (Lowell) said the next morning he wasn't that sort of person." Morning-after regrets are weak excuses. But after having thrown Yaddo into an uproar, Lowell conveniently checked himself into a mental hospital. Lowell was right that we were a bunch of "subversives." We were all out to subvert restrictive, conventional attitudes, and in spite of his breakdowns, shock treatments, and loosening up his disciplined poetry, he remained an uptight bastard.

Yaddo was wonderful for meeting all kinds of artists, though not particularly academics. Academics generally went to the MacDowell Colony, which was somewhat looked down upon in those days by Yaddo-ites who, on the whole, were freelancers and bohemians, creating for art, not money. You didn't go to Yaddo to write a nonfiction book, but to MacDowell. In the room next door to mine was elderly Jean Starr Untermeyer, a high aesthete of a poet, once married to Louis Untermeyer, whose anthology had turned me on to poetry in the army. Unaware that his wife wrote poetry, Untermeyer had come upon her poems hidden in a box on her vanity table and got them published. Now she was working on a book about Schubert and Keats, who, she pointed out to me, were contemporaries and had surprisingly parallel lives, both dying young. She had also hoped to become a lieder singer and studied in Vienna. The Untermeyers' one son, Richard, went to Yale during those days of quotas for Jews at Ivy League colleges—Yale was even more restrictive than Harvard, and only two were allowed in each class. A friend of mine, who was the other Jew admitted to Yale that year, told me that the Untermeyer youth felt ostracized in that WASP bastion and asked my friend to room with him, but my friend refused. And shortly afterwards, the boy committed suicide. When Jean Starr heard the news in Vienna she lost her voice forever. Evenings, in the Yaddo music room, she would croak out for us the famous Schubert

51

songs, sounding like a worn-out record, but nevertheless with great artistry.

Another elderly writer in residence was Mary Miller, a tall, imposing, woman who wrote under the name Isabel Bolton but was a Chapin and a relative of the Princess Caetani. The Chapins, much like James Merrill's clan, did not approve of anything so dubious as a writer in their midst and she was ostracized, though I heard later that it may not only have been being a writer that made her the black sheep—as a young woman she had gone to Italy and may have given birth to an illegitimate child. That would have been unthinkable back then, especially in such a stuffy, Main Line family.

Her pen name, Isabel Bolton, sounded so romantic that, when one of her books was published to excellent reviews, critic Edmund Wilson, famous for his priapic tendencies, asked to meet her. Nervous about this, she arranged the meeting in Central Park on a bench safely near Fifth Avenue. Seated there, she observed him walking by her several times, unable to believe that this old lady was the glamorous Isabel Bolton of his fantasies, before she greeted him. She always laughed when she told the story.

The ritual of the Yaddo day was much like that on an ocean liner. And as on a sea voyage there were sudden love affairs that often ended in broken hearts before the arrival in port. Clifford Wright, resident stud, helped to console those unfortunates by listening to their miseries or, if possible, with his fat prick. Like on a ship, we came from our rooms to a buffet breakfast in the dining room—overlooking a sea of grass sweeping down to the trellised rose garden—to sit at the half dozen tables lively with the bright chatter of "voyagers" thrown in together, except for one "silent" table set aside for those who wished to husband their first energies for their work. After breakfast, there were newspapers in the lounge, and on leaving for your studio, your lunch pail, the kind workmen carry, was waiting—the kitchen staff had it down to a science. Even though it was already spring, it was still chilly upstate and in my studio I would light the stove with chunks of firewood and kindling. Sitting at my desk I could look out at the woods and watch squirrels and chipmunks, and once a fox raced by pursued by dogs. My poems weren't going very well, even in this shrine dedicated to the arts, but I kept working at them—that's what I was there for. Though it was discouraged because of insurance reasons and we were told there were snapping turtles, lunchtimes, I sometimes rowed one of the rowboats out on the pond to eat my sandwiches and two fruits disconsolately, and took long walks through the extensively wooded grounds that abutted onto the famous race track where horses were exercised. I sometimes bicycled or even walked the five miles into Saratoga Springs, a sleepy town that only came alive during the summer racing season. Like some of the other horny Yaddo-ites, I too considered cruising the park, but I didn't see anyone lurking in the bushes.

After being completely cared for for two months, I was faced with the problem of leaving the safety of the "ship" and returning to "shore," a panic I had equally felt crossing the ocean or even getting out of the all-embracing army. It meant the same old problems of getting a job and an apartment. Back in New York City, still true to the ideology of the left, I pursued what I considered working class jobs, until I was taken on as a machinist apprentice in the factory district of lower Manhattan—it was a grimy collection of cast-iron buildings with loading platforms that has since become artsy and fashionable SoHo. The machine shop did subcontracting jobs for big arms contractors, parts for missiles and weaponry of all kinds. I liked my fellow workers, who were mostly refugee Jews, many of whom had been in concentration camps, attested to by the numbers tattooed on their forearms. I was living at home again and had to get up at 5:30 in the morning to catch a train to get to work at 8:00, six days a week. Though it was my favorite job ever—it made me feel very butch—I saw after six months, during which I had graduated to lathe work, that I'd never be able to get back to writing, and quit.

Getting and keeping a job was one thing, writing was another. I tried writing in some of the cafés on the Lower East Side where the immigrant card players reminded me of the Europe that had so nurtured my poetry, but everything I wrote was tight, manipulated, showed the effort. Still, when Harry Goldgar, one of my Café Pergola pals in Paris, sent my manuscript to the New Directions editor, David MacDowell, he showed it to poets William Carlos Williams and John Crowe Ransom, who were enthusiastic, and MacDowell, when he moved to Random House, got me a book contract. Unfortunately, this staggering development, a contract with a major publisher, had the effect of inhibiting my writing even more. I really was only a beginner in the literary world.

It helped a little to be meeting other young poets who were already part of it. Jerry Rothlein of the old NYU cafeteria crowd, now a grad student in art history, introduced me to Stanley Moss (a distant relation to *New Yorker* editor Howard Moss via a complex genealogy) — Jerry was having an affair with the husband of one of Stanley's girlfriends. Stanley was a beanpole of a man with black curly hair like a horsehair mattress — David MacDowell, with his Southern sense of humor, called him Mattress Moss, though I think that referred more to Stanley hitting the sack every chance he got. At that time Stanley, too, was working at New Directions Press, which had been founded by steel-heir James Laughlin and had offices in the Village, attesting to its noncommercial literary ambitions. My generation devoured New Directions's New Classics series, and its thick annuals of avant-garde literature, which my poems were appearing in.

Jerry Rothlein got it from his boyfriend's wife that, indeed, Stanley was not short-changed where it counted. A true heterosexual and passionate lover of women, Stanley adored every part of woman, and once told me he could look at a woman's cunt for hours. At twenty, Stanley had become the lover of the beautiful, even legendary, Group Theater founder, actress Stella Adler, the only one in the company, it is said, who actually went to Moscow and studied with the originator of the Method — the great Stanislavski himself. A story I heard was that the forty-year-old Adler, married to director Harold Clurman, with all her experience with men had never had an orgasm — until Stanley Moss.

Like many Jewish men I've known, Stanley didn't have an iota of homophobia and was completely comfortable with gay people. He even described his nighttime prowling for women as "cruising." He was so cool about it he once shared a basement room with the lesbian poet Jean Garrigue, who was later to become the "great love" of Stanley Kunitz as she had long been of Josephine Herbst and who knows how many others—she had a marvelous independent spirit, something like the free-living Edna St. Vincent Millay. Stanley and Jean used the apartment in turns to bring home female partners at night.

Shortly after I met him, Stanley fell in love with an exotically beautiful Barnard undergraduate, Ana Maria Vandellos, whose father had fled with his family from Franco's Spain, and we would pick her up at her dorm to go out to literary parties as a threesome—Barnard had a curfew for it's students, but Ana Maria was often late returning and had to sneak back in. Waiting for her in the dignified lounge of the dorm, Stanley, in full bad-boy mode, printed "MARY KELLY EATS HAIR PIE" on the bulletin board.

The literary parties had a somewhat predictable crowd, with the sculptor Shari Dienes, famous for her suitcase full of shards of a broken mirror, symbolizing her shattered dreams, I suppose, and George Reavey, a Brit who translated from the Russian, and anthologist Oscar Williams, always in attendance. Ana Maria and I were photographed together at a reception at the Gotham Book Mart for Christopher Isherwood on the occasion of the play-version of his novel, *I Am a Camera,* opening on Broadway, and one of the pictures turned up shortly after in a Leica camera manual.

Stanley particularly admired poets like Dylan Thomas, whose motto was Gargantuan Excess—eat the whole roast, drink all the wine or brandy, read the whole shelf, or the whole library, of books. This sensuality went along with a fascination with Talmudic lore that inspired many of Stanley's poems. The skin on his hands seemed to symbolize these two aspects of his nature—it was remarkably fine and sensitive to earthly pleasures, while also representing his spirituality. His obsession with the minutest detail in his poetry was Talmudic. Like we all did then, Stanley was into the endless rewriting of his poems, which in his case was useful, since he arrived at what he wanted only after going through this process, which, much like his years in psychoanalysis, certainly straightened out the seeming muddle of fragments he started out with. I always watched with fascination as the poem, through its innumerable drafts, started to cohere and emerge. His obsessiveness about his poems resulted in his revising them up to the moment of publication—he told me that he even kept making changes over the shoulder of the typesetter.

I once heard that when Stanley quit New Directions, in a fine demonstration of the poet's disdain for money, he picked up the blotter on the desk of his boss, the millionaire publisher, which was covered with checks he was signing, and threw it all out the window to flutter down eight stories over the avenue and across the Village. If this never happened it should have, it sounds so much like Stanley.

To support his poetry, Stanley began selling fine art prints to high schools—it was the framing of the prints that brought in the commissions—driving around the boroughs of New York in a battered car filled to the windows and above with sample frames, prints, dirty clothes, books—I doubt he could see much in the rearview mirror, even if the rear window had been clean enough to see out of. When he drove Ana Maria and me to the beach, a wild stretch at Point Lookout called "Cannibal Beach" because of the gay action in the dunes, I had to shove aside the mountain of junk to get into the back of the car. Stanley's apartments were equally appalling. When he cooked—he's a marvelous, inventive cook—food dropped to the floor and he never noticed. After he gave parties he'd just shove the used plates, glasses, and cups into the corners until the apartment became unlivable, and then move out. Though she was a good student, Maria was equally feckless, seemed to accept the mess, which in her world the servants would undoubtedly have dealt with, and carelessly pinned up her petticoat with safety pins—it was an age when a woman's slip showing caused titters. When Stanley broke things, as he often did, he couldn't fix them himself and just bought replacements—in his garage, when I visited him in the country years later, was a large collection of his broken fishing reels. I felt that two such sloppy people, beautiful as they were, could never last in a long-term relationship, and indeed they ultimately lived out their lives with different partners. His next wife was an extraordinarily neat and organized woman whose efforts to control the damages have been heroic, if often fruitless. It was obvious that Stanley would have to become rich, because he could never live bohemian poor, and he did.

Stanley once told me that his analyst said anybody in America who doesn't get rich is a masochist. Still, it would have been hard to believe then that, over the years, Stanley would become a dealer in Old Masters, whose sales to major museums would be front page news in the *New York Times*—but a dealer who never stopped his obsessive writing and rewriting of his poems.

7

I was finding it harder and harder to force myself out of bed to look for a job, and there was no way I could afford to return to Paris. In 1952, in despair, I started in a form of Freudian-based therapy called Group Analysis that took over my consciousness for several years, and influenced my life for years after that.

Various critics have interpreted the title of my first book, *Stand Up, Friend, With Me*, in different ways, as referring to my mentor Robert Friend, or, as Richard Howard interpreted it in a Freudian manner, the "little friend" as a synonym for my penis. Actually, the "friend" of the title addressed the downtrodden like me, the underdogs, even the exploited Third World countries, inviting them to join me in my new pride in myself, my new-found courage to stand up against all oppressors. This title was taken from a poem I wrote, when, as a result of my therapy, I had a startling experience. I *stood up*.

Though in the long run, Group, as we called the therapy, turned out to be largely destructive, early on in the opening-up process I went through a critical episode, a remarkable, though brief, period of what I can only describe as a state of "expansion," of wholeness, and which perhaps could be clinically labeled as a manic phase of my manic-depressive nature, except that it was like nothing I had ever experienced in mood swings before. What I actually felt was almost Olympian in its openness and calm and I would like to have remained in that euphoric state forever. The title *Stand Up, Friend, With Me* was the final line of the poem that I wrote after I "stood up" myself, a poem that I've never included in any of my books.

What happened to me was very much like the plot of Dostoevsky's novel *A Raw Youth,* in which the illegitimate son is recognized by his natural father and experiences a tremendous burst of energy and exhilaration. The plot spins out of control after this early section, but like Richard Strauss's tone poem "Thus Spake Zarathustra" it just needs its spectacular opening to be forever memorable. In my case, one afternoon, when I was leaving my parents' house in Lynbrook for a Group meeting in Manhattan, out of the blue my father offered me money. For some reason (money equals love? the love from him I never got?), I walked away from the house toward the Long Island Railroad station in a state of emotional turmoil. I felt I was coming apart, but choked back the sobs heaving in my chest. Somehow, I held myself together, the mile to the station, waiting on the platform for the train, the half-hour ride into the city, and the two changes on the subway, my panic rising the whole time. And I made it without cracking to the analyst's office for the meeting, when, in the waiting room, I realized I had miscalculated. I was an hour early and the previous group was still going on. I couldn't hold back any longer, and wedging myself into a corner of the room for support, I let go and started screaming, until he came out and I sobbed out how terrified I was and was able to calm down.

An hour later when my own group met, I could barely wait for everyone to sit down in the circle of chairs when I "stood up." Literally. I was shaking violently as I forced myself to my feet, while the whole group started shouting at me to stop doing that to myself. But even crying and shaking all over, at that moment it was the most important thing for my survival to "stand up." I can't remember what I said to the group—perhaps I just shouted back at them to let me do

59

it, that I had to do it. But I *stood up,* and at the end of that session walked out of there, healed. Whole.

As I say in my poem "The Journey," it was as if a fist inside me had opened. Wonderful to be able to breathe so easily, to feel part of other men, when I had always felt separated from them. Different. I felt sane for the first time in my life. I was perfectly normal!

I started writing like mad, composing a poem called "It Is Dawn and the Cock Is Crowing," the one that ends with "STAND UP, FRIEND, WITH ME"—yes, all caps—which I mimeographed and mailed to friends all over the world, asking them to have it published—I guess that sounds crazy now. At the next group meeting I high-handedly passed out a copy to everyone in the room, which enraged the group further, as if my new state of being threatened them. It was clear to me by now that they were my enemies, not my friends. I was very sure of myself. Poetry flowed out of me during the following weeks. I felt like Shakespeare, but what was wrong with that!

I still have a tattered mimeographed copy of "It Is Dawn and the Cock Is Crowing," with its final line, "STAND UP, FRIEND, WITH ME," that I used as my book title. The poem has many interesting qualities, but its amalgamation of Marxism and Freudian psychology seems naive and reductive to me now, where once, briefly, I thought I was speaking ultimate truth like a prophet. After I came down from my initial exhilaration, I gradually felt uncomfortable with it and revised it. Unfortunately, I loaned my one copy of the new version to Ernest Jones, a *Nation* writer I'd met at Yaddo, and never got it back. He claimed his cat had eaten it. This was just before Jones went through a voluntary lobotomy to cure himself of homosexual tendencies, after which he never wrote again, and retired from his teaching job at Queens College. But perhaps it was a successful outcome in medical terms since he married his department chair. The only poem of that time that I included in my first book was "Prologue," which ends with the line, "Look, friend, at me," echoing "Stand up, friend, with me," my aria of freedom.

The deadline in my book contract with Random House had long passed and it turned out, as David MacDowell informed me over an extravagant, alcoholic, expense-account lunch at the East Side watering hole where he took his authors, that Random House had never intended to publish my manuscript as it was, and was waiting for me to write more poems for it. I was quite aware that the poems I'd been writing were not up to the ones in my original manuscript from Europe—but I'd lost my way in the difficult transition back to New York. Then after I stood up in the group, the poems I wrote were so different from the ones in my manuscript I could tell that MacDowell was embarrassed by them, especially my "Stand up, friend, with me" poem.

After the "standing up" experience, I didn't know if I'd gone straight, as I should have done according to the group's half-baked Oedipal theory that we had to kill our father and marry our mother. The father part of that equation seemed to be resolved, at least for the moment. The one thing I knew was that there was nothing wrong with me anymore, whatever that meant. No longer feeling any separation from other men, no difference—if that meant marrying and having children, I was ready to do it, in a spirit of male community, though I still didn't have any sexual drive towards women. Or towards men, for that matter. My sex drive must have gone into limbo while I explored my new condition—perhaps I should have been suspicious of that. Anyway, I had no chance to try anything, for, unfortunately, this gift of wholeness, connectedness, didn't last more than a couple of weeks. From there on, it was all downhill. The wonderful state of being faded away, never to return, and I sank into a fearsome depression that the therapy group, with its continual attack on my homosexuality, only made worse. The therapist had little to offer except his prescription for psychological health—first, a job, to be able to afford an apartment, and then get a girlfriend. There was no question of encouraging me to get a boyfriend, even though I pursued homosexual experiences ever more desperately now. I was shocked—and my first doubt about him arose—when he urged me to drop poetry, which he said could never be the basis for a satisfying life, and turn to prose.

I did allow myself to be persuaded to try a white-collar career job. In the *New York Times* regularly were full-page ads for Gimbel's Department Store with an insert calling for Phi Beta Kappas to work in their advertising department. I wasn't even a college graduate, much less Phi Beta, but I applied to the formidable, no-nonsense advertising director, Bernice Fitz-Gibbon, a tank of a woman. At the interview, I spoke up nervily to her, which she liked, and on the basis of my publication record, was hired, though the canny Fitz-Gibbon said dolefully, "First spring day, you'll probably up and leave." I and plump, rumpled Rollie Hochstein did flunky work in a windowless cubbyhole, clipping ads and delivering copies of the paper to all the offices, where Phi Betas, who had been through our apprentice stage, were rising in their careers. Like them, our future escape, too, would be promotion to Production or Copywriting, or, if we turned out to be duds, exile to the dreaded basement, which had its own advertising department and where cluttered ads for basement bargains were churned out for the tabloids.

After two months, I was slated to be promoted to Production, with a lifetime career in advertising ahead of me. But on that Monday morning in spring, true to Fitz-Gibbon's prediction, when I arrived at Penn Station, instead of walking the few blocks to Gimbel's, where I'd take the next step up the ladder to being a full-fledged advertising man, I turned away and jumped on the first train for Washington, D.C., where I checked into the YMCA and sent a telegram to Fitz-Gibbon with my regrets. I met Rollie forty years later, after she had become a widely published short story writer, and learned that, after my departure, an enraged Fitz-Gibbon consigned her to basement hell. She also returned to me a sheaf of my early poems that I'd left behind with her, many of which I thought I'd lost.

In my post-high misery, the ease and fluidity with which I'd been writing vanished and I was back to struggling. But if I was dissatisfied with these poems, I still got them published in magazines. It didn't help, though, that leftist friends criticized them as decadent and negative. They certainly reflected my depression, but how dogma ridden, how rigid was that period of leftist thought, as if the more it was attacked, the more undeviatingly they had to hold on to its positions! The New Left that came along in the sixties was a breath of fresh air.

8

My mother always lamented that her children couldn't "cash in" on their looks, sharing the popular belief that being good-looking should get you somewhere. I don't know if I could have profited from it if I had set out to—actually, I felt unattractive—but in any case, I had strict ideas about such things. I was going to make it on my poetry. I did, of course, respond to the flattery of anyone showing interest in me, but nobody ever suggested exchanging my body for some benefit, like a book contract or a screen test.

Ralph Pomeroy was different. Talented as he was, Ralph was not above using his remarkably durable childish beauty, and in fact was quite a little hustler, but though he later claimed that it did not actually help him much in his striving for success, it certainly gave him entrée into the world of prominent artists and writers, art collectors, editors, and patrons. I don't have the expertise to vouch for his artwork. But whether or not his looks made it easier for him to show his paintings and get published, whatever success he had as a poet was entirely due to the quality of his poetry itself.

If he could speak of Gore and Tennessee and Truman familiarly, it was just as important that he had a refined sensibility and exquisite manners and taste, not qualities I cared about much, but I could admire them in Ralph. And it was natural that a young man of such gifts was invited on millionaires' yachts and to country houses, which gave him a glamorous life periodically, but left him high and dry in between. For, as a number of my women friends have observed about their rich, successful lovers, the one thing they won't give you is a job.

When I was in my gloomiest years, the early fifties, Ralph had a glorious top floor-through apartment with a skylight in a Greenwich Village brownstone. He always lived on what I can only call a professional level, and giving an impression of success is absolutely necessary for a successful career. Again, this level of luxury was being paid for by a lover, Monroe Wheeler, who like his name was a wheeler-dealer at the Museum of Modern Art, and was the lifetime partner of the novelist Glenway Wescott.

Ralph was interviewed by Wheeler when, after his return from Paris, he went to the Museum of Modern Art looking for a job. Charmed not only by his looks but by his talents and intelligence, Wheeler invited Ralph to dinner at the Park Avenue apartment he shared with Wescott, beginning a love affair and later a friendship that lasted until Wheeler's death. Wheeler's affair with Ralph created a triangle that seemed to be recurrent in the Wheeler/Wescott relationship where a third person was always involved. A friend of Alfred Kinsey of the famed Kinsey Report, Wheeler held parties in Ralph's Village apartment to allow Kinsey to observe urban gay life for his study of homosexuality, although back in Indiana Kinsey had plenty of first-hand experience himself with the provincial variety. It was through Wheeler that Ralph met such figures as the photographer George Platt Lynes, who snapped him at the height of his youthful glory, and writers Katherine Anne Porter, Louise Bogan, Edith Sitwell, Thornton Wilder, and William Inge, several of whom became his friends.

Glenway Wescott, like his contemporaries Thornton Wilder and Somerset Maugham, was always frightened that his homosexuality would become known, and though he was one of the foremost men of letters of his period, this eventually silenced his writing. It was ironic that in the upper-echelon world he frequented it didn't matter in the least that he was queer, as it was mostly called then, just so long as you didn't mention it. Even as an old man, he was afraid to publish his revealing journals. But after his death, *Glenway Wescott Personally*, a biography by Jerry Rosco, from a younger, more open generation, spilled the beans Wescott was so successful in sweeping under the rug.

With the recommendation of several of his fancy new friends, Ralph was accepted by Yaddo, a visit that coincided with my second stay in 1955. This group turned out to be much livelier than on my previous visit, when the atmosphere had been fraught with hostility between the Rocks and the Flits—this time the Flits outnumbered the Rocks. Ralph, never one to waste his time, quickly threw himself into a steamy affair with the host Clifford Wright, who was completely besotted with him.

In my usual state of confusion about my life, I didn't make any attempt to work and, rebelliously, refused to join the starchy director Elizabeth Ames at the main table in the dining room. There was no problem between the gays and straights this time, and I made friends with Seymour Krim, who had the battered face of a prize-fighter and was officially a Rock, but he was a peaceable man, and besides, his super-bohemian status as a writer of essays for the *Village Voice* put him above categories. In any event, he was completely comfortable with us gays. He had already given up writing fiction, but I couldn't forget a harrowing story of his in a *New Directions Annual* about a teenage boy who borrows a pair of panties from his mother's dresser drawer and masturbates into them. When she comes home she immediately suspects something, discovers the panties gone and demands of her son where they are. The boy locks himself in the bathroom, as her ultimatum hangs over his head like an axe. Obviously, it's the story of a crack up, as Seymour must have experienced it himself—and indeed I learned that he had done time in mental wards. I was told that when Seymour was crazy he picked up men, but went straight again when he came back to himself. After all he had gone through, he looked like a punch-drunk boxer, but was a kind, gentle man, whose suffering found echoes within mine. By the evidence of that panties story, fiction had proved too painful for him, but his book of essays, *Notes of a Near-Sighted Cannoneer,* was brilliant social commentary.

I was particularly impressed by Howard Griffin, one of Clifford's closest friends, a poet with a sly grin, who had been secretary to W. H. Auden, and published an account in *Poetry* magazine of their daily conversations. Out rowing on one of the little lakes on the Yaddo grounds where we would take our lunch boxes, Howard told me that, every night after working with Auden, he came home and transcribed the poet's words into a notebook in a tiny private shorthand, as he did all his conversations with friends. He seemed to have total recall, and after his death in 1975, his notebooks were left to the painter Nell Blaine. When I heard of this, I suspected that they also contained transcriptions of his conversations with me, and curious about this record of our talks together in my by-then faraway youth, I asked Nell if I could see them. She told me that they were indecipherable, and when I persisted and said I'd like to try to figure out the script, she replied that, in any case, they were inaccessible in a warehouse.

On a trip to Greece, Nell Blaine had caught polio and had to be flown home in an iron lung, at which time she fell in love with her marvelous Welsh nurse, Dilys Evans. Miraculously, Nell emerged from the iron lung and went on with her painting career, and I used to see her in her wheelchair at various events with her nurse lover. What happened to her things, and the Howard Griffin notebooks, after her death I've never been able to learn. But the notebooks, deciphered, might be a treasure trove of verbatim transcriptions from that era.

Herman Rose, a painter friend from New York whom I've always considered one of the two geniuses I've known in my life, the other being Alfred Chester, showed up, and Clifford, who equally admired his painting, made an extra effort to make sure he was comfortable.

Herman was not easy to please, but he was the kind of person everyone tried to cater to. I had noticed in New York that when he sent food back in restaurants, as he continually did, or demanded a change in his order, waitresses never minded. He had been in one of my psychiatrist's groups, so I'd heard a lot about him in my own group because he had been included in a show called Fifteen Americans at the Museum of Modern Art, and was a minor celebrity among us. He was known for his New York cityscapes made up of tiny painstaking daubs of color, like jewels.

I first met him at a party thrown by one of the groupniks, where he was lying drunk on the floor, waving an arm about, saying "Take my rose," which endeared him to me immediately. I joined him on the floor and he invited me to sit for a portrait. He was an indefatigable worker with all those meticulous little dabs of paint and for the following year, which it took him to finish the painting, I bicycled every Sunday the twenty miles into New York from Lynbrook to his Union Square studio where he posed me in a plaid flannel shirt holding my guitar—I sang my union and social protest songs to him.

A child of ignorant, immigrant Russian Jews, Herman had the kind of looks that could be homely or handsome, according to his mental state. When he felt good about himself he presented a noble Renaissance head to the world, and when he felt neurotic he was a shambling Chaplinesque figure with baggy drawers. In fact, he is brilliant, but dotty. A complete New Yorker, his idea of nature, he once told me, was a weed pushing up through a crack in the pavement, and he saw the traffic coming down the avenues as a herd of buffalo. So when he arrived at Yaddo, so different from everything he was used to, it boded no good. Trying to paint outdoors, he was attacked by clouds of mosquitoes that infested the woodsy, marshy grounds. Even with years of therapy, he tended toward melancholy and vagueness, which Elia Braca, his wife, a high spirited actress, could bring him out of with her lively chatter, hysterical flights and quarrels, which kept him from sinking into his usual fog. But unable to paint in the bucolic world of Yaddo, where he couldn't run out to the corner coffee shop or see a movie, he soon terribly missed his wife and his New York life and had to leave. He had lasted all of a week, but it was with considerable regret and assurances that he was welcome back at any time, that Clifford and even Mrs. Ames bid this saintly innocent goodbye.

Though we were all dedicated to one art or another, over the years some of the people I met there would go in unexpected directions. Richard Olney, a fair-haired Midwesterner, in those days was a painter who did portraits using the wooden tip of the back of his paintbrush dipped in inks, rather than the brush end, to draw with, which sounded, when I posed for him, like chalk on a blackboard. But he soon moved to France, became a culinary expert, and wrote the classic cookbook *Simple French Cooking*.

Painter Tobias Schneebaum was an even more startling example of switching careers. Tall, slender, and graceful, he trailed around after studly bantam rooster Dudley Huppler, a painter he was having an affair with. Toby didn't exactly give up painting, but a year later on a Fullbright in Peru, his life took an almost fictional turn when he walked into the Amazon jungle and discovered, or was discovered by, a group of naked cannibals, who, to his delight, stripped him of his clothes and led him to their village where he slept with them in uninhibited "body piles" in the men's house—all of which he chronicled vividly in *Keep the River on Your Right*. From then on Tobias was hooked on cannibals, who inexplicably saw this Brooklyn Jew as one of them, rather than someone to be eaten. He would work for Tiber Press in New York for part of the year, silk screening Christmas cards to be sold in elegant department stores like Lord & Taylor, and when he had saved enough money he took off for the remoter and more primitive parts of the planet, traveling through deserts and jungles, and became an expert on "sex among the savages." He finally found his Eden among the stone-age Asmat people of New Guinea, who unlike his Amazon tribe had recently abandoned headhunting and cannibalism. But there was some backsliding on their part, notably in the case of Michael Rockefeller, who unaccountably "disappeared" on an expedition to collect artifacts there. Tobias, who once again escaped this dire fate, learned first hand about the

Asmats' unusual bisexuality—kept secret from the missionaries, of course, which he reveals in his book *Where the Spirits Dwell.*

On this visit, when I wasn't happy with myself or my writing, I was grateful for Clifford's reassuring presence and patient ear. For all his good cheer, he had a mournful streak himself. He was an orphan, raised by foster parents and never knew his origins. But he was content to live peacefully and paint at Yaddo until some friends encouraged him to write to the Red Cross and ask if they could find his real parents. Several years later, out of the blue, he got a call from California—it was from his father, an old Finnish carpenter, who had had to put the children into foster care when their mother died and, through a bureaucratic mixup, had lost contact with Clifford. After flying out for a reunion visit with his newly discovered family, Clifford told me, his father gave him the money to go to Finland where he could get acquainted with his Finnish relations and his Finnish heritage. Leaving the safety of Yaddo, he set off on the trip with a muscle-bound boyfriend—he had a weakness for showy muscles in both men and women, especially female lifeguards. When the hunk deserted him in Denmark with the rest of their funds, Clifford, stranded, got in touch with a Danish writer, Elsa Gress, whom he had known intimately at Yaddo in the course of his duties, when he had ended up in her bed after a boozy party. At that time, Elsa, who was no beauty, had been in the United States on a fellowship, but then an academic lover denounced her as a Communist and, in spite of her being pregnant with his child, she was deported. Reunited in Denmark, Clifford and Elsa, a decidedly odd couple, got married and had two children. Clifford lived there the rest of his life, going on with his painting, as Elsa became a prominent arts celebrity, her gnomelike face much caricatured in the Danish papers.

These were the years when it seemed that Ralph Pomeroy could not fail to become successful. He had the fair WASP looks that are adored in Jewish New York, knew all the right people, and was publishing poems in the glossy pages of *Harper's Bazaar* and the *New Yorker.* Andy Warhol, not yet a superstar, collaborated with him on a book of drawings and poems. He even landed a bread and butter job as travel and entertainment editor for one of the Condé Nast publications that could have led to a substantial job in publishing, but that wasn't the kind of glamorous career, the fame and glory, he dreamed of. So in 1956, he left New York for San Francisco, where Freddie Kuh, who had started a restaurant, could help him get settled.

In our high bohemian days, none of us would ever have predicted for Freddie that he'd become a restaurateur. The youth who lolled in the bathtub at the Hotel Montana in Paris for hours turned out to be capable of putting in the hard work necessary to make his restaurant a success, as he could not devote the same effort to being a writer or painter. But he did put his talents to work in creating the Old Spaghetti Factory and Excelsior Café, so named because he took over a burned-out Italian pasta factory in North Beach. It became a national institution, and its antiques barn décor that Freddie created was widely imitated. He quickly became a typical restaurateur, portly, bearded, and jovial, but, untypically, opened a theater in one wing of the restaurant where the successful hippie musical *Beach Blanket Babylon* got its start, and after it moved on to a larger theater, Freddie invited a flamenco troupe to become the resident company. The restaurant, which served cheap but wholesome Italian food, attracted a large public, though the bar was always AC-DC. Eventually, he branched out and bought the Savoy-Tivoli restaurant around the corner, which he decorated wittily with faux marble columns—he knew an artist who was a skilled marbleizer—and here, the bar section became completely gay. He liked to brag that he had a gay bar. But even with success he never had a lover—once he had money he was afraid of being taken for a ride—and Ralph remained the most significant person in his life, though there was to be a terrible rift ahead for them.

9

I have come to see my depression of that era, in large measure, the result of my psychiatrist and fellow groupniks targeting my homosexuality as the cause of all my misery, seeing it as "simply" the result of an unworked-through "oedipal situation," which the group dynamics would resolve. Ludicrous as it now seems, I bought it, lock, stock, and barrel, and was even willing to go straight, if that would solve my problems—except that I was gay. Therefore, it is ironic that three years of several group meetings a week, a treatment that was supposed to help me, had left my ego and life in tatters. But I finally caught on to the brutal punishment I was taking, and in 1955 I walked out. By luck this coincided with my second two-month fellowship to Yaddo. For I was not only broke, but desperately in need of being taken care of, in order to think about how to go on with my post-therapy life.

I was in a very confused state and again doing little writing in my Yaddo studio, when I discovered the poetry of Frank O'Hara.

$\mathcal{L}$istening to Maria Callas in Bellini's *Norma* on the radio recently brought back to me my brief affair in the fifties with the late poet Frank O'Hara. Frank adored *Norma,* particularly those dizzying vocal duets between the ladies. But he dismissed all the fuss over Callas, whose performance in the title role was getting raves, considering her an unnecessary and expensive import, when "we" had "our own" Zinka Milanov, as he put it. This was part of the Frank O'Hara mentality I found unusual at first. He was always using that phrase "our own"—"our own painters," "our own actors," "our own galleries," even "our own duo piano team," which turned out to be Gold and Fizdale, whom I frequently heard on a classical music station. What I came to understand, when I got to know him, was that his crowd, with its "own" poets, painters, museum curators, and so on, comprised a new arts movement, of which he was clearly the center.

On that visit to Yaddo in the spring of 1955, when I wasn't walking moodily in the surrounding woodlands, where, a century before, Edgar Allen Poe, in a black suit, was said to have wandered shouting "Nevermore!"—presumably the inspiration for "The Raven"—I spent much of my time in the library, which spilled out from one of the oak-paneled rooms onto shelves lining the halls of the dark, cluttered but imposing mansion. It was in this unreal atmosphere, disoriented by the grim oedipal struggles I had been engaged in in my therapy, that I came across Frank O'Hara's poems in *Poetry* magazine.

I had been hopefully, if unsuccessfully, submitting my poems to *Poetry* myself. The poetry world back then, in contrast to today's, was terribly limited and the periodicals that did take poetry were restrictive, even prudish, about what could be published. I was too informal, too far out, too Jewish, or too openly queer, though they all published me eventually. But now in stuffy little *Poetry* magazine I was electrified by Frank O'Hara's swishy, surrealist, almost zany poems, so fresh and funny. I had to admire anybody who could write like that and get away with it. Frank O'Hara had gone to Harvard, I read in the Contributors Notes, where so many other poets seemed to have gone, including Dunstan Thompson—it was the world of the silver spoon, to which I could never belong. When I read Frank's poems enthusiastically to the other guests, who had gathered at the cocktail hour in Yaddo's baronial hall for predinner drinks and chat, the listeners were offended at their irresponsibility, their flaunting of homosexuality, their sparkling decadence, and let me know it with yelps of outrage. No one felt neutral about them. My bell jar lifted a little, as Sylvia Plath put it about the effects of her first shock treatment.

When I returned to New York at the beginning of that summer, I slipped into the back row of a poetry reading by Frank O'Hara and John Ashbery at the Egan Gallery. The walls of the room were lined with distorted self-portraits by the artist Earl Kerkam, grotesquely descriptive of the way I was feeling about myself. O'Hara and Ashbery, looking like the young Harvard graduates they were in button-down shirts and ties, were seated on folding chairs before the crowded room, heads bent over their manuscripts and without any concession to performance, as they read heavily romantic poems about Venice. Smiling occasionally with appreciation at their own clever bits, they would flick a look now and then at the audience, which sat listening with a kind of awe, typical of poetry audiences in The Presence of Poets, participating in a sacred rite. And with fashionable poets it's even more so. Enjoyment has nothing much to do with it, since poetry readings are not entertainments, though the poems we were listening to in the Egan Gallery were, in this case, quite charming.

Afterward, I went up and introduced myself to Frank, who left no doubt that he wanted me to stick around. Though he was not my type, as we used to say, I didn't have anything better to do in that grim postanalysis period. And though I wasn't looking for a lover, I was definitely intrigued by his aura of confidence, and grateful that he went for me.

Frank was somewhat younger than me, perhaps in his mid- or upper-twenties. He wasn't conventionally good-looking with his beaky nose, petulant lips, long-lashed round blue eyes, and a big brainy skull, which was emphasized by receding fair hair that he wore short in those pre-Beatles days. But he had a nice enough body, slender and with the almost transparent, lightly freckled skin of the ginger man. Full of high energy, Frank lived in a casually bohemian style, as I learned that night, sharing a ramshackle apartment in an Upper East Side tenement with a writer friend, Joe LeSueur. This was long before the neighborhood was gentrified, and shortly before I met him, Frank had even been shot in the arm in a stickup in the grubby hallway entrance of his building.

Frank and Joe, who were not exactly lovers, each had a bedroom off the sizable main room, with its expanse of splintery wooden floor, featuring a life-size plaster sculpture by George Segal, I think, on which the boys casually draped their shirts and ties and coats. Frank said he wished he had a piano, but luckily didn't, since he would be practicing all the time and never get any writing done. In any case, I never saw him working at anything. But he had music on constantly, and besides operas like *Norma,* he particularly loved the Russians, Glière and Scriabin, but also flamboyant romantics like Rachmaninoff, as well as the poets, Pasternak and Mayakovsky.

Frank took lightly the cockroach problem in the apartment, which was crawling with them. When he had made an attempt to exterminate them, he said a delegation of roaches waited for him on his pillow when he came home at night to complain.

I admired how Frank made his life in New York, where I could never feel I had one, especially after the therapy group that had filled up my life with meetings for years, most of them in the evenings, and my social life dwindled. The city was his playground, whereas I drifted around it, feeling out of place everywhere. My friends were scattered, each in a different world, none connected with the other. Frank's friends, and there were enormous numbers of them, were a cohesive group that revolved around him. Once I started staying over at his apartment, I met many of them, some of whom would become famous—artists Larry Rivers, Grace Hartigan, Jane Freilicher, Jane Wilson, and Fairfield Porter, gallery director John Myers, art critic John Gruen, book editor Michael de Capua, playwright Arnold Weinstein, poets Kenneth Koch, John Ashbery, and James

Schuyler—tons of friends. He even had curator friends in all the museums, as well as pianist Alvin Novak and painter John Button who presided as a couple over the front desk of the Museum of Modern Art, where he himself worked upstairs. His world also intersected with Julian Beck and Judith Malina's Living Theatre, which had put on plays by John Ashbery and Frank. The two poets had even played dogs in a play by Picasso at the Cherry Lane Theatre.

After my therapy, which looked on homosexuality as sick, and I myself had accepted that judgment, it was a relief to be in a world where it was accepted as normal. Frank made no bones about being gay, and some of the seemingly straight painters were bisexual. Fairfield Porter, the landscape painter who had six children, was hopelessly in love with him. The darkly handsome Larry Rivers always resumed his long-term affair with Frank in between wives and girlfriends.

Like many young New Yorkers, Frank went out every night, but always got up in the morning for work at MOMA, where he was an assistant curator for traveling exhibitions. He said he wrote his poems on his lunch hour, though on fine days went into Central Park and ate hot dogs—even back then, my Jewish dietary instincts would never have let me eat junk food so casually. His careless attitude toward his writing also surprised me. He said if a telephone call interrupted him, the poem ended there, perhaps an aspect of "chance" composition he and John Ashbery had picked up from John Cage. This spontaneous method, much like the Beats who were also against revising and rewriting, turned out to be a convenient solution to the pace of his life, his necessity to be constantly active and in a social whirl.

He also was a proponent of surrealism and French literature as antidotes to the academic poetry then in vogue. Prefiguring Pop Art and Andy Warhol, who was still drawing women's shoes for the advertisements of fashionable department stores, Frank and John Ashbery never denied the role in their lives of the pop culture they had grown up with—the funnies, movies, radio, popular songs, and slang. They were unashamed in their admiration for trash. High class from the start, they knew who they were: They were trashy *and* high class. How different I found Frank from my bohemian world, for whom being a writer or artist meant being an outsider. Frank belonged to a new breed, who were not alienated from society, even if they were avant-garde. Their avant-garde was about to become the fashion.

New York, that summer when I met him, was still pretty much mired in the witch-hunt atmosphere—after caving in to McCarthy and HUAC, the arts and intellectual community was generally sunk in a bad hangover. There were glimmers of light, though I didn't see them at the time. If only a few depressed Villagers continued to patronize traditional hangouts like the San Remo Bar on MacDougal Street, the Cedar Tavern just north of Washington Square was humming with a whole new nonpolitical scene around painters like Jackson Pollock, de Kooning, and Kline, a scene of which Frank O'Hara and John Ashbery seemed to be the prophets. It was a movement that was gathering force and definition, even benefiting from the witch-hunt. Like the Russian poet Boris Pasternak, who stood aside from the Soviet political arena, Frank exhibited a similar detachment toward American political events. He and his artist friends were starting fresh, without the burden of the compromised politics of the thirties and forties, with its party-line simplifications and its naive populist idealism. I sympathized with that, but they also appeared indifferent to the victims of McCarthyism. It was something new in bohemia not to identify with the victim.

According to this new arts movement, poets and painters were considered to have a special affinity, and Art News regularly featured poets writing on painters. Richard Miller and his wife Daisy Alden, along with Miller's lover, Floriano Vecchi, published them together in their magazine, *Folder,* and in beautifully printed collectors' editions by Tiber Press, the same one that employed Tobias Schneebaum as a silk-screen printer. Even though I had appeared in the magazine myself, I was largely ignorant at the time of these new developments in the arts world. For me, *Folder* simply was a place to publish my poems.

That was the year of Elia Kazan's film *East of Eden,* and Frank and his friends went to see it again and again, especially for James Dean and his dance in the bean rows. And though it didn't make a huge impact in New York, which is never impressed much by what goes on in the rest of the country except for Hollywood, it was the year of Allen Ginsberg's historic "Howl" trial in San Francisco, which helped release poetry from its petrified standards and made the Beat Generation famous. New York did not really pull out of its witch-hunt gloom until the end of the decade, when Barney Rosset of Grove Press went to court and won the right to publish *Lady Chatterley's Lover* and *Tropic of Cancer.* In 1955, the arts scene in New York still seemed dead to me, and only the Frank O'Hara world offered a glimmer of life.

The fifties was an age when, if you were "sensitive," you had to be "neurotic," which meant you had problems of "guilt" and "anxiety" and "adjustment," which always had "sexual problems" at the root. Sex, itself, was usually looked on as a sickness in those moralistic years. In fact, almost everyone I knew in New York was in therapy of one kind or another and many gays beside me were driven to try to go straight. Frank was tolerant of all that, but he himself would have none of it. And there was no evidence that he needed it, even if he had a problem coping with his widowed mother, an alcoholic, and was concerned about his younger sister in a private school. But he lacked any interest, even in his poetry, in self-exploration, or self-analysis. That was unusual for that Age of Therapy, but may have accounted for his tremendous outward energy. Somehow, his family did not keep him tied up in knots of guilt, as mine did, and ruin his life. But then, he wasn't Jewish. He gave me an image of a different possibility, that of an adult male with a circle of friends, enjoying the city and his job, functioning as poet and art critic and even culture czar, having lovers, living without my obsession with neurosis, without torment about being gay. It seemed very grown up to me, and desirable.

In contrast, everything I did seemed arbitrary. My years in the therapy group had disconnected me, not only from a social life, but even from the literary world. Frank must have seen what a mess I was. His attention boosted my ego tremendously, and I was grateful to him for that, even if I wasn't in love with him. I squirm to think of it now, but I remember saying to Frank that I needed to become "a unified person," and he simply couldn't understand my not accepting myself as I was, as me. But I saw Frank's personality as unified, and mine as fractured. When you are unified, I felt, you don't question your poems, you just write them. *Because they are you.* You write out of what you are. You write what you are. And what Frank wrote was entirely *him*.

Frank's idea, which I found exciting and new, was that you didn't have to assume any "stance" to write a poem, you just started from whatever you felt like at the moment. In other words, you didn't have to put on an act. A poem could even be what you might say to a friend over the phone. This free and easy approach was a liberating influence, and I was soon able to start enjoying writing again.

He was also generous, and had been supporting his roommate, Joe LeSueur, who was writing a novel. Frank knew how broke I was, and in the morning before he went to work, showed me the art book where he kept his spare cash, and told me to help myself. But there, too, I had scruples, perhaps out of fear of becoming dependent, too attached.

During my period with Frank, Joe LeSueur frequently had a boyfriend staying over, too, a hunky actor, unverbal in the Method-actor Brando-style of the decade, who like me had "problems." Le-Sueur, like Frank, seemed neurosis-free. He had fled his Mormon past, but it appeared to be a successful and complete escape. Earlier, he had gone into therapy with Paul Goodman, the poet and social scientist, who had developed, along with Frederick Perls, Gestalt Therapy, which was particularly popular with artists because it was nonjudgmental about sexual tastes. LeSueur was the perfect blond WASP with a straight spine that I, who was always collapsing, admired. Like Ralph Pomeroy, he couldn't help but be attractive to New York Jews. Paul Goodman, who was largely gay himself, was crazy about him. Goodman openly proclaimed the virtue of a therapist having sex with patients, insisting, in opposition to the social norm of the time, that sex was good for people. This caused an out-cry from the psychiatric establishment and endless controversy, but Goodman stood his ground. At the drunken end of a cocktail party at the Gotham Book Mart, I saw Goodman kneeling over a visiting Welsh poet, who had apparently passed out, masturbating him, explaining to onlookers that the poet needed "relaxing."

Though I knew Frank wrote reviews for *Art News,* and was influential, my ignorance of his world was nearly total. But it soon became alarmingly clear that one of the principles of the new movement was that the United States was no longer provincial, but had its own culture to be proud of, and even its own art form, Abstract Expressionism, that was superior to anything Europe had to offer. In other words, along with economic supremacy, we had become the world's art capital, surpassing Paris, where the arts were said to be in decline and artists mired in outmoded leftist thinking. "America has come of age," would soon become the slogan of corporate America, and especially *Time Magazine,* which would champion abstract art, to the dismay of older realist artists who were being shut out, losing their galleries, collectors, and museum purchases. Nevertheless, Frank's circle included realist painters, too, but these rejected the social concerns of the previous generation and concentrated on "painterly" qualities.

I never heard Frank badmouth *Time Magazine* and its glib Cold War simplicities, but I don't think he would ever have taken a job at *Time,* the fast track for literary success, which he could have done easily with his Harvard degree. He didn't join any establishment, unless you consider MOMA as one. He was out to create a new, more tony art world, springing up in the wreckage left by HUAC. Meanwhile, bohemia for him was a playground in which to be young and sexy in, and also orient himself for the seemingly inevitable position of power he was not exactly aiming for, but seemed inevitable. And it was obvious to me, and to everyone, that he was destined for it.

Ralph Pomeroy was never in this league—he lacked the intellectual fiber. It was new for me to meet someone who was poised for fame and saw fame for his whole crowd, since being a real artist, according to my old bohemian philosophy, meant opting out, not joining in. Many of the artists in a movement beginning to be called The New York School had already moved out to the Hamptons, an enclave of the rich. Perhaps for painters it's important to hobnob with the people who can afford to buy your work. It's nice to have money, but as a natural rebel, I couldn't help being contemptuous of an arts world that allied itself with the rich, snobbish, and fashionable, even if it was a reaction against the discredited proletarian views of the previous generation. The few years gap in our ages made all the difference, and Frank's generation didn't see being taken up by the media and the wealthy as a sellout. This change must have been in the air, because on the West Coast, too, the Beats were getting on the bandwagon and courting the press, even if their act was to portray themselves as scruffily defiant of bourgeois society. But that group was also reaching for celebrity status. Bohemia was dying.

I had already gone to gallery openings, bohemian village bars, and literary cocktail parties on my own, but with Frank I had an entrée to the inner circle. At the San Remo, one evening, we were joined by the poet Chester Kallman, puffy-faced, flabby, and balding, but legendary for his association with W. H. Auden. In 1939, Kallman, a student at Brooklyn College, and his fellow student Harold Norse, had concocted a plan to seduce Auden and his friend Christopher Isherwood, who had recently immigrated from England to the United States, and were giving a reading in New York. I heard this story from Robert Friend who was also at the Auden/Isherwood reading where the seduction was to take place. Although he had graduated Brooklyn College earlier, Robert knew the two student poets who told him about their scheme. It turned out to be a historic moment. Blond Kallman and swarthy Norse went up to the two Brits after the reading and asked to interview them for the school paper. Auden, who went for blonds, was reported to have said, when Kallman arrived at his apartment for the interview, that he was "the wrong blond." But in no time, he turned out to be the right blond after all, whatever trouble Kallman would cause him. And no doubt about it, Kallman was a royal fuckup and troublemaker, but one who would occupy the space in Auden's soul that we all have waiting within us for our true mate. Harold Norse was not so lucky with Isherwood after the interview, though he became a confidant to Auden, who definitely needed one, as he struggled with the difficult task of keeping track of his wildly promiscuous young lover.

That night at the San Remo, Kallman brought us back for a drink to the musty apartment he shared with Auden in the parlor floor of a brownstone on St. Mark's Place, though, to my disappointment, Auden was out for the evening. Kallman, interested in rough trade, had previously been entrapped by detectives—at that time, a plainclothesman on the morality squad would wave his dick at you in public urinals and if you grabbed the bait his partner outside slapped handcuffs on you. Unfortunately, shortly after our San Remo meeting, Kallman picked up a tough number who again turned out to be a cop. Auden bought off the judge, as was common in those days, for five hundred dollars, and, on the advice of the judge, shipped Kallman to the safety of the more tolerant Mediterranean world, where he lived off and on for the remainder of his life. Except for the opera libretti he wrote with Auden, Kallman's own poetry career faded away. Or perhaps it was the association with such a powerful and successful poet as Auden that has overshadowed his work.

At the Tibor de Nagy Gallery—one of "our" galleries, as Frank put it, where many of his friends showed their work—Frank introduced me to the large, supercilious-looking director, John Bernard Myers. Putting on a performance for us in his queeny style, Myers treated the gallery's backer, Tibor de Nagy, with bitchy contempt. Tibor, used to the role of whipping boy, seemed to enjoy this as a clever display, wincing theatrically under the barbed lashing. For Myers, too, was becoming a power in the art world and could do no wrong. Another time that summer, one of Frank's closest painter friends, Jane Freilicher, drove us to what was then called the Coast Guard Beach at Riis Park, a section populated by artists and gays that would later, for a time, go legally nudist. Driving home, Freilicher pointed out the Brooklyn neighborhood of her youth, which

I'm sure appeared very exotic to New Englander Frank O'Hara, much as I must have been to him, with my dark Semitic looks.

Frank was not a demanding lover—luckily, since I wasn't comfortable with my sexuality. Typical of the guilt-ridden, I wasn't keen on having sex with anybody I knew, preferring strangers, and liked keeping my sex life a secret. So being public in a love affair was difficult. Anal sex, particularly, was not something I felt easy about. Reacting to my generally inhibited state, Frank wondered once whether it would help me loosen up if I fucked him, and if he should just take the initiative and pop me inside him, so to speak, but it embarrassed me to talk about it. In the state I was in, I couldn't pick up on this suggestion, and he didn't pursue it further. He was obviously completely uninhibited, and I couldn't help but notice that there was a suspicious darkish stain on the bedsheets, that may have been skidmarks left by an earlier lover, God knows how long before, for he and Joe LeSueur never did the laundry.

Frank was painted by a number of artists, but none captured his penis as I remember it. Though nothing to be ashamed about, it was remarkable not for its size, but for his long, loose foreskin, which seemed designed for a much larger organ, and gave it the appearance of a horse cock. As someone who was circumcised, this was intriguing to me. It was as if he had enough for both of us in that department.

Among what appeared to be a number of best friends, John Ashbery was clearly Frank's best friend. As poets, they were linked from Harvard days, sharing ideas, giving readings together, and at that time even writing very much alike, as I had noticed at the Egan Gallery. Neither had a better reputation than the other, and both wrote art criticism of the same bewilderingly opaque, surrealist/impressionistic variety, as if reflecting the abstract art they promoted. But Frank was obviously becoming the power center of their world in New York, and he was the one everyone was talking about. So there may have been more competitiveness on Ashbery's part than anyone was aware of, or that he ever expressed, and tensions may have been building. The situation had to be intolerable for someone equally ambitious, and I got the impression that John, who was in therapy then, worked out with his analyst the solution of him going to France and salvaging his ego by making his career there, leaving the New York scene to Frank. Just before he left that summer for a Fulbright fellowship, which would lead to a decade living in Paris, Frank and I met Ashbery at the San Remo, where he read us his latest poem, a marvelous love poem much unlike his later, maddeningly evasive work.

My affair with Frank, which was by no means stormy or passionate, ended abruptly later that summer, though with considerable regret on my part. Frank broke it off. Before catching the train to the Hamptons, where he was going to stay with Fairfield Porter and his family, he checked a valise in a coin locker at Pennsylvania Station, assuming it would be safe for the weekend, but by some fluke the lockers were cleaned out by the staff before Frank got back to the city and could retrieve it. The loss of this bag, which contained not only manuscripts but, he said, his diary, and letters discussing drug deals, threw him into a panic over the possibility of it falling into the hands of the police. I had never noticed in him the least interest in drugs, and assumed this had something to do with the Larry Rivers crowd, full of druggy jazz musicians. From his panic, though, it had to be more than letters, and I suspected that Frank might have been stashing drugs for Rivers. Frank began avoiding me, suggesting that it was because of his anxiety over a possible scandal, even arrest. I couldn't quite understand this, and there might have been another explanation—a new lover, perhaps, or more likely, a dissatisfaction with our low-key sex life.

If I suffered over our breakup, though, it was brief, and I soon found my life taking a new direction, one that had nothing to do with this crowd. I had never belonged there anyway. But I had gotten from Frank some new and liberating ideas about poetry and life that during the next several years would help me reorient myself. Every so often you have to shift gears and start writing differently, and Frank O'Hara showed me the way. Or gave me the courage to follow my instincts and accept what was happening already—a pity

I'd thrown away all those poems that seemed to come too easily. The transitional period can be difficult, and there are sometimes years of uncertainty until you find the new voice or subject matter or direction and move forward again. Now I found that I could just write my poems and, as Frank did, let them be the poems of their moment, an expression of that impulse—risking the danger that you reveal yourself as you are, in his case charming and brilliant, in my case a jerk. But that's okay—Woody Allen has built a career on being a schlemiel. Thanks to Frank, I was able to get through my block and start writing again, even accept what I was writing.

A couple of years later, I was at the St. Mark's Baths, a seedy, late-night sex scene that was tolerated by the police, perhaps because it was part of the old Bowery, kind of a moral no-man's-land, when Frank came in with his friend, the poet Jimmy Schuyler, in tow. Jimmy was a sweet, helpless man who seemed constrained by gentility from showing his rage, and cracked up periodically. Leaving Jimmy to wander the halls by himself, Frank and I ducked into one of the empty cubbyhole rooms to talk. Sitting on the sagging cot with its drab sheets, unchanged from the last occupants, he said he wanted to start up with me again, but by this time I was warier about getting involved in his world, and begged off. Though I was still in a troubled state, I didn't need him anymore. After that, whenever we met each other at parties or other events, he was always friendly, his most charming self, to me, even though I heard that with his growing fame he had lost his simple, unassuming manner. At parties, it was said, he could be quite arrogant and play the star, enthroned in a chair, receiving tributes from admirers. But I never saw that side of him. Nor was he the heavy drinker he was later said to be.

I'm sure it was he who got Donald Allen to include me in the seminal anthology, *The New American Poetry, 1945–1960,* published by Grove Press, in which the poets were divided into several so-called movements. I found myself grouped with The New York School, all of whom had been in Frank O'Hara's circle, a qualification I barely fulfilled, though I was as much a New York poet as any of them.

But not everyone in the inner circle was pleased that I'd been included. After Frank's death in 1966, a student in the notoriously bad-tempered Kenneth Koch's poetry class at Columbia University reported to me that he had proposed writing about me for a term paper. "Not in my class!" Koch snapped at him.

So it is ironic nowadays that I frequently hear my name linked with Frank O'Hara's. And in James Schuyler's journals, published after his death, he writes that when Frank started to go with me, Jimmy was relieved that his friend had found someone nice at last.

10

The editorial offices of New Directions Press, the awesome publisher of avant-garde literature, were in an odd triangular building in the Village, with the Avenue of the Americas on one side and a crooked lane, Cornelia Street, on the other. The Cornelia Street side of the building was notable because W. H. Auden lived across the street there for several years before he moved, in 1953, to St. Mark's Place across town. I used to walk by his building as if by a shrine.

It was at New Directions that I met the poet May Swenson, though she wasn't at a publication party I went to at the editorial offices in 1950. The party was given for *A Family Romance,* a first novel by Elizabeth Pollet, the blonde, perfect *shiksa* wife of the crazy poet Delmore Schwartz, who, she later wrote in her memoir of the marriage, had tortured her sexually, to the point of burning her vagina with a cigarette. I knew no one at the party except editor David MacDowell who was still working there before he moved to Random House and got me the book contract. But whatever literary celebrities I managed to meet at this event—and because Elizabeth Pollet was married to Schwartz the whole *Partisan Review* crowd, the

New York Intellectuals, had to be present—all is overshadowed in my memory by the agonies of embarrassment I suffered over having stuffed several books from the wall shelves under my jacket, and then, as I left, having to shake hands at the door with the publisher, James Laughlin, a tall, forbidding, aristocratic figure, while trying to keep the books from tumbling out with my other arm. He had to have seen them, but gent that he was, didn't say a word. I must have been blushing scarlet, for I really wasn't good at lying or stealing.

I still have a vivid picture of May Swenson in my mind from our meeting a couple of years later when she was working at New Directions as a manuscript reader and came out to greet me one afternoon in the shabby, cluttered editorial offices. May was a small, charming woman in a white blouse with crisp, pointed collar and gathered dirndl skirt in the Villagey fashion of that time. Her face with its honest, broad cheekbones reminded me not so much of her Swedish ancestry, but of the Lapps of the Scandinavian far north, or even perhaps some American Indian connection. Her eyes were gleaming slits as distinctive as a cat's, and her small retroussé nose and mouth also had something of a cat's meow to them. Distinctive, too, was her cap of shining gold hair, like a Nordic medieval pageboy.

Her first book had already been published, and as one of the more promising young poets she had gained entrée to that exclusive circle that in the years after World War II comprised the aggressively parochial, even snobbish, poetry world, before the populist Beat revolution of the late fifties changed the shape of American poetry forever.

My poems came to May's attention from the manuscript I had submitted to New Directions. I'd always looked younger than my age but, as I approached thirty, I was already feeling a little seedy. And after the fiasco with Random House, my manuscript was getting rejected by one publisher after another. If May was first attracted to me by my poetry, after meeting me I think she responded to the lost soul I was and tried to help by bringing me into her world.

May had gotten to New York a decade before me, after graduation from college in Utah. For someone from rural America and a religious environment, she was extraordinarily capable of making her way in the city, even in the dark years of the Depression. Needing a dress for a job interview, but penniless, she told me, she didn't hesitate to steal one. She went into a department store, slipped on a dress from the racks in a try-on booth, and, putting her old dress over it, walked out of the store. Probably her youth and innocence fooled the hawk-eyed guards. But even if she had been caught, I believe she was the kind of person the world would forgive anything. In fact, once when she was hungry and broke, she said, she went into a restaurant and ordered a meal. When the waiter presented her with the check, she told him she couldn't pay, thinking she would at least have to work it off washing dishes. The waiter looked at this unworldly waif and let her go.

For years she worked in offices as a temporary typist. She wrote a brilliant, futuristic story about her experiences as a temp, in which the typist is strapped into a machine, something like a space capsule, and has to keep up with the pace the machine sets for her. But by the time I met her she had graduated to her part-time New Directions job, and was living in the Village with her friend, Pearl Schwartz, very much the New York Jew and the complete opposite of her. They were as much a wildly contrasting couple as Delmore, the other Schwartz but no relation, and Elizabeth Pollet.

Unable to hold a job myself, except sporadically, for most of the fifties, and with all my money going into my therapy group, I was again with my parents on Long Island, when I was first invited to May's apartment at 23 Perry Street, one of the quiet, residential streets in the West Village, as opposed to the more obvious touristy and nightlife areas of Christopher or Eighth Streets. She and Pearl had a floor-through in a brick and brownstone building dating from the 1840s, owned by St. John's Episcopal Church around the corner. In warm weather, parties could spill out onto her terrace in back, overlooking the lush church gardens. Besides constant trouble with the church over her legal right to the rent-controlled apartment, May had to remove her name from the mailbox, because of eager young missionaries arriving from Utah to try to bring this lapsed Mormon back into the fold.

I first came to May's literary parties, and only later was invited to the other parties May and Pearl gave together for their gay friends. It was a time in my life when meeting literary figures, and especially poets, was a major thrill, and at May Swenson's was a generous sampling, gay and straight: Babette Deutsch, Howard Griffin, Jane Mayhall and Leslie Katz, Jean Garrigue, Arthur Gregor, Sandra Hochman, the painter Hyde Solomon, Margaret Marshall, then the literary editor of *The Nation,* the *New Yorker* poetry editor Howard Moss, John Wheelright, and many others. They were all high aesthetes. At one of the parties, I remember, indelibly, Jean Garrigue, always intense, whose affairs with both men and women were legendary, taking the young Sandra Hochman's face between her hands, staring into her lovely eyes and kissing her passionately on the lips, then calling to Babette Deutsch across the room, "Babette, isn't twenty-six a wonderful age to be a poet?" The ancient poetess called back in her cracked, warbly voice, "Any age is wonderful to be a poet, Jean." On another evening, Babette Deutsch was quite disturbed to hear that I was not an admirer of Rilke, whom she had translated, and said she would read him with me. But this was shortly before the sad deterioration of her last years, and I let the brief opportunity slip by.

During these literary gatherings, Pearl, who was studying for a college degree that would eventually qualify her for a civil service job, would come in from her night classes, greet people briefly, and retire to a back room. But she was very much there at the parties for their crowd of gay friends, some of whom overlapped May's literary list—the poet Bob Hutchinson and his painter friend, Bernie Rosenquit, novelist Alma Routsong, also known as Isabel Miller, and her economist lover Betty Deran, and a whole slew of women with shifting alliances.

At the early parties, I remember Pearl announcing with pride that she and May had been together sixteen years, and May trying to shush her, as though something about that enduring a relationship sounded absurd in the world of more evanescent affairs around them. But at some later get-together, Pearl seemed to have changed, and complained openly that she didn't want to spend the rest of her life with someone who didn't take care of her properly. I thought at the time that this was just Pearl being a kvetch. Since Pearl worked at a job and May no longer had to, it could have simply been resentment that May was enjoying herself. One of Pearl's beefs with May was that before going off to her job, Pearl, who did the cooking, regularly assigned housekeeping duties to May, and these were often not carried out properly or at all. Later, after getting to know Pearl better, I understood that Pearl was particularly unhappy about the lack of sympathy she got from May for the series of ailments she was suffering from—allergies and sinus attacks, and her elbows wrapped in elastic bandages (from lesbian elbow, I was told). Pearl liked to repeat balefully, "You know, May, after forty, it's one thing after another." But May, like most people who enjoy perfect health, as she did then, had little patience with what looked to her like hypochondria.

I began to sense intrigues among the women invited to the parties. Apparently, May and Pearl had come to "an arrangement," whereby May accepted Pearl's necessity to search for a partner more sympathetic to her needs. With May's increasing literary reputation, there may also have been an element of competitiveness. Pearl, never shy about revealing the most intimate details of her affairs, complained that one of the women she had gone to bed with confessed that she was only there to get closer to May. Furious, Pearl kicked her out of bed.

During this last phase of the relationship, May was on firmer economic ground—she got a retainer from the *New Yorker*, which published her regularly, and was being sought after to give readings and workshops at universities around the country. After working at her desk mornings, she used to go out for lunch to the nearby Bigelow's Drug Store, which had a counter, where she would meet old literary friends like Jean Garrigue, novelist Marguerite Young, and Ursule Molinaro, editor of *Chelsea Review,* who wore black lipstick and fingernail polish. May also spent a lot of time (instead of cleaning the windows, as instructed) on her own activities, like making little "sound collages" on her tape recorder. These had the effect of compositions by one of the more extreme modern composers. On her tapes, she would alternate ordinary noises from the street or apartment with highly magnified tiny sounds, in a way that made none of them easy to identify. These compositions had some of the interest of her riddle poems, and luckily, they were short, when we were forced to lend polite attention. They were not much different from the concerts of atonal "modern music," which I endured out of loyalty to the avant-garde we all nominally belonged to.

May liked creating puzzles and games. Besides her book of riddle poems, *Poems to Solve,* she "made" (her word for writing) a book of shaped poems, designed eccentrically on her typewriter, and at her reading from the book at the Kaufman Auditorium of the YMHA a slide machine projected the poems onto a huge screen so we in the audience could see them as she read them, to enormous effect. But the published book, *Iconographs,* the size of a typewritten page to accommodate these quirky poems, reproduced exactly as typed, ran into trouble because it didn't fit on standard shelves.

Her cats were also an important element in May's life. One of them had been rescued newborn from the gutter in front of the house, where possibly an inexperienced mother cat had given birth to it, or had been frightened off before she could eat up the placenta and free it from its birth-sac. May and Pearl carefully snipped open the membrane with scissors, and out popped tiny Zeebeedeebee, as they named it, who grew up to inspire a number of May's poems.

May's sensibilities were always in tune with the cats', as if they were her teachers, instructing her in minute observation of the world around them. She came up with precise images, as in her description of a cat "still as a jug." In fact, her poems were solidly grounded in particulars, for like a cat, she trusted her senses. But she also had an intellectual toughness that gave her poetry structure and strength: She was opposed not only to established religion, but also to the kind of vaporous spiritual talk common among Village bohemians. She would not loosely employ certain words like "heart," "soul," "God," and derided their use in poems—even in one of mine, I must admit. But at the same time, she told me, along with most of New York's arts community, she had been impressed by a demonstration of Gurdjieff's dervish dances when he brought a group of his students to America years before. That seemed to be as far as her interest in the spiritual went. But it was not so simple. When I was a guest at the Ruth Stephan Poetry Center in Tucson, Richard Shelton, the director, drove me out into the surrounding mountains, dotted as far as one could see with the giant saguaro cactuses, like noble, primitive figures with upraised arms—an awesome sight. Shelton told me that when May was in residence at the poet's cottage at the Center, he had taken her out to witness the spectacle of a desert dawn, and she was so carried away that she fell to the ground and rolled around. I, myself, had only seen anyone react like that once before, outside of an epileptic seizure. This was at a midnight prayer meeting in a dervish house in Central Asia, where one of the dervishes was so transported during a climax of the chanting of the name of Allah that he fell to the ground in religious ecstasy.

In the early sixties, New Directions submitted the manuscript of my first book for the Lamont Award, which would have made publication possible—I was sure that May had a lot to do with it. It didn't win but I was runner-up. It was only after that, when I was well into my thirties with about two dozen rejections of my manuscript, that May advised me to make multiple submissions to publishers, a practice which at that time was unacceptable. Even though publishers could hold on to your manuscript for up to a year or longer while they decided, it was not until they relinquished it, often with only a printed rejection slip, that you were free to submit it to another. I think that May identified with me, feeling that she had had an over-long wait for her own first book.

Her advice was sound. It turned out that after I submitted the manuscript to five publishers at once, Grove Press entered it in the next year's Lamont Award competition, and this time I was the winner, making possible the publication of *Stand Up, Friend, With Me* in 1963. May's faith in my work always meant a lot to me. Later on, talking about her state of disillusionment with the poetry world and her feeling that critical standards had deteriorated, she told me that I, at least, was a real poet.

In those years, neither the women's nor the gay movement had yet crystallized and May's reputation was simply as a poet, not a woman or gay poet. Moreover, she would have firmly rejected any such labeling. Though she was perfectly comfortable being a lesbian in her own world and her poems were often based on that experience, if not explicit, poetry for our generation was not to be divided into compartments like that. Poets were poets. Even when she was an established poet, May was never one of the celebrities of the literary world—she would scorn to seek that kind of fame: The work was everything. Though for a time, in mid-career, when the poetry world was in upheaval, even she had difficulty finding a publisher.

If May Swenson did not then seem the impressive figure she has since become, it must be remembered that some of the giants, the founders, of modern poetry were still alive, and next to them everybody who came along later seemed lesser. The style and scope of these masters had a mandarin, outsized authority, making our own poetry "merely" human-size. So it was not until they were gone that May's poetry could be seen in its true uniqueness, and since her death, in its almost Elizabethan grandeur.

But even before May received the prestigious honors of her later life, she had the authority that comes from years of good critical reception and a lifetime dedicated to the highest standards. I once witnessed her meeting with the novelist Hortense Calisher, who was much more widely known than she, but could recognize a peer when she saw one. It was at the apartment of the painter Nadia Gould and her art historian husband, Philip. The two powerful women, Hortense Calisher, tall, dark, and gorgon-like, the other, May Swenson, short and fair, but each a unique phenomenon, appraised each other across the room for a time, until both at once started, "Aren't you . . . ?," and moving together to a sofa, were soon rapt in conversation that revealed their mutual admiration.

In May's private life, the relationship with Pearl continued to deteriorate, and when May went off to Purdue University as poet-in-residence, Pearl urged her to have an affair during the long separation, as she intended to do herself, in her continuing attempt to find a more compatible lifetime partner. I didn't actually take this threat seriously, since they had been together so long. But I retain an image in my mind from this period of a newly independent Pearl saying goodbye to me on the street after dinner at painter Bernie Rosenquit's apartment, tucking her cigarettes into her t-shirt sleeve and a five dollar bill into one of her socks, and setting off bravely for a women's bar up Lexington Avenue with long strides. May's departure had liberated her from any constraints their relationship had formerly imposed, and she was out on the town, determined to find her new, more satisfactory, more caring mate.

May had a monogamous nature, but she finally understood that her life with Pearl was finished. It was at Purdue that she met blonde-haired, athletic Zan Knudson, with whom she lived the rest of her life. Unfortunately, after much experience with new companions, all unsatisfactory, it didn't take long for Pearl to regret the breakup, and she began to see May Swenson as the most important person in her life.

11

$\mathcal{I}$ had never thought of doing anything but writing poetry, but that was not in itself a full-time occupation. After the affair with Frank O'Hara had ended, with no group therapy meetings to fill up my life anymore, I hardly knew what to do with myself. Elia Braca, the actress wife of Herman Rose, was playing the lead in *The Heiress* for a small company in the Village, and when I met the director after a performance she suggested I play a part in her next production, *The Imaginary Invalid* by Moliére. This experience before an audience was a revelation to me, and I decided to become an actor.

I started studying the Stanislavski Method with a shrewd dumpling of a woman, Vera Soloviova, who had been a member of the Moscow Art Theatre. Suddenly, my life was filled with classes, rehearsals, auditions. I had less time to think about myself, and, indeed, Method acting is a kind of therapy in itself, in some ways even an improvement on talk therapy, since it makes you use your body, and with the added advantage that you play characters different from yourself, the loser you're thoroughly sick of. It was also liberating to study speech and start speaking differently from little Eddie

Field with his Brooklyn accent. I remember the nerve it took, the first time I had to open my mouth with my new vowels in front of my family. It announced that I had the right to be separate from them, be my own person.

Madame Soloviova told us right off, "If you want to be an actor, learn to type." In my ambitions to be a "poet of the people," I had always resisted working in an office, but she was right—it was the best kind of work for an actor, especially doing temp typing, which allowed for taking time off for auditions and rehearsals. When I relented in my opposition to it, I found being a typist just as enjoyable as my other jobs. For truly, the work isn't what mattered, it was getting to know all kinds of people. It was at one of my temporary office assignments that I started to write a lot of poetry again. I didn't write poems at lunch, as Frank O'Hara did, but the first thing in the morning, when I sat down at my desk. Out the window was a spectacular view of the Hudson River and the New Jersey shore, and I found myself writing a new poem each day over the months I worked there, usually starting with that view out the window, and without expecting the poems to be masterpieces. Each poem felt like a small victory, a thawing.

I never made acting a lifetime career, but I had the experience of being a leading man, if only in summer theatres. It certainly was part of my development as a poet, and helped me keep audiences awake at my readings. But as the theater became less compelling, I applied for a fellowship at the MacDowell Colony in New Hampshire to concentrate on my poetry.

It was winter of 1958 and we, the "colonists," walked through silent, snowy woods to our studios, where we lit fires in our iron stoves and worked at our typewriters or easels or pianos. All night long we heard the snow plows clearing the roads linking the studios with the main house. My cheeks were so red from the cold that a Chinese painter in residence accused me of wearing makeup!

Jimmy Baldwin, whom I hadn't seen since Paris, was also a "colonist," and had the studio across the road from mine, so we often had lunch together—the lunch boxes were dropped off at our studios during the morning. Even during the day, Jimmy was a steady drinker and liked a glass of scotch and water by his typewriter as he worked—he picked icicles hanging from the roof for ice. This did not prevent him from being a hard worker, and he often went back to his cabin after dinner, through the pitch black woods, to continue with his novel-in-progress, then named *Deep Sea Diver*, which would become *Another Country* when it was published.

Jimmy was a strange looking man with his bulging eyes and spaced teeth—he was later described, accurately, as looking like a "startled bush baby." At the MacDowell Colony, he was nervous about going to the barber in the nearby all-white village of Peterboro, sure that the man had never cut the hair of an African American, so I gave him haircuts. He wore his hair in a short Afro, and I tried to shape it to minimize his oddly shaped, almost pointy, large skull.

He was quite open about having been an illegitimate child, an infant when his mother got married, and talked about his cruel stepfather. But Jimmy was also a boy preacher, which squares with his ability to mesmerize audiences later on when he became a spokesman in the civil rights struggle. It was the combination of a high school teacher who encouraged him to write and his adventures picking up men that liberated him from his religious environment. Plus his voracious reading—he told me that he had read Dickens's *A Tale of Two Cities* many times. He even did some teenage hustling on Times Square, but found it distasteful—if the john paid him before sex he would sometimes manage to get away before going through the act. After high school, he left his family in Harlem to live in the Village, where, in the bohemian arts community, he was acceptable as a black man, but his attempts to work in wartime factories were disastrous—he was once chased by a white mob down a street in a New Jersey factory town. Even later when he was famous, on visits to New York he was always being pushed hands up against a wall by police and patted down. It was to escape such humiliations and dangers that he had fled to Paris in the first place. His economic situation didn't improve until his books started to be published in the fifties.

Jimmy told me that when he was really broke in Paris he would write to Marlon Brando, who always sent him money. They had met in the men's room at the New School in the Village, where Brando was studying acting with Irwin Piscator, before he went on to Stella Adler's drama school and stardom. Jimmy was always vague about what happened between Brando and him at that "meeting" in the john, but from then on Brando never failed him when he needed him. Jimmy himself was generous with his money and supported his family, as well as old friends like the painter Beauford Delaney, who barely scraped by in Paris. For by the time we renewed our friendship at the MacDowell Colony, Jimmy had already become a successful author. In fact, he was frequently away from the MacDowell Colony, flying down to New York with rewrites of a play that Elia Kazan was working on at the Actors' Studio, after which he started calling Kazan by his nickname, Gadge.

He was always very open and straightforward with white people—essentially everybody was just people to him. When we visited a liberal white family who lived in a nearby town, he earnestly tried to make them understand what black people went through in racist America, especially what his mother went through, worrying about her children. One of the points he always made about the difference between whites and blacks was that blacks knew whites intimately from the viewpoint of the kitchens where they worked. But he made it quite clear that it was the whites who had to change.

He became a superstar of the Movement very quickly and I didn't see him much after that winter, though when I applied for a Guggenheim Fellowship, he wrote a support letter for me. And when he came to dinner once, he complained that he didn't see the people he really wanted to see, but mostly the people who pursued him.

At the MacDowell Colony I wrote a lot of poetry, and when I returned to New York that spring, I gave my first reading at the Poetry Center of the 92nd Street YMHA, in the Discovery series, with Ruth Stone and George Garrett. Madame Soloviova was there in the front row, and afterwards when she congratulated me, she said she just didn't listen to the dirty words.

I was keeping busy as an actor on the fringes of show business, filling up chinks of my time with every variety of sexual adventure, and being generally miserable and complaining about it to my long-suffering analyst, Leah Schaefer, who had been in show business herself and had finally stopped trying to turn me straight—a relief after my group experience! Working as a temp again, this time in the typing pool of an advertising agency, one day the supervisor assigned the typewriter next to me to a new temp, a sturdy, intelligent young man from California named Neil Derrick. It was a case of immediate attraction between WASP and Jew. Too bright and adventurous to remain back home on the cattle ranch in the Central Valley, he had escaped to the city the first chance he got—first going to college in Berkeley and then to New York to pursue some vague idea of a Madison Avenue career. He looked like an up and coming young professional in his trim Bloomingdale's basement suit, but though he would be hired anywhere at the drop of a hat, he really had no interest in that. He worked as a temp until he saved up enough to go to Europe and live there as long as he could, which is what he really cared about. If he said he wanted to be a writer, he did nothing more than keep a journal, but that's as far as it went, so my active literary career made me even more attractive to him. We started a non-stop conversation that led the supervisor to switch him to another typewriter several rows away from me.

We were soon going out together, and in a few weeks I moved into his cold-water flat on West 47th Street in Hell's Kitchen off Times Square. Cold-water flat didn't mean cold water anymore by then, and even central heating had just been put into the building, though the toilet, which we shared with a large, noisy neighboring family, was still outside in the hall. Leah Schaefer was greatly relieved by this development in my life and, when I brought Neil to meet her, gave her approval.

"The Garden," the last poem in *Stand Up, Friend, With Me,* is a celebration of how finding my life partner—and I had no doubt this was a miracle—changed everything. Before this, I had only thought of myself as a poet whose role was to be a public figure, but had never seen myself living a private life. Unfortunately, I wasn't at all successful at this. But when I finally connected with somebody, it meant that I didn't have to go on being the scapegoat/victim and the voice of suffering mankind, which I wasn't really suited for anyway. I also abandoned my theatrical career and concentrated on writing again. Here, I was able to latch on to one important aspect of Neil's character, one I totally lacked—he kept an orderly schedule, with regular waking-, meal-, work-, and bedtimes. I'd always written sporadically, when the spirit moved me, if I had an idea, or if I could bear to sit at my typewriter. But now, following his lead, every morning I was free I went straight to my desk. Of course, to write fiction, which was Neil's ambition, you have to be disciplined, but even for poetry, which needs such intense concentration, it helps to be there every day, even if you just write letters—I always found letters a good warm-up. And under my influence, or perhaps having to live up to my belief in him, he started writing short stories.

After our ad agency jobs ended, he landed a permanent half-time afternoon job at the front desk of the Museum of Modern Art, which allowed him to keep a morning writing schedule, while I settled into a long-term temp job at the Magazine Institute, a correspondence school in Rockefeller Center that advertised blatantly that anyone could earn good money from their writing and offered a free "aptitude test" that no one failed, unless they couldn't pay the tuition. It was in a back office that I met, hunched over a pile of students' assignments, a novelist I had long admired, a mild little man named Millen Brand, the author of *The Outward Room* and the screenplay of the harrowing film *The Snakepit,* set in a mental hospital. A saintly idealist of an old lefty but by no stretch of the imagination a "security risk," he had been interrogated by the House Un-American Activities Committee. He refused to cooperate, was blacklisted, banned, and, unable to find an appropriate job, was now uncomplainingly working for pennies per manuscript corrected, with eyes permanently red-rimmed behind his thick glasses from long hours on the job. He also had terrible woman trouble, with a hysterical ex-wife who stormed in screaming for him one day and, when she found him absent from his back office, smashed a bottle of champagne sitting there, a gift from one of his students, over his typewriter.

I'd been working there a couple of years when I got a telephone call that would make a huge difference in my life—the fulfillment of my ultimate dream.

12

*I*n 1960, a few months after I moved in with Neil, Alfred Chester returned from Paris and our old acquaintance immediately turned into firm friendship. He, too, had changed into a new person during his decade abroad. He was still strange-looking with his ratty wig, but now was charged up, high-powered. If he was a callow youth when I last saw him, the years abroad had given him enormous self-confidence. He was widely published, had won a Guggenheim Fellowship, and his stormy, live-in relationship with the handsome Israeli pianist had lasted a decade, even while carrying on other romantic affairs. In Paris he had impressed numerous literary Americans, French, and British with his brilliance. Over the next few years I could observe how he operated, as he became one of the hottest figures on the New York literary scene.

It had been his growing literary success that gave him the courage to return home. The American publication of his novel *Jamie Is My Heart's Desire* in 1958, in tandem with a short story, "As I Was Going Up the Stair," in *The Best American Short Stories* of that year, prepared for his return. And the sale to the *New Yorker* of his short story, "A War on Salamis," for the then enormous sum of three thousand dollars, provided the funds. In this story, he told about escaping from a Greek island after adopting two wild dogs, considered untamable, even dangerous, by the backward islanders, which put him into conflict with them. In reality, the two dogs, named Columbine and Skoura, accompanied him back to the States and fully justified the apprehensions of the villagers by biting people everywhere and refusing to be house-trained. Later, on the ferry across the Straits from Gibraltar, when Neil and I accompanied Alfred to Tangier for the first time, I watched with horror as Columbine, the larger and fiercer of the two, lunged forward and sank her teeth into the leg of a woman passing by on deck. The dog's fangs caught in the elastic fabric of the woman's pedal pushers with an alarming snapping sound. Alfred was not fazed in the slightest—she did that all the time, he said, proudly—and when the husband of the tearful woman came over to berate him he merely thrust out the dog's papers at him to show she had been tested and inoculated against rabies.

The first thing he had to do, he told me on his return to New York, was find somewhere to live, not just for himself and the dogs and a pair of cats as well, but for Arthur, his Israeli pianist boyfriend, who would be coming to join him from Paris, and would need a place big enough for a piano. With half of New York apartments rent-controlled and solidly occupied, and the decontrolled rents out of sight, this wasn't going to be easy, especially with those dogs. I got an immediate example of how Alfred had learned to operate when he located a spacious floor-through penthouse in a handsome wreck of a building in the Village, south of Washington Square. The only trouble was that the rent the landlord quoted was three hundred a month, which was half of all the money he had left. Undaunted, Alfred looked up the real estate records in City Hall, and found that the building was still listed as rent-controlled at sixty-six dollars a month. Then dressing himself up as an eccentric millionaire in an old velvet jacket from the Marché aux Puces, and with a friend posing as a professional decorator, they went over the apartment pointing out to the landlord the improvements they would make, tearing out walls, putting in a Hollywood bathroom, a marble fireplace, and a farmhouse kitchen. The landlord was dazzled. In his greedy mind the place was already magnificently renovated and decorated without him having to invest a penny.

As soon as the lease was signed and Alfred had turned over his last six hundred dollars, one month's rent plus a month's security, he immediately applied to the municipal rent control office to have the rent reduced to the legal sixty-six dollars a month. After this sleight-of-hand the landlord did everything in his power to get Alfred out, of course, but Alfred repeatedly took him to court, and even had the rent reduced to forty-four dollars a month when the landlord failed to provide adequate services.

He now not only had a great Village apartment, but the run of the roof for his dogs, which freed him from the onerous duty of taking them out, for they could shit up there too. When he had a roof-top party, he would simply sweep the turds into piles in the corners. Cleanliness was never one of his concerns. When I'd come over, everything was covered with New York grime. Once when Neil and I were between apartments, we accepted his invitation to stay there for a few weeks, but first came and scrubbed the place down. Of course, as soon as we moved out it returned to its usual state.

Now he set about getting his boyfriend into the States. Though born in Germany, Arthur had grown up in Israel and was an Israeli citizen, but while living in Paris with Alfred, he had reclaimed his German citizenship to avoid military service in the Israeli army. Unfortunately, the American immigration quota for German citizens was filled. The simplest method of circumventing the restrictions was to get him an American wife. So Alfred started interviewing women to marry Arthur, which would give the lucky bride two weeks in Paris, all expenses paid, and a divorce in Juarez after a decent interval of a year or two. He proudly displayed for me the fiancée he had chosen for wiry, little Arthur—a fat, good-natured Hunter College girl with an incipient mustache, whose Middle-Eastern family despaired of her ever finding a husband and welcomed the arranged marriage. To prove her talent for the job she eagerly demonstrated how she had played a buxom wench in a Shakespearean production at college, hands on hips, spouting, "How now, Mistress Quickly" with a fine rolling of the eyes. Alfred beamed. But a few days later he informed me that he had broken off the engagement, because her large, ethnic family had joyfully made plans to welcome the new groom, who had been sent by heaven. They had already started furnishing the bridal apartment in the basement of their home and buying gifts for the happy couple.

Alfred soon found the perfect temporary bride in a neurotic girl in psychotherapy whose analyst thought that breaking the barrier and getting married on any terms would be a healthy step in her life—once she had done it she could move on. So she flew off to France, married Alfred's boyfriend, and though Arthur's police dossier detailing his stormy life with Alfred made the American Embassy suspicious that it was a phony marriage, the visa was eventually granted. Arthur's head, however, was turned by the wedding bells, and he fell in love with his bride. A cablegram arrived to an outraged Alfred informing him of the fact, followed the next day by an equally emotional cablegram begging Alfred to ignore the cable of the day before, saying he had come to his senses.

The first time I met Arthur in the Sullivan Street apartment that Alfred had filled with cast-off furniture and a grand piano, I felt that he was a nasty little thing. Dark and handsome, I suppose, but the kind who looks out of his eyes at you suspiciously. He hated all of Alfred's friends, and usually retreated to the bedroom when any of us came over. I'm pretty friendly, myself—irrepressible Eddie, my high school yearbook called me—so I'm never prepared for that. But Alfred was used to it, after being with him through all the Paris years. And since it was Arthur who had pursued him, I suppose it was no wonder Alfred put up with it—most of us would be grateful forever.

Though Alfred's scheming had succeeded and he and his friend were reunited, it was not to last. In chilly, friendless New York the displaced Israeli was miserable. While Alfred's star was clearly rising, Arthur's career was going nowhere—in fact, friends who had heard him perform told me he was dreadful. Within a year the young bisexual pianist found comfort playing duets with a pretty female violinist who had been introduced to him by the poet Jean Garrigue, whom Alfred had known in Paris. Jealous, Alfred kicked him out, which only forced the young duo into each others' arms. The pianist later claimed that he had never liked "the homosexual thing," or maybe getting married the first time, even if it was just to get into the States, had switched him over. But this marriage took—and eventually Arthur and his wife had six children, while he settled for giving piano lessons to support them.

Alfred faced one of his familiar scrambles to survive with no income. Here again, he didn't consider getting a job. As the electricity, telephone, and gas were being turned off for nonpayment of bills, he had to fight his landlord's frequent eviction attempts tooth and nail in court, resulting in ever-lower rent for reduced services. The electric company even broke in through the fire escape to rip out the meter, and he held dinner parties by candlelight. When the phone was turned off, he called the telephone company and said he was in bed with hepatitis. They were sympathetic and turned it back on, but almost immediately he made a call to a friend in Mexico City, and the phone went dead again.

Though bereft of love, Alfred's literary star was rising. He knew everybody on the scene, for many of his Paris expatriate gang had also returned to New York and moved into strategic editorial jobs. He had never seriously considered turning pro, for like many in our generation he was an extremist about Literature, a believer in Art as redemption. It may sound strange to today's generation that one should write for posterity, rather than immediate recognition and money, but, in that not-so-long-ago-time before it became perfectly acceptable to aim at money and celebrity, we all shared a general contempt for writers who sold out, and expected a true artist to disdain fame even if pursued—on several occasions Alfred rebuffed *Time Magazine* reporters who persisted in trying to interview and photograph him (yet afterward, how bitterly he resented his book not getting more attention). Occasionally, though, his scorn of writers we knew who turned out television and movie scripts seemed less idealism than jealousy. As he once wrote to his old friend Theodora Blum: "[It] is kind of unpleasant to be getting nowhere what with Eugene [Walters, who had a short story done on television] and Manny [Rubin, an old classmate who was writing movie and TV scripts] and James Baldwin (to Hollywood yet for 25 G's) rolling it in hand over fist." Generally, after thirty, a milestone he had passed, one can't help beginning to feel like this, especially if you're still living in poverty, struggling to pay the rent, while around you your peers are advancing their careers, or at least settling down to the adult business of raising a family.

When he returned to New York from his decade in Paris, fiercely committed to fiction, but with his novel, *I, Etc.,* after years of work still an enormous, shapeless manuscript, the irony was that the minute he allowed himself to be persuaded to write reviews, he was faced with the shocking but undeniable fact that as a critic he was a winner. His life became hectic, and his phone, when it was on, rang constantly with editors pursuing him, hoping to get him to write something, submit something, review something, or show them the novel or story he was working on. He began popping pills to stay awake as he strove to meet deadlines for *Commentary, Partisan Review, New York Review of Books, Paris Review,* and other intellectual magazines. Though flattering, this was very hard for him to swallow, especially since he still couldn't pay his bills, and the novel remained unfinished.

Editors soon expected from him more than book reviews, they wanted controversial reassessments of major literary figures. He was willing to oblige them, and produced, one after another in the next two years, essays on Updike (a famous roasting), Nabokov, Burroughs, Rechy, Albee, Salinger, Genet, and others. "All I ever do is try to show the writers up," he complained to me. "I am campier than Rechy, beater than Burroughs, more brainy than Nabokov, more zen than Salinger, etc., etc. All you have to do is turn the dial and I'm it." He had been accused of having a different style in every story. This was true, to the extent that in writing fiction he was in continual development, though I'm afraid he saw this as evidence that he didn't have a real "I." But when he wrote reviews, his prose was high powered, racy, and iconoclastic. A magisterial critical voice sprang from him fully developed, the same in all his essays. To a certain extent one could call his approach to reviewing, Literary Criticism As Entertainment.

But the high-intellectual *Partisan Review* was too dignified to accept some of Alfred's more outré remarks in a review of Henry Miller. Where he quoted Miller's boast, ". . . having taken on [my] six-incher, she will now be able to take on stallions, bulls, drakes, St. Bernards," the editor deleted Alfred's camp response, "Six whole inches? Eeek! Ooh-ooh! Help!" I was laughing so hard when he read it to me in manuscript, I may not have gotten the exact words, but that was the idea. His attacks on some of these major authors was not just grandstanding. He continued to express doubts about them in his correspondence. A year after the essay on Salinger had appeared, he wrote that "his [Salinger's] spiritual quest leads nowhere." And his put-down of Burroughs (whom he would get to know in Tangier) was confirmed in a letter: "My review of *Naked Lunch* is true. . . . I don't like his easy assimilation of the vocabulary of Industry and Wall Street. Remember, remember, he is the Burroughs Adding Machine."

One review had unfortunate consequences. During a newspaper strike in 1963, a group of New York editors, including Alfred's old Paris friend Robert Silvers, had the brilliant idea of launching the *New York Review of Books* to fill the gap of the suspended *New York Times* "Sunday Book Review" section, and for its premiere issue Alfred reviewed *City of Night,* John Rechy's daring Genet-esque novel. To some extent Alfred saw himself as Jean Genet's heir, and in a fit of pique he gave it a savage review, one that is so brilliant and has been reprinted so often that it has haunted Rechy's whole career, but as Gore Vidal has written, "[Chester's] review . . . is murderously funny, absolutely unfair, and totally true, a trick that only a high critic knows how to pull off." Yes, but *City of Night* was also brilliant, daring and original, and a milestone in gay literature.

For these productions, he labored for long hours through draft after draft, often resorting to dexamils, a then easily obtainable version of speed that gave him *sitzfleisch* at the typewriter. But he kept resenting the diversion from writing fiction, which he felt was the important work his energies should be devoted to. Still, every publication was an event, and within a year or two, he found himself, according to *Esquire* magazine's annual charting, at the "red-hot center" of the New York literary scene.

Though he possessed a similar Talmudic intellect, Alfred Chester never quite belonged to the world of the New York Jewish Intellectual, with its political focus and clubby sensibility. He was a generation late for that, and unlike many of them, he had been raised, in spite of the Depression, in relative comfort and, even though his parents were also immigrants, without the struggle to enter American life from a quasi-alien world. Perhaps more important, though he lived in a perpetual state of crisis over his identity, he suffered no serious conflict over his Jewishness. It was his homosexuality, and in his own eyes at least, his wig, that set him apart, kept him marginal— even though important figures among the New York intellectuals were also homosexual, Paul Goodman among them. Clinging to a disappearing bohemia, Alfred Chester never entered the academic or publishing establishment, and therefore lacked the power base to be more than a peripheral figure on the literary scene. He was considered a "sport" for his original, off-center, ruthless, and devastating analyses—brilliant perhaps, but an oddity.

Several of his short stories were on homosexual themes and unapologetic about it, in that era before the gay liberation movement. The publishing world, even after the Supreme Court decisions that liberated publishers from most restraints, still maintained a taboo, with exceptions, on homosexual writing. It is interesting to note that though Alfred's essays and reviews were published in the leading journals, he could only publish these openly gay stories in small literary magazines. Again the *Partisan Review* disgraced itself by rejecting his story about a promiscuous Spanish homosexual, "In Praise of Vespasian," with the editor, Philip Rahv, saying, "Our objection is not to the subject or its detail but rather to the rhapsodic treatment. The piece is very well written, but the writing is more celebratory than analytical or just plain fictional-prosaic." This is so obvious an evasion it doesn't need analysis. But it was typical of the hypocrisy of the time, even in intellectual circles. The story was published, with a flurry of excitement, soon after, in *Second Coming*, a magazine that had the usual tiny, if hip, readership and a brief life.

The tone of this tale about an inveterate cruiser is indeed rhapsodic. In the manner of Jean Genet's *Our Lady of the Flowers*, it follows the protagonist's almost religious, if strenuous, pilgrimage through the *pissotières* of Paris and New York. Another landmark story, "From the Phoenix to the Unnamable Impossibly Beautiful Wild Bird," is a fictional treatment of the breakup with Arthur. As an analysis of the complex games that develop throughout the years between two people, it could apply to either homosexual or heterosexual relationships, but is unique in homosexual fiction. Another story, "Ismael," tells of an intense but brief passion for a young Puerto Rican, who easily gives himself, but dismisses the hero just as casually. It's a realistic and ruthless account of the protagonist's pursuit of a sensual but indifferent youth.

It is a sad truth that jilted lovers are attracted to similar types as their lost loves, an unavoidable mistake, I suppose. And for a time Alfred was considering as a replacement for the faithless Arthur twenty-five-year-old Jean-Claude Van Itallie, who, just out of Harvard, was working as an editor on the *Transatlantic Review* to which Alfred had submitted a story. Van Itallie, with his dark good looks, struck me as a dead ringer for the absconded boyfriend Arthur without the glower. Jean-Claude was born in Belgium and his wealthy family had emigrated to the United States ahead of the German invasion. Jean-Claude didn't learn that he was Jewish until his twenties, and, in fact, was one of the few Jews I've known who was never circumcised, another being Allen Ginsberg, whose parents, being atheists and communists, didn't believe in it. I remember Alfred telling me that Jean-Claude had loaned him evening clothes so they could go to the opera together in style. Beyond opera-going, Alfred's friendship with Van Itallie, who was already writing the plays for which he would become known, was creatively significant for him, since Alfred now wrote *Divertissement de Coin de Rue*, a playlet/near-ballet that is dedicated to Van Itallie—"from whom I stole the idea," he typed on the title page. The relationship never went further, which one might infer from the plot of the play, in which two youths play elaborate court-ship games but never manage to connect.

As the play demonstrates, Alfred saw relationships as fierce prim-itive contests. The partners were animals in a cage, and no lovey-dovey stuff meant anything, love allowed no tolerance of occasional indifference, of the boring patches. The way you kept a relationship fresh was high-handed hysterics. His commentary on couples was that one of them was always miserable, according to who was on top, and he could invariably point out which one was on top among the couples he knew. When he mentioned me in letters to other people, he always said "Edward is miserable . . . ," when I was perfectly happy with Neil. At any rate, his own relationships seemed to prove his theory by following an exhaustingly stormy scenario.

But the play itself deals with the courtship phase alone, with its unreal expectations, and represents Alfred's view that two people really can't get together. This was not his own experience, for he not only had the long-term relationship in Europe, but several others later on, including a blissful period in Morocco, which is not a bad record for anyone. But perhaps because of his wig, he continued to believe that he didn't have a chance, and even when he had estab-lished a relationship, never could quite get the reassurance he needed that he was loved. Unfortunately, he never learned that he was a person of impressive magnetism and power. The play does not, of course, go into his own particular difficulties in the mating game. It is an elegant, and somewhat schematic, representation of the fairly standard situation of everybody looking for what they can't have.

The Sullivan Street Playhouse, long the home of the hit off-Broadway musical, *Fantasticks,* was on the ground floor of his build-ing. However, I doubt if Alfred, or anyone we knew, ever went to see it, for it was clearly middlebrow, and we were terrible snobs. *Divertissement de Coin de Rue* is relentlessly highbrow and sophisti-cated. It has entirely French dialogue, but is clearly labeled on the title page as "A One-Act Play in French for the American Stage" and the stage directions are in English. He told me with glee at the time, as though it were a great joke, and it is certainly a clever idea, that anyone in America could understand it since it is written in high school French—perhaps overestimating the linguistic ability of Americans. It is true that the sexual highjinks going on on stage between the boys would be no mystery to any viewer, even without understanding a word. However, his fearlessness in writing about the subject so openly, years before the gay liberation movement, is quite remarkable.

Divertissement was never to be staged. Nevertheless, *Fantasticks* aside, he took an interest in what was going on in the New York theater, On-, Off-, and Off-off-Broadway, as we all did, and the plays of Ionesco and Beckett that were the current rage in the avant-garde. I remember him telling me about going to Village and SoHo artists' lofts to see dramatic productions called "Happenings," an invention by an artist friend, Allan Kaprow, which was a subject much discussed in the popular artists hangouts of the time like the Cedar Street Tavern, where Alfred sometimes met friends. It was a theatrical form that escaped the control of the professionals, for Happenings were staged by amateurs, the painters and writers themselves, even including the audience for whom activity, usually aimless, was programmed. Surely, those performances also had something to do with his playlet. He never wrote plays again, though for a brief time he did become drama critic for *Partisan Review,* which had forgiven him for his campy Henry Miller review. Several years later in Morocco, he spoke of doing another play, this one about Pinocchio. The puppet without a soul who becomes human must have seemed an appropriate metaphor for his own experience in Morocco, a golden period in his life where he became fully alive.

In his single, often miserable state, I watched Alfred go through a succession of pickups and affairs with good-looking guys. Speaking of Alfred's fiction, Gore Vidal later remarked, in his "quest for Love . . . . Cock is often settled for with unseemly haste." Well, of course, you have to live for today—and today's erection, if you're a man. Alfred Chester wasn't the kind to waste his time moping about.

And he was living proof that it is a lot of baloney that you have to be a beauty to have a sex life. Of course, he suffered over being gay, as we all did back in those self-hating, homophobic days. When lonely, he hung out at the Catholic Worker settlement house off the Bowery where an old boyfriend from Paris, Walter Kerell, was now a volunteer worker and gave him clothes from the donations. Walter even sent over to Alfred's apartment one of the many aimless young men who landed at the Catholic Worker hostel while passing through the city. The blond drifter from Canada with the invented name of Extro had shown up at Alfred's door one evening, proved willing to play, and soon moved in with his toothbrush and not much else for a year's stormy relationship in which he suffered Alfred's recriminations for not "giving" enough and was repeatedly kicked out and forced to return to the Catholic Worker. Extro had a girlfriend and child in Canada, but had a weakness for guys, he told Alfred, ever since he had worked as a fruit picker and was bedded in a three-man bunk between two other workers who quickly inducted him into the club. Extro had a penchant for wearing women's underwear, which Alfred went shopping for, and whenever he came home to find Extro on the bed wearing panties, he knew he wanted to be fucked. Alfred was always joking about Extro's "little twidgen," but in spite of what sounded like a strenuous sex life, he constantly complained that Extro didn't love him enough.

He used Extro to exact revenge on the traitorous Arthur, when with Extro's help, he took the cats he and Arthur had raised and knocked on the door of Arthur's apartment. The door opened and there, dumbfounded, was Arthur, who had always been lean and wiry, now ballooned up into a caricature of himself out of which came his squeaky Arthur voice. Behind him in the hallway, his wife, heavily pregnant with their first child, on seeing Alfred, started screaming, upon which Alfred and Extro threw the cats into the apartment and got out of there. It was a kind of closure.

In the summer of 1962, Alfred had a brief, disastrous stay at the MacDowell Colony, which had a stuffier, more academic roster of guests than Yaddo, and where bohemian Alfred was decidedly an oddball. He was seething at the distinguished anthropologist Hortense Powdermaker for her refusal to give him a lift in her car to his distant woodland studio, when hers was just beyond, and every day she drove airily by him trudging along. So, one morning at breakfast in the dining room, he stood up and, before all the colonists, denounced her as a cunt. Called on the carpet by the dignified director, he refused to apologize and was "flung out," as he put it, for antisocial behavior. He then spent the rest of the summer on the island of Vinalhaven, Maine, as the guest of Leah Knoepfmacher, a gorgon of a Viennese psychoanalyst, who in her youth had been a girlfriend of Wilhelm Reich. She confessed to me that she collected grotesques, explaining, I suppose, her taking up Alfred. He must have suspected this, because he exacted his revenge after she went back to the city, leaving him in her seaside house. Nobody could wreak destruction on a place like Alfred and the two wild dogs from Greece with whom he traveled everywhere. In the month he spent alone in the house after Knoepfmacher's departure, he comforted himself by telephoning all his friends around the world, billing the calls to the number of Senator Saltonstall's mansion on a neighboring island. A number of the calls were to Mexico, where playwright Maria Irene Fornes was on a *beca,* a literary scholarship, from the Mexican government. She urged Alfred to apply for one, too, and join her there, but he kept putting it off. Shortly after, I was working at my clerical job at the correspondence school when I received a call from the telephone company in Maine, attempting to track down the culprit who had run up the Senator's phone bill and questioning me about the lengthy long-distance calls I had received. Unfortunately, my memory was notoriously poor.

Dunstan Thompson in 1945. Photographer unknown.

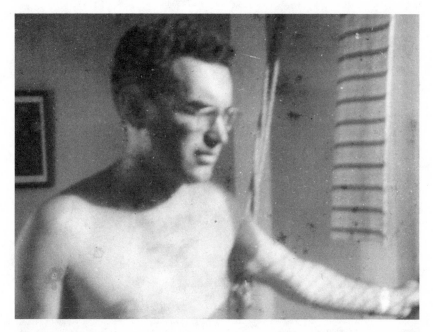

Robert Friend. Photographer unknown. Courtesy of Jean Shapiro Cantu.

Ralph Pomeroy in Paris, 1948. Photographer unknown. From the collection of Edward Field.

Drawing of Yaddo Mansion, by Tobias Schneebaum. By permission of Tobias Schneebaum.

Edward Field with Maria Vandellos at a literary cocktail party, New York 1953. Photo by Paul Berg. By permission of *St. Louis Post-Dispatch*.

Frank O'Hara. Photo by Alvin Novak.

May Swenson at forty. Estate of May Swenson. By permission of Roseanne Knudson.

James Baldwin in Paris, 1953. Photo by Leslie Schenk.

Paul Bowles and Alfred Chester. Photographer unknown. By permission of Allen Hibbard.

Susan Sontag in Seville in 1958. Photo by Harriet Zwerling.

Alma Routsong (right) and Betty Deran. Photographer unknown. From the collection of Elizabeth Deran.

Fritz Peters at eighteen, 1932. Photographer unknown.

Neil Derrick. Photo by Cynthia Stewart.

13

It was another telephone call to me in that office in Rockefeller Center that changed my life: The Academy of American Poets informed me that I had won the Lamont Award for Stand Up, Friend, With Me, *and it would be published by Grove Press the following year. This, after it had gotten dozens of rejections from publishers. So in February 1963, Neil and I celebrated by going off to Europe, hoping to stay at least a couple of months. I'd be away when the book came out, but one advantage of being out of town was that Alfred documented his doings in his marvelous letters, beginning, that winter, with a dinner party where, though we couldn't know it then, his fate was sealed. He was thirty-four years old, at the top of his form as a critic, and one of the darlings of the New York literary establishment.*

Paul Bowles, the author of *The Sheltering Sky,* a book that had eclipsed his reputation as a composer, was in New York writing music for a Tennessee Williams play on Broadway, *The Milk Train Doesn't Stop Here Anymore,* when Alfred was invited to a friend's apartment to meet him. Over dinner, Bowles spoke of the advantages of life in Morocco for a writer, and urged Alfred to come and see for himself.

Our generation, Alfred included, was in awe of the famous expatriate, the resident guru of Tangier. In the late forties, we had been electrified by his short story, "Pages From Cold Point," with its homosexual theme, that came out in a New Directions Annual and set off endless debates about whether the boy, who had gone around seducing all the men on a Caribbean island, actually seduced his own father as well at the story's murky end (Bowles later confirmed to Alfred that he did). But even before that publication, we were aware of Bowles as a figure on the international arts scene, hobnobbing with the legendary Gertrude Stein and Alice B. Toklas in Paris, before, following their advice, he settled in Morocco.

When he met Alfred in New York, Bowles was in his lowest period of creativity from the exhaustion of years of coping with his wife Jane Bowles's psychological and physical problems. Her decline, through breakdowns, shock treatments, strokes, and alcoholism, is chronicled in painful detail in Millicent Dillon's biography, *A Little Original Sin.* That winter in New York, Paul Bowles was in desperate need himself, and must have recognized in Alfred Chester a brilliance similar to his wife's, the "food" his own creativity needed. For like Jane Bowles, Alfred was Jewish, homosexual, self-destructive, even masochistic, and also had a physical "defect"—her crippled leg, his hairlessness—that would allow Bowles to be the golden boy to their "monsters," a withholding role he had played earlier to various men who were in love with him, like Aaron Copeland.

The attraction between Alfred and Bowles was never sexual. A tall, dry stick of a man, though sexually active all his life, Bowles was a complete closet case, whose Moroccan lovers, in the eyes of the world, were able to pass as servants, and indeed he employed them. Now he seemed to need the stimulus of Alfred's energies, as he had

130

once needed, and used, perhaps used up, his wife's. After a successful career as a composer, he had shifted to fiction in the forties, psyching himself into writing stories by tuning in on Jane's quirky craft, making it his own, and, as her infantile psyche probably interpreted it, taking writing away from her. Her difficult behavior, in the years of her decline after her writing became overshadowed by his, when she continually interrupted his sacrosanct writing schedule, might be seen as her only means of getting even, as well as a kind of "left-over life to kill," when she was unable to write anymore. So perhaps another explanation for Bowles's invitation to Alfred to come to Tangier was that he also saw him as a companion for his wife Jane, to look after her, amuse her, lighten the load on him that her mental illness had caused.

Bowles always claimed that he never invited anyone to Morocco, yet after returning to Morocco that winter, he wrote again and again urging Alfred to come. But Alfred was playing hard to get, nervous about falling under Paul's spell. According to a letter I received from Alfred on March 13, 1963, "[Paul] wrote me a fascinating gossipy letter and insists I come there. He and I are linked together in the new *Transatlantic* [Review] — we both have fables. It made me feel good." But Alfred was not ready for Morocco. "If I get the Guggenheim I'll come to Europe." Again, on April 3, he wrote, "If things work out with Random House I'll come to Europe, although Paul keeps writing and saying come to Tangier. It sounds so full of Beats that it makes me nauseated." On April 17, he was weakening. "I had a letter from Paul Bowles today and he makes me want to come to Tangier like mad. What if I went at the end of May?" But by April 22, he was backing off: "Whoever thought the day would come that Paul Bowels [*sic*] would be anxiously awaiting my appearance in Tangier and I would be thinking what an asshole fucking place it seems to be."

Paul Bowles was famous for being close, if not tight-fisted, with his money, as well as with his privacy and his emotions. Therefore, it is particularly revealing that he offered to loan Alfred passage money and even to put him up, dogs and all, until he found a place of his own. In response, it was with untypical considerateness that Alfred wrote back that Paul had better rent him a place nearby. Paul would learn soon enough that the dogs were large and barely manageable mongrels that tore up apartments, bit people everywhere, and were never quite house trained.

But still, Alfred held off. He bought a battered Chevy and, after subletting his New York apartment to his friend Susan Sontag, drove to Mexico with his dogs and his young hippie lover Extro, vaguely expecting to meet up with Fornes in Mexico City. But he and Extro never got there, and lingered in the province of Vera Cruz, with Alfred's letters full of complaints about Extro's inability to love, a spiritual failing that had nothing to do with what seemed to be a satisfactory sex life. So it was no surprise that the trip ended badly, with the harmless young man abandoned in the wilds of Mexico, a pattern of behavior Alfred seemed doomed to repeat.

Back in New York, it was with a feeling of loathing for the literary marketplace and a desperate need to return to writing fiction that Alfred accepted his long-suffering landlord's offer of six hundred dollars to leave the apartment. In June, 1963, after burning all his furniture in the fireplace and throwing a wild party during which he "bit Jerry Rothlein, tried to throw George Broadfield out the window," and generally behaved abominably, Alfred turned his back on his New York success. With dogs and a footlocker containing his ancient Underwood and his manuscripts, he sailed on the liner *Jerusalem* for Tangier where Paul Bowles and his wife Jane were eagerly awaiting him.

Neil and I had arrived in Paris in February, and for me, it was the first time back in Europe since my shattering return to New York in 1949. We had very little money and lived frugally because Paris had become much more expensive in the intervening years. But in the spring, coinciding with the publication of my book, the windfall of a Guggenheim Fellowship of four thousand dollars came through, and we shot off on a tour of Europe.

Among our stops was the schoolhouse in Denmark where Clifford Wright, the ex-host at Yaddo, was living with his wife, Elsa

Gress, and their children. In fact, they had set up a miniature Yaddo in their home in the rural hamlet of Glumsø, and welcomed artists from all over the world. Neil and I stayed with them for a few nights, along with a German writer, Ruth Yorck, one of the benefactors of Ellen Stewart's La Mama Theatre in New York. In her youth Yorck had appeared in Carl Dreyer's celebrated silent film *Joan of Arc,* had gone on to become a successful popular novelist in 1920s Berlin before Hitler, and was now writing plays. A tall bony woman in her fifties, her hawk-like profile and chopped off dyed-black hair went with a barking voice, as she called out "Renata! Renata!" in a heavy German accent to her traveling companion and lover. A complete eccentric, Elsa Gress was by now a leading figure in Danish cultural life. Though burdened with raising several children and dealing with guests, Elsa was also the breadwinner of the family. In the midst of the turmoil around her, she managed to sit down at her typewriter on a movable work stand in the kitchen and work away at her journalistic pieces and books. To her chagrin, her son by the traitorous American academic chose to live with him and adopted his right-wing father's politics.

Clifford and Elsa were living on a shoestring, though I didn't realize it until we offered them the rest of our Danish money when we left, and Elsa called out happily, "Clifford, we can buy gas!" Clifford seemed perfectly content in Denmark, in spite of the fact that he never learned to speak Danish. I didn't see much evidence of Clifford's gay side, except in his paintings, which were still campy fantasies, though when he took us to a local glass factory his eyes sparkled as he pointed out some hunky workers.

Neil and I returned from Denmark by ferry and a train through East Germany to Berlin. It was our first trip through the Iron Curtain to an Eastern Bloc country, bristling with guards and guns. But both sides of the border had an arsenal aimed at the other. We crossed over it without peril numerous times through the years. At that time, my sister Barbara was living in West Berlin with her Dutch husband, Ack Van Rooyen, a jazz musician, who had a bread and butter job playing trumpet in the radio station orchestra. With

Ack's help negotiating the red tape of German bureaucracy on both sides of the wall, Neil and I bought a second-hand Volkswagen and took turns driving south to Spain. We were going to rendezvous with Alfred, whose ship was letting him off in Gibraltar, and from there we'd continue on to Morocco by ferry.

14

I'd caught a bug and lay feverish in our Gibraltar hotel room, while Neil went down to the docks to meet the *Jerusalem.* Crossing the Atlantic, Alfred had an affair with a woman for the first time. In this he was following the advice of his women friends, Maria Irene Fornes, Harriet Sohmers, and Susan Sontag, all sexually ambiguous themselves, that he was "really" straight. His partner in this experiment was a young woman going to Israel to study at Hebrew University for a year. She had ambitions to be a poet, and when she heard that Robert Friend, who was on the faculty there, had taught me to write, she planned to appeal to him to perform the same miracle on her. Enlaced with her on the deck, Alfred had basked in the approval of the other passengers, a pleasant change from the usual reaction he got with his male lovers. But Alfred described the sexual act itself with a mixture of hilarity and disgust, as feeling "like a bowl of oatmeal."

The day after his arrival I was miraculously well again, and together with Columbine and Skoura on leashes and the weighty footlocker, the three of us took the ferry across the Straits to Tangier, a two-hour trip from the modern world to a place that might be described as medieval but is essentially timeless. As picturesque a country as anywhere on earth, the populace swarms through the streets in biblical hooded robes and skullcaps, the women still mysteriously veiled, the medina a movie set of whitewashed cubist dwellings clustered on the slope above the harbor, with mysteriously twisting alleys leading up to the casbah, the walled fortress, at the peak.

Alfred was nervous about being alone with Paul Bowles, and begged Neil and me to accompany him to the house that Paul had rented for the summer. This was in Asilah, a fishing village about twenty miles from Tangier on the Atlantic coast, which was not then the artsy resort it is today. We would have to take a taxi, and Alfred, slipping into Spanish, the alternate language of Tangier at the time, easily negotiated with the driver over the price. Tennessee Williams had visited Paul in Asilah and had used it as the model for the town with rapacious boys in *Suddenly, Last Summer*. Though I loved the play, after experiencing the real Asilah I can attest that one aspect of the script is ludicrous—the contention that the boys needed to be aroused by a beautiful woman like Elizabeth Taylor before they would have sex with the poet Sebastian, for Asilah boys were born hustlers and, as Jimmy Baldwin used to say to me about his own sexual voraciousness, "could fuck a snake."

Much as in the movie version of the play, as our taxi arrived and the boys on the beach below spotted the three of us getting out with our luggage above the ancient sea wall of the picturesque town, they raced up the crumbling stone stairways to surround us, and were only prevented from "devouring" us, as Sebastian had been in the movie, by Paul Bowles coming out of his house and shooing them away in the local Arabic.

Overlooking the sea, Paul's rented house was built into the ramparts of the town's old fortifications that also incorporated a derelict palace. He was obviously not happy that two unexpected guests had come along with Alfred, any more than Neil and I were comfortable about showing up uninvited. But with Alfred's longed-for arrival, he agreed to put all three of us up for the night. Alfred was going to stay on as planned, and Neil and I would go back to Tangier the next day. Paul had Larbi, his manservant, serve us lunch, though after several severe bouts with typhus, he himself would only eat a can of salmon, and when I questioned him about the delicious looking goat cheese I had seen in a market stall on the way—round white cakes nesting on fresh grape leaves—he dismissed them as "typhoid pie." I had always thought of Paul Bowles as an adventurer, but this was the first indication to me of his complexity, the paradox of his self-protective nature, while at the same time choosing to live in a place that he saw as dangerous. But quite the opposite of him and never cautious when it would have been wiser to be, it could be argued that both his wife, Jane, and Alfred fully embraced, and were destroyed by, Morocco.

Alfred and Jane's lives followed a similar path. Enthralled with Morocco and its exoticism, they both threw themselves into the life there with abandon, living for the moment and to the hilt, as a more cautious Paul Bowles had never done. They had fairytale relationships with Moroccan lovers (though in Jane's case she married the witch), used alcohol and drugs immoderately, went crazy, and died in exile within a few years of each other.

Jane, though devoted to Paul, described him as a spider, referring to the spider's talent for capturing his victims in a web and draining them of their fluids—and indeed "dryness" was a quality, a physical characteristic even, of Paul Bowles. (Later, he would learn a less destructive, more creative use of the same devouring impulse, by taping the stories of Moroccan illiterates, which he transcribed and translated into English.) To play the kind of psychic games he craved, Paul had to have a "receiver" who could read his subtext, those messages that can be conveyed underneath the surface level of the conversation, requiring a sensitivity enhanced by the use of kif, the Moroccan form of marijuana. This took a special kind of person, a borderline psychotic perhaps—like Jane, or Alfred. At the New York dinner party where he met Alfred, Paul must have unconsciously recognized a perfect foil for his mind games, yet another reason why he invited him so inscrutably, so insistently, to Tangier.

Lending weight to my supposition that Alfred had been invited as a "playmate/nurse/companion" for Paul's troublesome wife, Jane seemed to have been primed to meet Alfred, and almost immediately showed up from Tangier with her Moroccan lover, Sharifa, a silent, saturnine butch in Levis. We all sat on Paul's terrace overlooking the Atlantic Ocean, as Jane chattered on in a tone of sophisticated mockery that I found quite unnerving. She stunned us right off by proudly announcing that Sharifa carried a doctor's certificate attesting to her virginity. Jane was obviously performing not for Neil and me but for Alfred, who immediately fascinated her.

Alfred and Jane soon became intimate friends. Perhaps he brought out her maternal instincts. She got him to a doctor when a fungus sprouted on his eyelids, and loaned him money when he was broke.

After Jane and Sharifa left, we all lay on mats on the terrace and our first kif pipe was passed around, leading to a strange reaction on Alfred's part, in which he saw my face distorted hideously—he looked at me, his best friend, with horror—indicative of his ultra-sensitivity to drugs. Throughout his stay in Morocco, he was both alarmed and fascinated by the effects of the kif, and wouldn't stop taking drugs, even if they brought on terrors and panic.

Alfred's initiation into Morocco under the tutelage of Paul Bowles continued when, in the late afternoon, our host led us down the long flight of steps from the terrace to the beach where the town's fishing fleet had come in, the boats drawn up on the shore, and where the fishermen spread the day's catch on the sand to sell to the townspeople. We had barely descended from the sea wall and started across the sand to the fish market, when a young fisherman left the crowd haggling over fish and approached us, a large fish dangling from one hand. He was tall, muscular, and graceful, with a face almost Greek, but too rugged to be classical, and a little fierce-looking. Paul introduced Alfred to the young fisherman, whose name was Dris, and thus began a passionate, stormy, and exalting relationship that Alfred described to me in his letters during the next two and a half years, and the loss of which he mourned for the rest of his short life.

But the meeting on the beach was not as accidental as it looked. In a letter to me many years later, Paul described how he had set up this relationship in advance: "The first time I met that young man," he wrote, referring to Dris, "I decided never to have anything to do with him. He struck me as bad news, and I admit I was afraid of him. His conversation consisted solely of accounts of assaults he had made on European men, and this seemed to me a very bad sign. So (this may sound like a non sequitur) as soon as Alfred wrote me he was definitely coming to Morocco, I began to coach Dris on how to behave with him. We would meet for tea every afternoon in the public garden, when I'd tell him all I knew, and what I surmised, about Alfred. Reason for this behavior: I was curious to see what would happen. . . ."

This gives a good idea of Paul Bowles's strange preference for setting up situations (in both his fiction and in life) that he can stand outside of and watch impassively while the characters, fictional and real, destroy themselves. In this case, Paul was surprised to learn that the New York Jew was more than a match for the tough Moroccan fisherman, who quickly fell under his spell.

Alfred was not like so many expatriates who never learn the language of the country they live in. His French was fluent and idiomatic, and "having a pride in languages," as he put it, meant he made the effort to learn to speak the language of any country he was in. Perhaps the Jewish tradition of exile has a good deal to do with this. Like Paul and Jane, he learned to speak Moghrebi, the language of Morocco compounded of Arabic and local dialects, a rare feat in the foreign colony. Paul Bowles said he never saw anyone adapt to Moroccan life as fast as Alfred Chester. And indeed, Morocco was paradise for Alfred from the beginning. Even with periods of extreme poverty, psychotic episodes, and a variety of exotic diseases, Morocco was the high point of his life.

15

When Neil and I returned to New York in the fall of 1963, I found myself a minor celebrity. *Stand Up, Friend, With Me* was receiving such good reviews, especially for poetry, that the hardcover edition of 1,000 quickly sold out, with the Gotham Book Mart offering the dwindling copies at five times the cover price. In the spring Grove Press brought out a paperback edition that went through several more printings. But this never impressed Grove, and when I went in to see the editor, Richard Seaver, an intimidatingly handsome man, he left me standing there hangdog like a truant schoolboy before the principal. Once I asked him why he didn't ever invite me to sit down, when my book had done so well, and he put me in my place by snapping out that I hadn't earned my share of the overhead.

Perhaps it is just as well that I hadn't succeeded in getting a publisher earlier, since the book ended up the stronger for it, as I added and subtracted material over the years. And by the time the book came out, the airless little poetry world had opened up and my poetry was generally praised for those very qualities that had made it so difficult to find a publisher, its colloquialism and openness, its off-beat subject matter. But years of rejection had taken their toll, and even with my new success, I told myself, "I will not be consoled." However, the unloved little boy in me enjoyed all the attention. But this did not make it easy for Neil. The phone rang constantly, and whenever he answered, it was invariably for me. When we entered a room, he was ignored as people rushed up to me. But he accepted this with good grace, and escaped to his job at the front desk of the Museum of Modern Art where he got plenty of attention of his own.

One result of the book was that making a living was much easier now, and I never had to temp again. Odd jobs came my way. I was hired to translate a book of Inuit poems for a fifth-grade teaching program about the Eskimos that was being developed in Boston. The editors said they chose me because I was the only poet they found whose poetry could be understood by ten-year-olds. I think most poets enjoy translating, not only as a technical exercise, but also as a way of getting into the head of the foreign poet and trans-muting his vision into your own—in this case, I found the Inuit sto-ries familiar, with the same earthy quality as stories my mother told me about the *shtetl* of her childhood in Poland. Or as my sister Bar-bara put it, "Ethnic is ethnic." This Eskimo project along with a project about the Bushmen, funded by the National Science Foun-dation, went on for years, keeping scholars busy. But both were sud-denly terminated, when it was revealed that the CIA was the real source of the unlimited funds behind them, a cold war exercise to keep the scholars of Cambridge out of mischief. My translations were later published as a children's book, *Eskimo Songs and Stories,* and still later, a smaller selection as *Magic Words.*

I next was asked by a filmmaker, Francis Thompson, to write the narration for his new documentary *To Be Alive,* which was shown at the Johnson's Wax Pavilion of the New York World's Fair in 1965 and won many prizes including an Academy Award. But my main source of income for the next decade was giving poetry readings at colleges. I set these up myself. Readings were then looked on as honors to be bestowed on the poet, and the fee was called an honorarium, but I knew that English departments had budgets for visiting writers, and didn't see why I shouldn't get my share of it. In any case, I wasn't invited, so, following the shameless practice of actors who send out resumes to producers and agents as I had done myself in my acting days, I wrote to the chairmen of English departments, listed my book and awards—my "credits," as an actor would call them—and told them I was available. It took a lot of letter writing, but this way I managed to set up small reading tours in different parts of the country two or three times a year. I'm a good performer, but, initially, it was a surprise when audiences responded, often laughed at my poems—I hadn't thought of them as funny. I'm sure that people were laughing in surprise at my unexpected subject matter plus language that was more informal than usual for my formalist generation. Mostly, they never expected to understand the poems, much less enjoy a poetry reading. Nowadays, it's nothing unusual.

When I started going on tour, my canny show-business analyst, Mrs. Leah Schaefer, suggested that I sell books at my readings, and I reacted with indignation, protesting that I was not a salesman. In the face of her insistence, I had to admit that I was ashamed to sell my books—part of the snobbishness of poetry then. So I tried it. When I'd set up a tour, I'd go down to the Grove Press warehouse and buy a box of books, which I'd lug around from gig to gig. It would get lighter, of course, as I sold books. I used to rate the success of my readings by how many books I sold. I'd set up a stack of books on a chair with a hand-written note to "take book and leave money." Afterward, it was such a pleasure to find the books gone and a tangle of money on the chair. It became my favorite part of the readings. A reading is evanescent, but a book is something you leave behind.

Passing through San Francisco on my frequent tours around the country, I would often stay with Freddie Kuh in the Spaghetti Factory in North Beach, where he lived on the top floor above the restaurant amid a clutter of Victorian house furnishings and art works he bought at auction from the mansions that had survived the devastating earthquake of 1906. Huge paintings of himself and Ralph Pomeroy as young men hung on the walls. These he had commissioned, for he could now be something of an art patron himself. A layer of dust lay over everything, though in San Francisco, unlike New York, it's clean dust, and I had to climb over piles of things to get to the corner bedroom he put me up in. Fred had a coil of heavy rope to escape with in case the grease-soaked walls of the kitchen below caught fire, as had occurred when the building was a real spaghetti factory. Jolly restaurateur though he seemed to be, Freddie sometimes sat up alone in the dark, drinking and listening to nostalgic old records of chanteuses. I would come in late and hear a husky, mournful voice singing, *J'ai perdu ma jeunesse, en perdant ton amour.* . . .

16

If Paul Bowles said that he had never known anyone who dared throw himself into Moroccan life as fast as Alfred Chester, Jane Bowles added that Alfred had gotten more from Morocco than anyone she'd ever known. And, indeed, from the first day, he not only started picking up the language, with its cognate relationship to his childhood Hebrew that he learned in school, but his involvement with Dris and Dris's family also gave him entrée into Moroccan life. His letters to me and other friends reveal a Morocco as seen from the inside, as well as his often stormy, mostly blissful, relationship with Dris. They're full of his transatlantic battles with his family, agents, and publishers (sometimes resulting in lawsuits), plus reports of his complex negotiations with Paul and Jane Bowles and, woven throughout, portraits of the expatriate, literary, and beatnik colony, both in the Tangier Medina, where the hippies lived, and on The Mountain, the fashionable suburb where snobbish, titled Englishmen like Cecil Beaton and The Honorable David Herbert had luxurious homes. At that time, the richest of all the foreign colony, though, was not a Mountain resident but the heiress Barbara Hutton, who grandly claimed to live in the Casbah, the ancient walled fortress dominating the town, when actually her house, made up of a group of houses joined into one, was just below the Casbah, in the lowlier Medina. Alfred's epistolary style was neither that of his fiction nor his essays, but a livelier, more informal amalgam that went beyond both. The charm of these letters, and what makes them his most important writing, I believe, is that the voice of his entire being is expressing itself, the demanding, impossible, brilliant, and entertaining Alfred Chester, the voice he was always seeking in his prose, all the while lamenting the fragmentation of his "I." He was just being himself.

After a few days with Paul Bowles in Asilah, Alfred had escaped his clutches, he wrote me, by renting a house nearby, also on the sea wall but simple and unfurnished. Dris soon moved in, bringing his bed with him. Expected to rise at dawn to go out with his fishing boat, Dris often slept late and was fined by the Spanish company that owned the fleet. His family depended on his earnings, and Alfred had to make up for the loss. Dris finally gave up his job after the couple moved to Tangier.

Although Alfred had hoped to escape the New York literary scene by coming to Morocco, even there he had to eat, and if he could basically live on one hundred dollars a month, there were all kinds of extra expenses, and the windfall of the six hundred dollars from the New York landlord did not last long. Luckily, Richard Kluger, the editor of *Book Week,* a supplement of the *New York Herald Tribune,* offered him one hundred dollars for a monthly column. And he continued to write reviews, though less frequently than before. He reviewed *Candy* by Terry Southern and Mason Hoffenberg, originally published in the porn series, The Traveler's Companion, followed by an enthusiastic piece on *In Cold Blood* by his early idol, Truman Capote, for *Book Week,* and most notably, a long study of Jean Genet for *Commentary.*

A vivid picture of him at work on the Genet essay (during the holy month of Ramadan) is given in his letters to me:

Jan. 20, 1964 . . . My Genet essay tears everything down, the whole of western civilization. . . . [It] says that when Christ died in the 19th Century, Europe woke from a sweet dream with a bloody knife in its hand. It couldn't face its guilt, 2000 years of godless murder. . . . "Freud comes briefly to Europe's rescue with his brilliant diversion . . . making it possible for a man to ignore history in favor of his childhood. . . . What a relief to be guilty of nothing worse than coveting mama. (And what a perfect totalitarian weapon psychoanalysis potentially, if not actually, is. It reduces all opposition to expressions of personal and misdirected hostility. It makes all protest infantile.)" On and on goes my inexorable logic, until the coup: "Hitler had the genius to turn Christianity inside out, to make that of which the Christians were most guilty into the ideals of a new order."

The fascinating thing about this and the following quotes from the piece he was writing is that all this material was deleted from the published essay by the editors of *Commentary*. Unfortunately, the original manuscript, which Alfred said was three times as long as the published version, has disappeared.

"When one looks back at the slaughtered of Christendom—the American Indians, the Negroes, the Moslems, the Christians themselves, the Asiatics and Africans—six million Jews are a drop in the bloody bucket. Hitler was no uncouth accident in the ladylike history of Europe. He *was* the history of Europe, he *was* Europe merciless up to its very last gasp. And if we don't know of the crimes of the humanists, it is probably only because the humanists won the war.

"To a melody by Mozart, enter Jean Genet, whom François Mauriac has accused of being in league with the devil."

And later:

I finally ran out of dexamils and to my surprise I went right on working, just as many hours and just as clear-minded. Lots of coffee though. I don't need liquor either, though I might if I started on a novel. I can't write at all with kif except analytical horrors.

Tuesday. . . . "A state executes in order to disavow everyone's guilt. The execution of Eichmann, for example, makes all the rest

146

of us seem innocent, when in fact the only honorable and honest thing would be to have the whole human race hanged in Jerusalem." Do you think *Commentary* will be amused by that?

And on January 29, 1964:

> It is eight p.m. and I've been at the Genet since eight in the morning and yesterday and forever and it is supposed to be there this week and I'm exhausted. It gets more and more brilliant, but I hate it more and more. And the letter comes from Irving Rosenthal in Marrakech saying money is absolutely the only justification for writing essays and book reviews in which case you don't tell your friends about it. So I've written him a letter (Hitler being his favorite hate) beginning *Mein lieber Adolf* and telling him I didn't know the law. And that if he was cold there was a surplus of fuel at Auschwitz. But it's made me depressed because it's true and I'm working like a dog. What I say in the Genet is just telling the truth. He (Genet) is making the real Christian ideals—murder, pillage, treachery and robbery—into his own ideals. As he's in jail he has nothing to lose. It takes me thirty pages to say it, but that's a good sign. I'm beginning to get my wind back. I don't come out in farts now, but in streams of shit. Note how long my letters are.
>
> From last part of essay: "America is Europe's knight in shining armor. But the love-starved maiden needs something a lot warmer in her arms than a coffer of jewels. Beauties have been known to fall in love with beasts before; or, as Confucius said, a hot dragon is more fun in bed than a cold dollar bill."
>
> I really need a rest after this.
>
> Dris woke me at five this morning and I finished the Genet in time to get it to the post office before noon when it closed for the weekend. The Genet is called, "Goodbye to Christendom." [It was published as "Looking for Genet."] I do hope they print it. It will bring me $300 and cause a little stir.

It is easy to see from these excerpts why he called it "Goodbye to Christendom," and why *Commentary* had to rename it when they threw out that whole aspect of the essay. Besides the unlikelihood of a Jewish magazine publishing an attack on Christianity, they probably did not appreciate that he was writing from outside the Christian world, from the liberating vantage point, for a Jew, of a Moslem country.

I read it over this morning and could hardly believe how good it was though it reads like I'm in the middle of a nervous breakdown. It must be the dexedrines I use to keep going. I alternated between dex and librium as you can't get dexamils here. At night I had gin and kif to unwind with. The Genet is really an apologia per mia vita. It tries to explain my dybbuk. The essay is really such a vicious attack on everything except Genet, you, God and myself, that I don't even know whether they'll have the nerve to print it.

By the way, my Genet ends up talking about Kennedy. I quote Mailer's passage about the subterranean river of American life, [then go on to say] "It was out of this river that the assassin's bullet came, regardless of who pulled the trigger or why. We accept, with the authorities, the guilt of the lonely psychopath because it tells a truth if not a fact. It dramatizes the refusal of Unreason to be silenced any longer by man's, Europe's, idea that he, Reason, rules the world. Humanism, however pretty, isn't for us because nature isn't human, and man willy-nilly is of nature. Nature is unreason and God. It is the madness that runs through our lives and connects us to the stars in a way no rocket ship can ever duplicate. It connects us to all living things and to ourselves. To name this madness Holy doesn't promise peace or prosperity; it promises only a reason for being, a reinvestment of life into the dead matter of which the universe is now composed." Nice, yes?

But in a later letter, he adds: "I feel as if mama's going to slap me hard for writing such mean things."

One could live on very little in Tangier and writing reviews and the column brought in enough; still, when Alfred got a check he'd splurge, maybe buy an old car that would demand continual repairs, and soon he'd be broke again. It was feast or famine with him. As he had done in his Paris days, when he had worked a scam to bilk insurance companies by "losing" insured luggage, he succeeded in pulling the trick off successfully again, and even recommended it to friends. Now, in that difficult first winter in Tangier, he conceived another "surefire" plan—to blackmail Paul and Jane who, he reported to me, were supported by patrons he called "Jane's millionaires"—not only old friends like Truman Capote, Tennessee

Williams, and Libby Holman, but also the wealthy and titled expatriates from the Mountain.

While the Bowleses were freely homosexual in their personal lives, their marriage and the remoteness of Tangier had protected them from scandal for several decades of an era that was quite intolerant about such things. Alfred quickly spotted that they were terrified of anything coming out publicly. The world would see through their glamorous façade and they'd be shunned, no longer welcome at parties and receptions in the fashionable milieus they enjoyed. Nor, with their high-class artistic reputations tarnished as known homosexuals, would they continue to get grants from prestigious foundations, as Paul had been doing for years. (When Paul became a successful writer, fellow composer Virgil Thomson, known for his wicked wit, said that after Paul had gotten all possible grants as a composer, he had switched to writing to be eligible for writing fellowships.) But perhaps Paul's fear of being known as gay in that benighted age was primarily grounded in his WASP tradition of presenting a conventional appearance to the world, which meant a marriage, no matter that it was a sham and no matter what you do in private.

The idea for Alfred's blackmail plot, that Jane later referred to as "The Mistake," grew out of a reference to Paul in an article by Irving Rosenthal in a forthcoming issue of medina-denizen Ira Cohen's magazine *Gnaoua*. The offending sentence, an oblique reference to Paul's dry mouth making him an undesirable cocksucker, now seems almost innocuous, but it did out him in print, which Paul saw as threatening and he demanded that it be deleted. When Ira Cohen resisted censoring the piece, even William Burroughs got into the act to appeal for its removal. In the resulting tempest in a teacup, Alfred and Ira, thinking they had Paul over a barrel, got the idea of demanding ten thousand dollars from him to remove the line, and even after Ira backed out of the infantile plot, Alfred went ahead with it on his own.

Faced with Paul's ice-cold eyes and icier reception as he made his extortion pitch, Alfred suddenly became terrified at what he was doing. A letter Paul had previously sent Ira, in which he said he was going to have Alfred Chester "rubbed out," no longer seemed so innocent. This had been written by Paul a few months before when he was fed up after one of the stormy fights Alfred provoked, probably for the pleasure of getting a rise out of Paul. And during the blackmail attempt, Alfred became fully conscious of the fact that Paul Bowles was part of a world where murder was no big deal. After all, Jane's good friend, the singer Libby Holman, had killed her husband, and the novelist William Burroughs had killed his wife, accidentally in both cases, and neither was convicted. But as Alfred told me, Paul himself, perhaps indulging in drug fantasies, liked to brag how easily you could arrange to have anyone done away with in Tangier for a pittance. It sounded as if in Morocco, under the influence of kif, the exotic culture, and Paul's powerful presence, Alfred started living in a fantasy, and he could no longer distinguish between fiction and reality.

Alfred had the note Paul sent Ira and had the presence of mind to mail me a copy. Fear for his life sent Alfred into a tailspin, and he wired me in New York to come get him out of Morocco and take him home. This was really nuts, and I went a little crazy myself with worry over him, trying to reach him by telephone. Eccentrically, Paul never had a telephone, but Jane who lived in her own apartment in the same building did, and I eventually got through to her, shouting over the crackling transoceanic telephone lines that were routed through a switchboard in Paris. Not really remembering me, Jane put on her usual act to the outside world, reassuring me blithely that nothing was wrong, and that there was nothing to worry about. In fact, Alfred, in his panic, even went to the U.S. Consulate about the death threat from Paul, who then had to smooth things over by convincing the Consul that the note was a joke and Alfred was unbalanced to have taken it seriously.

Daily use of kif by itself may not have been the culprit that ultimately destroyed Alfred's sanity, but in combination with dexedrine, liquor, and occasional LSD and opium use, it was dangerous. In his first letter to me from Morocco, he had already complained that

150

"there isn't any me now. . . . There is no one or thing around to establish my past." I had felt the same culture shock when I lived in Greece in 1949 and was completely immersed in Greek life. There is also the possibility that Dris, who cooked for Alfred, put into his food mind-altering substances, prescribed by a witch to keep his Nazarene faithful. Alfred and Dris frequently resorted to the local witch, who once gave them a vial of mercury to blow under the door of a troublesome upstairs neighbor and did spells to influence Alfred's mother to send him money or get manuscripts accepted by editors in New York. There is a scene in "The Foot" where Alfred awakens in the night to find Dris performing magic before the fireplace, chanting and inscribing eggshells. Much as Sharifa, Jane's lover, was said to use magic to keep control over Jane, Dris might have used it to keep Alfred.

Another factor in Alfred's crackup was his recognition, in the midst of his "disgrace" from the failure of his blackmail plot, that his collection of short stories, *Behold Goliath,* which was about to be published, would not be the success he fantasized. And he was right about that, as it turned out, for the book included several openly gay stories, which were a red flag to critics in that homophobic era. It didn't help that he again barricaded himself into his apartment when *Time Magazine*'s reporters and photographers showed up, trying to get an interview and a picture. Susan Sontag, mistress of spin more than camp, bluntly wrote him that he couldn't expect to get good reviews when he had made so many enemies through his critical attacks.

But he emerged from this crisis apparently more stable than before, when a crucial event occurred that I'd have thought would be devastating—the wig he had worn from childhood burned up by accident on the kitchen stove. Surprisingly, he did not fall apart, and it looked as if his growing maturity allowed him to reveal his baldness for the first time in his life. He even invited the Bowleses to lunch in order to display his newly bald head.

When Alfred's letters arrived I found myself overwhelmed by his orders of Things To Do for him. I suspected he made these inordinate demands on all his friends, but I tried to fulfill as many as I

151

could. Being somewhat shy myself, I was not too successful confronting and fighting his battles with formidable publishers like Jason Epstein, and dealing with lawyers and agents. He was furious with Epstein for not promoting his book *Behold Goliath* as vigorously as he wished, and even broke with his devoted agent, Candida Donadio, switching, on Norman Mailer's recommendation, to Scott Meredith, a tough cookie who Mailer said would make his fortune, but who turned out to be equally unsatisfactory. For the truth was that Alfred was not a mass-market writer, though it was remotely possible that he would have evolved into one. He was also convinced that his family had swindled him out of his father's inheritance, and laid out his case repeatedly in obsessive detail. I was required to get him a lawyer, and found an old NYU cafeteria friend, Si Perchik, who had become a lawyer and a poet. A simpler chore, one would think, was to buy construction worker shoes for Dris, whose foot was traced on a sheet of paper. It turned out to be the largest size available, 13, but when they arrived they were so enormous that Dris took offense!

Writing the *Book Week* column, aimed at a mass readership, was at variance with Alfred's image of himself as a writer for the literary few, and it disturbed him. He wrote me, in February 19, 1964: "Edward, am I going mad or is it possible that people do actually write nasty things about me in newspapers? Someone called Jimmy Breslin writes: '[Brendan] Behan at least tries to write for the entertainment of the reader. He is not some outlandish homosexual trying to sound off on human destiny between paragraphs about his boyfriends.' I just read that and I thought that man is talking about me. I keep thinking I am mad. I mean, suddenly I think, How can I write about being poor, and Dris, in the Herald Tribune?" But the columns brought him some diverting correspondence: A psychiatrist wrote, "Dear Scabrous Fungus Collector. I'd order you to douse the glim of your horrible light of darkness if I had the power and if I didn't like the twisted macabre stuff."

Alfred had now become the ultimate authority on Moghrebi sexuality, and when some of the resident foreigners complained to Alfred that their Moroccan boyfriends wouldn't kiss them and make love, just wanting to fuck, Alfred went to bed with them and reported back that the boyfriends were very tender lovers. He saw this problem as having to do with the foreigner's attitude. Reflecting his expertise in this area, his first "story," if one could call this non-narrative piece of writing a story, was "Glory Hole," in which some boys of Tangier discuss their foreign lovers. The "story" should be required reading for anyone going to Morocco and expecting to make out.

It was fascinating to hear Alfred talk about Moroccan sexuality, admittedly of the lower classes. The boys, it turned out, had a fear of oral sex, worrying that their dicks would be bitten off, though Alfred's own boyfriend, Dris, soon overcame this fear. Dris repeated a story to us about Paul blowing one of the boys, who held a large rock over Paul's head, in case he bit off his cock. But it was certainly not all oral sex. After living with Dris for a few months, Alfred wrote me that his asshole was so large a family could move in. He said that Dris knew he wasn't Marilyn Monroe, but if the person in his arms felt good, that was good enough for him. Dris certainly seemed happy with him, and confessed to another friend that making love to Alfred was like fucking a large, hairless baby.

But the street boys have their own rules and hierarchies, Alfred said. When boys don't want to be fucked anymore they grow a mustache. According to Dris, between good friends, sex was all right, but no more than the head of your friend's cock must penetrate your asshole. Another rule is that the older one fucks the younger, and the older pays the younger. The exception to this was sex with Nazarenes—the Nazarene is always the one who pays—naturally enough, since the local boys are poorer than the foreigners. Alfred also said that in their love affairs, the Moroccan never leaves the Nazarene, but vice versa. One Moroccan youth Neil and I talked to said he would never go with a Nazarene again because they always went away.

Besides "Glory Hole," Alfred completed only one other short story in Morocco, "Safari," full of dark reflections of the psychosis he was already in the grip of. It tells of a scorpion hunt he went on with Paul but was really an essay on the demonic power the older man had over him. Indeed, his whole stay in Morocco from 1963 to his expulsion at the end of 1965 and even beyond was dominated by Paul, and to a lesser extent by Jane. When we arrived in Tangier, his nervousness about being alone with Paul and asking Neil and me to go with him to Paul's house in Asilah, turned out to be justified. "Sometimes I think Gerald is God," Alfred wrote in the short story, "Safari," disguising Paul as Gerald:

> at least a local god, or more exactly, a local demon. Africa is not the same as other continents, despite its revolutions, and Gerald has lived here so long that magic and sorcery are more part of his nature than science or the ten commandments. I do actually hear drums at his approach; I can see the bone and the ring through his nose; I can see the hideous paint on his face. He is a witch doctor using the body of a mild English missionary. I believe his mind can create things, can make them up as he goes along, real things (so to speak), like this road we were on, or the valley we'd just crossed over, or the mountain above us. If the world is illusion, why shouldn't Gerald be the cause of some of those illusions? I know this sounds insane. I probably am insane. Still and all, can't a madman be logical and right?
>
> If I see too much of Gerald, he spreads insidiously through my life like ink on blotting paper. I go out at night and hear a strange bird cry in the trees, and I think: that's Gerald. Or a dog baying. If I'm with someone else—but it is rare that I am—I might easily say, "Listen! Do you hear that bird? It's Gerald. He can turn himself into a bird . . . a demon bird . . ."
>
> One summer afternoon I went bathing at the vast empty beach on the cape. After a while I started feeling strange, maybe a little sunstruck—giddy and nauseated, but yet exultant. Trying to calm myself, I paced around in the sand; Gerald was much in my mind, like a huge dirty joke. Then suddenly I was looking at the towering sand cliffs to the east, and I felt sure—without fright, mind you, with laughter, rather—that Gerald's smiling head would appear above those hills like a gigantic puppeteer over his stage, like a dripping leviathan surfacing out of a swimming pool.

As Gerald, Paul is portrayed as a wizard-like demonic figure, sometimes benign but more often satanic, his behavior arbitrary, speaking in an unsettling subtext, perhaps part of Paul's druggy mentality. Paul later denied he ever spoke in subtext, as Alfred claimed, and treated it as one of Alfred's inventions, but it is this view of Paul that also comes through the many letters I received from Alfred, the Bowles that presided over Alfred's Moroccan years.

The Paul Bowles myth with its image of the unruffled, imperturbable, neutral facade is shattered by Alfred's letters, which reveal a more human Paul. Yet he strenuously denied Alfred's reports of his throwing tantrums and smashing things. I conjecture that it is likely that for a brief time Paul, uncharacteristically, was trying out being like Alfred, imitating his unleashed self-expression, a mode of behavior he later felt uncomfortable about and wished to deny. But if Paul was suffering from a writer's block, as Alfred reported to me soon after settling in Morocco, his experimentation with erratic, loosening-up behavior and Alfred-like excesses would have made sense as a kind of therapy. But their relationship was more than that. Alfred would write that Paul was the only mind on his level in Tangier, but it must have been true the other way round also.

In the following summer of 1964, Neil and I made another visit to Tangier, although Alfred was somewhat disappointed in me this time, complaining afterward that I had become "old maidish." Of course, it would have been difficult to live up to the idealized image he had of me, and I was never going to throw myself into Moroccan life as totally as he had. I was relieved to find him so happy, living with Dris in a charming apartment in Tangier. They seemed very domestic and lovey-dovey, and Alfred had become a kind of housemother to the Tangier colony.

He had recovered from *Behold Goliath*'s bad reviews and, determined to stick to his ideals and drop out of the criticism racket to concentrate on fiction, had embarked on another novel, *The Exquisite Corpse,* named after the surrealist party game. If drugs disoriented his mind, it was also drugs that helped him find the perfect form for the novel, in which characters change sex and identity in each chapter—the novel as "a continually changing entity," as he had told Hans de Vaal in their interview in the early fifties—a web of shifting and multiple "selves," reflecting, often playfully in *The Exquisite Corpse,* his obsession with not having a fixed "I" and his suffering over this "situational" self, which was determined by whom he was with.

155

Alfred brought Neil and me to visit Dris's family in Asilah, our first experience in a Moroccan home. The women stayed in their own quarters, while we sat with the men, when Dris, who was holding his little nephew on his lap, grabbed the boy's crotch and said in his gruff voice, "He grow up and make money fucking Nazarenes." But when Dris's teenage brother ran away to hustle foreigners in Tangier, Alfred told us, Dris got inexplicably moral, went looking for him and dragged him home.

To celebrate our arrival, Alfred threw a cocktail party with martinis, a novelty to the beatnik medina crowd, whom he invited though he had complained about them frequently in his letters. Among them, Ira Cohen and his girlfriend Roz, who lived in a house in the medina called "Bat Palace," so named after a bat was cooked and consumed in a pseudo-satanic rite; "the King of the Beatniks" and his lady, Tatiana, who, after several tokes on the powerful joint passing around the room, broke our zonked silence with sudden shrieks of mad laughter; and Dale and Liz, another young couple who were opening a bar, where Dris worked for awhile and which was soon closed by the Moroccan authorities in one of their periodic sweep-ups, and expulsions, of the medina denizens.

Alfred drove us in his battered car on a hair-raising ride to the mountaintop village of Chauen, turning around from the wheel to speak to us in the back seat even while negotiating switchbacks on a road that allowed no passing room. Chauen, where water gushed from the mountainside, was considered a holy place that until recently had been closed to non-Moslems. As the magical night fell, we sat in the moonlit public gardens, set within the crumbling walls of an ancient palace, drinking mint tea among robed elders. Another time, he drove us out to an all-night religious festival at a Moslem saint's tomb on a stony hillside covered with the tents of families gathered to worship. There we crowded into a smoky tent to watch gold-toothed boys dancing to a *jilala* cult orchestra for an audience of men. The dancing boys had filed their teeth down and replaced them with gold, "to be beautiful," Dris told us.

156

All seemed to be going better than ever for Alfred, we thought. But the consequences of his giving up his wig were only delayed in coming, for he had a second breakdown a year later. The crisis came in the late summer of 1965, precipitated when his old friend, the beautiful and newly famous Susan Sontag, came to visit him in Tangier.

17

In the meteoric rise of Susan Sontag's literary career in the 1960s, little credit has been given to Alfred Chester, who was inseparably entwined in that period of her life. But for several years, their relationship was intense and complex, as all his relationships were.

Before women discovered their sexuality, it used to be said that many of them were attracted to men more for their minds than for their bodies. And in the long run, perhaps it is still the stimulation of another mind that keeps any relationship going. Susan Sontag, no mean mind herself, is reported to have called Alfred Chester the most fascinating man in New York. If inadvertently she played a crucial role in his final crackup in 1965, the effect of these two unusual personalities on each other was instantaneous and powerful.

It is remarkable that in the life of this shapeless, bewigged, odd-looking, pasty-faced, homosexual writer were a number of other beautiful and powerful women besides Sontag. I remember Alfred at a Passover seder he staged in his apartment in Greenwich Village, standing short, pale, and pudgy in his prayer shawl between the novelist Hortense Calisher, vivid as a geisha in her black wig, and stunning Art Students League model Harriet Sohmers, both women six feet tall, as they said the prayer while lighting the candles of the menorah.

After his mother, who was gypsyish and operatic in the style of Bizet's Carmen, came Theodora Blum, a girl of opulent, maternal flesh, over whom Cynthia Ozick, a classmate at New York University, was moved to a jealous fit fifty years later, bad-mouthing her rival for Alfred in a memoir, "Alfred Chester's Wig." In this essay Ozick expresses a remarkable theory about Alfred's homosexuality that dispensed with Freud and all the other deep thinkers Ozick usually pays tribute to. She recalls Alfred's teenage crushes on women and, taking them at face value, is convinced that her adolescent refusal to kiss him goodbye after a date—a kiss that might have given him a foretaste of heterosexual pleasures—caused him in reaction to become homosexual, since it was the final proof that he was too ugly to attract a woman.

Even if his friendship with the buxom Teddie, as Theodora Blum was called, was platonic, he was so obsessed with her that when he was living in Paris in the fifties he wrote letter after letter begging her to come to France, repeating that he was longing to lay his head on her voluminous breast. When she did answer his summons, finally, and the ship docked at Cherbourg, Alfred made a mad dash to get there ahead of a woman friend, equally eager to greet her. This reunion turned into a farce when, on Teddie's arrival, both contenders spotted each other indignantly at the dock, and on the journey back to Paris on the boat train the two rivals for a nonplussed Teddie refused to speak to each other. After Teddie got a look at the squalor of the cottage on the outskirts of Paris that Alfred expected her to share with him, his lover Arthur, and their dogs and cats, she wisely insisted on moving into a hotel. Alfred became furious, and his obsession with Theodora Blum waned.

During his decade in Europe in the fifties, he dazzled the Princess Marguerite Caetani, another large, imposing woman, who invited him to her husband's opulent estate at Nympha, outside of Naples, where they had lunch in a garden among marble ruins overgrown with tangled vines, as the bored Prince, Alfred told me, sat there swatting flies. For awhile Caetani even used Alfred as her literary advisor, until rival American novelist and poet Eugene Walter wormed his way into her confidence and beat out the competition to gain supremacy over her.

It was also in Paris that Alfred Chester met the boyishly slim, towering Harriet Sohmers, who was hawking the *Herald Tribune* in the streets, the inspiration, perhaps, for the Jean Seberg character in Godard's "Breathless." Harriet was a dead ringer for Prince Valiant with her large, handsome features and straight brown hair with bangs. Unlike many tall women whose unusual height was a curse that led to permanent round shoulders as they tried to stoop to the level of those shorter than they, Harriet seemed to enjoy the theatricality of her appearance, and strode dramatically around with immense confidence, attracting everybody's stares. No shrinking violet, her voice, too, had a rich, thrilling timbre that filled every room. It would be through Sohmers that Susan Sontag came into Alfred's life.

Harriet's friendship with a precocious Susan, already in graduate school as a teenager, began when Susan came into the Berkeley bookstore where Harriet was working, and while the tall, stunning, and dark-haired young scholar browsed the shelves, one of Harriet's gay fellow clerks leaned over and whispered, lewdly, "Go get her." Harriet, just out of the avant-garde Black Mountain College, where she'd had her first affair with a woman, was a good student and boldly carried out the clerk's whispered assignment—beginning an on-again, off-again affair, perhaps Susan's first. In the mid-fifties, when Susan, by now married and with a son whom she had parked with her in-laws, was studying at Oxford University, she came over to Paris where Harriet was living with a Swedish painter and reignited the affair. Like Alfred, Harriet kept affairs sizzling by making drama—which certainly monopolizes your lover's attention. Accordingly, when the two women gave a party, they had a terrible fight during which Harriet socked Susan in the jaw, leaving a visible bruise. Allen Ginsberg, also at the party, asked Harriet why she hit

Susan, since Susan was younger and prettier than she. Harriet, still simmering, answered, "That's why!"

In Paris, Harriet offered her shoulder to Alfred during a crisis with his lover, Arthur. The rift in the Alfred/Arthur ménage had occurred when a good-looking American named Walter Kerell arrived in Paris and fell in love with Alfred. Temporarily besotted himself, Alfred barely managed to stammer out to Arthur an implausible lie to cover up his leaving for a tryst in London with his new lover, and since Walter too had a wife, the escapade caused a rift there, too.

To give Arthur a chance to cool down, Alfred decided to escape for awhile to the Mediterranean island of Ibiza, still undiscovered by mass tourism and cheap enough to become a haven for impoverished artists. There, Alfred met Harriet's current lover, Maria Irene Fornes, a Cuban who was staying on Ibiza for the winter. Dramatically beautiful, Irene had the large, soulful eyes of a madonna and enough heartache of her own to understand him. She and Alfred immediately took to each other, and for years Alfred went around quoting her wise sayings, "Irene says . . .," until they fell out and he started quoting me, until I too got the axe. But that was not for quite awhile.

On Alfred's return to the States in 1960, after a decade abroad, it was through Harriet and Irene, also back in New York, that he finally met, at last, the brilliant young academic, Susan Sontag—"the dark lady of American letters," as she would be called—with her shining, straight, black hair, long legs encased in knee-high boots, Left Bank fashion, and perpetual dark glasses. From 1960 to 1963, during his period of celebrity on the New York literary scene, he maintained his friendship with these three extraordinary women, individually and in varying, sometimes dizzying, combinations. At a poetry reading in a Bowery restaurant, when I first met them, this trio of vivid young goddesses surrounded little Alfred Chester, his face beaming under the ragged wig, like handmaidens, or a phalanx of protective amazons. With Harriet he was a buddy, confidant, and after she got pregnant, protector. With Irene, he was romantically smitten with a concomitant holy feeling about her, perhaps aroused by her Spanish madonna looks. And with Susan he was mentor and, as earlier with Cynthia Ozick, rival, for Susan, with her unusual looks and mind, was already making the literary scene in a big way. But for now, Susan sat at his feet adoringly, soaking up the aura of success that he was enjoying—briefly, as it turned out, for he would throw it all away.

Susan had left her husband by this time and was living on West End Avenue with her son David. She was not to be alone for long. Harriet, under her married name of Zwerling, has published a memoir, included in *Notes of a Nude Model,* in which she reveals, masking the identities of the two women with initials, how Susan, in a particularly brutal way, announced to her over the telephone that Irene, who had been living with Harriet, would not be returning to her. This was such a painful shock that it caused Harriet to renounce lesbianism once and for all.

Susan and Irene and young David were living happily on West End Avenue, when the child's father sued for custody on the grounds that the lesbian household was not a fit place to raise his son. In spite of a story Harriet tells about Susan throwing a screaming David, frightened of the water, into the ocean to teach him how to swim, it looked to me then that Susan was a good mother, which was also attested to by their lifelong devotion. Once, when Neil and I were having dinner there, David came into the room and Susan immediately left us at the table, sat down on a sofa and devoted herself entirely to him. When the custody case came to court, Alfred told me, Susan and Irene appeared in dresses, high heels, and makeup—they were indeed stunning women—and the judge threw out the case, unable to believe that they were lesbians.

Alfred frequently suffered from a competitive spirit with such powerful women (see Ozick's memoir), even when he was their creative model, as he was for Susan. Seeing her as competition, though she was only beginning to find her way as a writer, and sensing that her beauty and brains were a winning combination, he liked to cut her down to size by bad-mouthing her legs as heavy, and her mind as academic and conventional. With her photographic memory, he told me, she might know everything, but only superficially. She spouted other people's ideas, he said, usually the fashionable kind derived from the French avant-garde, which she peddled in New York. But it was chiefly her beauty that he saw as giving her an unfair advantage over him, both in literary and personal matters.

Once, after Susan visited him at his apartment over the Sullivan Street Playhouse, Alfred went into a tailspin of jealousy, when his sexually indeterminate boyfriend Extro was smitten and went to call on her, provoking a near-breakdown on Alfred's part. In this, Susan was undeniably innocent—Extro had nothing to offer her and she wouldn't have wasted her time. Most likely, it was a device of Extro's to make Alfred jealous, for he was more taken with Alfred than he openly admitted, and if Alfred felt the youth was unloving, that was his own lifelong problem of feeling unloved rather than the reality. And feeling unloved had nothing to do with his looks, either. Magnetic as he was, Alfred hardly had to step out of his large, ramshackle apartment into the Village streets to be picked up by someone, as in his story "Ismael," where the young Puerto Rican falls happily into his bed.

At that period of her life, Susan Sontag was not yet much of a writer and had only published a few scholarly articles, though she claimed, according to Alfred, to have had more than a hand in her ex-husband Philip Rieff's magisterial work on Freud. By the time she came into Alfred's circle, she was teaching philosophy, first at Columbia University and then at Sarah Lawrence College and, using Alfred as an example, had embarked on her own first attempts to write fiction, as Irene was beginning to write plays. She belonged to a group of women writers that Alfred maliciously liked to call *La Societé Anonyme des Lesbiennes*. Irene told me that she and Susan would sit across a table from each other, each at their typewriters, stopping to read to the other a passage they were proud of. It was at this time that Susan began her first novel. And on the basis of what Alfred dismissed as little more than a collection of dreams, she immediately landed a contract with Farrar, Strauss for *The Benefactor*. Alfred, again jealous, claimed it was Roger Straus's hots for her that got her the contract. It is true that her publisher was a particularly devoted champion.

I hardly imagined at the time that the worshipful Sontag I saw so frequently at Alfred's apartment was an intimate of the likes of Hannah Arendt, William Phillips, and a whole panoply of iconic older figures on the New York intellectual scene. She actively courted "names," instinctively combining social life and intellectual discourse with career building. It was perhaps admiration for the way she operated via this social promiscuity, combined with his jealousy, that caused Alfred, unfairly, of course, to call Susan, invariably, "a whore" and "the enemy." "Susan is so famous," he wrote me. "Shows you how far you can get with a good memory, no scruples, a pretty face and an indifferent cunt." And again: "Susan is probably writing nice reviews for political reasons, in order to win a kind reception for her next book. (She is such a whore that it never occurs to her anyone might judge a book on merits; she probably imagines Shakespeare had the best press agent in Elizabethan times.)" And later: "How dare you say 'your friend S. Sontag'? You rat, she is my enemy. She is everybody's enemy. She is The Enemy."

But Alfred also had a healthy respect for Susan. When he left for Morocco in 1963, he turned over to her his job as theater critic for the *Partisan Review,* which she made good use of, resulting, a few months later, in the landmark publication in that journal of her "Notes on Camp," which created a sensation. And when he "glanced through her essay at Paul's," Alfred wrote me, he was surprised that she understood "about the true depth of a work being in the surface," a quality he was aiming for in his new novel. Perhaps it was natural that he agreed with her, since her ideas for the essay largely came from discussions she had had with him about W. H. Auden's article on Oscar Wilde, which had been published in the *New Yorker* the previous winter.

Before leaving for Morocco, Alfred had a jolting breakup with Irene, which was perhaps one more indication of the mental trouble to come. For this rift was inexplicable. On the face of it, it had to do with her choosing to stay on with a woman friend they were visiting, instead of leaving with him. One might possibly accept a tiff resulting from this small "betrayal," if one could call it even that, but hardly a complete break—especially considering that Irene was one of his closest friends and he quoted her all the time. The only other element in the break up was his involvement in her increasingly troubled relationship with Susan. He later wrote: "Irene says . . . that I broke her and Susan up. God, I have left a trail of blood behind me." The rejection of Irene could be seen as a foretaste of his rejection of me later on in his madness, when the "voices" in his head told him I wasn't "the real Edward" anymore. But in this earlier phase of his life he was apparently sane—Irene always called him one of the sanest people she knew.

However, he had mentioned breakdowns already. During his decade in Europe, Diana Athill, his London editor, had once received a letter from him explaining a mysterious silence as being caused by his terrified flight around Europe to escape nameless pursuers. Another mystery, a few years later, was a solitary trip to New Orleans and Houston, about which he would only say that a man had held him prisoner in a room. Taking this story as code for a strange love affair he didn't care to talk about, I discreetly let it pass without questioning him about it. Now, similarly, he didn't adequately explain his rejection of Irene.

On Alfred's arrival in Tangier, like so many of these other women, Jane Bowles, in her pathetic state after crackups and strokes, instantly cottoned to him, in this case as a fellow freak—she called herself "Crippie, the kike dyke." At Alfred's attempt to blackmail Paul, she responded with, "But, Alfred, we love you." Certainly, the upheaval surrounding this event was only a blip in the friendship between Alfred and the Bowleses, for completely normal behavior was not really expected in their world. The most extreme acting out was admired, and Alfred was a master of that.

We all applauded when Alfred gave up wearing the wig, and seemed to be living a normal life without it, not realizing that this was an illusory stability. For the final breakdown, from which he never recovered, had everything to do with his hairlessness, and was precipitated, inadvertently, by the visit of Susan Sontag to Tangier in late summer of 1965, when she settled into the Minzah Hotel, Tangier's most elegant, for several weeks. At the time everyone's attitude, irony mixed with admiration, when we heard she was at the Minzah was: Where else would Sontag stay? It looked to me that Susan was in a crisis over her career following the staggering success of her essay on camp, or maybe just in shock, and I wrote Alfred, perhaps heartlessly, that she was coming to pump him for ideas.

Though Alfred couldn't seem to get it into his head how really famous Susan had become, with her arrival in Tangier he was threatened all over again by her beauty, particularly in the light of what he saw as the stalemate of his literary career. He was convinced, as he had been earlier in New York when his hippie boyfriend Extro started to make afternoon calls on her, that Dris, too, would be smitten, an unbearable betrayal with someone he saw as his "enemy." As can be pieced together from his fragmentary and somewhat incoherent account in "The Foot," which he wrote later in New York on an overnight trip to the fatally beautiful mountain spa of Chauen, the one he always showed visitors, he was sure that this would be the inevitable setting for Susan's seduction of Dris. In a way he set it up, probably once again to prove he was unloved.

Though Dris was awed by Susan's dark beauty, nothing of the sort happened. But the fear of it was enough. Alfred's jealousy reached a critical pitch and triggered his madness. He began to hear voices and drums in his head, that, unaccountably, he believed in. Following the textbook formula of schizophrenia, which he would have recognized if he were sane, he was now convinced the authorities could beam into his bare skull, probably because it was no longer protected with the hateful but necessary wig. He was especially terrified in official surroundings like the American Consulate, connecting it to the cover up of the Kennedy assassination—this wasn't so crazy, actually. But he must have already been planning to return to the States and was afraid that he wouldn't be let out of Morocco with his old passport photo, showing him in the wig. Susan coped as best she could with his irrational behavior and even went with him to the American Consulate to get a new passport with a photo of him in his current wigless state.

Even without his madness, one basic difference between the two was that Alfred always felt the official world was his enemy, while Susan felt part of it and expected its approval, its rewards—her famous Sense of Entitlement.

According to Paul, Susan came to tea and reported that Alfred was crazy. "Of course," Paul, airily dismissing this as mere psychology, replied, "we're all crazy here in Tangier." "No, Paul," Susan said, "I mean Alfred's *really* crazy."

Before she left Morocco, Alfred's competitive feelings toward Susan must have gone ballistic, because the evening her taxi took her to the airport all the lights in his neighborhood went out, recalling the myth that New York lights used to dim when there was an execution by electric chair in Sing Sing, and he was sure she was being electrocuted by the Moroccan government.

With the onset of madness Alfred refused to have sex with Dris and, following the instructions of the voices and the drums in his head to go straight, he went out and slept with a whore. It was about this time that he turned against me, deciding I was not the "real" Edward, and in spite of my protestations, our correspondence ceased. According to Paul, with Alfred's behavior ever more erratic, both his landlord and the Moroccan government were at the end of their patience, and at the landlord's instigation, Alfred was expelled from Morocco.

When he returned to New York in the winter of 1965, I visited him in the apartment he rented at 71 St. Marks Place, where he was acting very strangely, indeed. He refused offers to write reviews, or even, full of paranoid suspicions, to see many of his friends, though he seemed to accept me as the "real" Edward again. I had once told him, when he was having trouble writing, to write two hundred pages and leave it at that, which he now set out to do, writing it down in his notebook. The title, "The Foot," refers to an ailment Dris had developed, a bone spur in the heel of his foot that made it painful to walk. Doctors could not diagnose it, but Alfred felt guilty that he had caused it when he had once kneeled down and kissed Dris's foot, presumably in adoration. Despairing of the doctors in Morocco, who tried one treatment after another to no avail, they even made an overland trip to London to consult doctors there. So Dris's foot dominated their lives for a long time.

"The Foot" is difficult to categorize as either fiction or nonfiction, though its transformation of autobiographical material by the imagination seems to place it more in the category of fiction. If it is literal in its description of the hellishness of his losing his hair, including the fitting of his first wig at the age of fourteen with his unforgettable description of this traumatic event as "an axe driven straight down the middle of my body," he also fictionalizes his bête noir Susan Sontag, as "Mary Monday," a character divided, though not by an axe, into two "Mary Mondays," either to make her less powerful and less of a threat, as a friend has suggested, or, more likely, as a representation of her narcissistic obsession and satisfaction with herself. Grieving for a lost, paradisiacal Morocco, the narrator tells in garbled fashion the story of how he went mad in Tangier, when Susan visited him and Paul Bowles (called, in a parallel pun, Peter Plate).

On his return to New York Alfred said that the "drums" were telling him to marry Susan Sontag—politically speaking, it would have been a shrewd career move. It was odd that he (or his voices) picked on Susan to marry, since he had always called her a whore, but an alliance between the two would have positioned him for the success he needed. Astonishingly—and I didn't know whether to believe this, considering that he was crazy—he reported to me that Susan did go to bed with him, though according to his version, this attempt was a fiasco. He said that there was no cuddling, kissing or romantic talk—hard to imagine that with La Sontag—and after she diddled him awhile and it was clear that he wasn't going to be able to perform, she gave up (probably with relief on both sides), turned over and went to sleep, after which he went on his way with dark mutterings about the "black hole of Calcutta," and the fantasy of marrying Susan Sontag seemed to evaporate. It is entirely possible, of course, that the whole of this episode was a figment of his disordered mind.

Perhaps this newly discovered sexual incompatibility was a factor, but the two came to a permanent parting of the ways shortly afterward when Alfred's novel, *The Exquisite Corpse,* was being published by Holt. Without Susan's permission, he gave his editor a quote from her to the effect that he was "the most brilliant writer in New York," perhaps a doctored version of what he claimed she said during their aborted fuck, that he was the most fascinating man in New York, and if she wasn't in love with a woman she was willing to go to bed with men. When Susan saw the quote splashed across the book jacket, she called her lawyers and the publisher was forced to reprint the jacket without the offending blurb. It is not clear why she minded him using the quote, considering her debt to him, but for some reason she found this damaging to her reputation, or was merely huffy that he was using her and hadn't asked for her approval. Perhaps at this stage of her career she wanted her name associated with more powerful writers. If he had the illusion that *The Exquisite Corpse* would be a best-seller, it was clearly "experimental" fiction, confusing to readers and reviewers alike, and after its publication in 1967, it, too, quickly disappeared without a ripple.

Alfred managed to break with each of his close women friends, except perhaps Harriet Sohmers, who by some instinct or understanding of primal psychological forces, knew how to handle him. A scene that will always represent for me Alfred's relationships with women is described in Harriet's memoir "Remembering Alfred." For a short while after he returned from Morocco, Alfred stayed at her apartment, and she tells how, nervous about his erratic behavior around her infant child, she confronted him. She held a knife behind her back and warned him not to act crazy again while he was in her house. In admiration, perhaps, at this Amazon of a woman with her eyes blazing in defense of her baby, his madness receded and he became a lamb. He paid tribute to Harriet and Irene and Susan in a story called "Trois Corsages," which was lost or destroyed, along with most of his papers, in his final years.

Alfred's behavior in New York remained problematic and there were a few more nasty episodes. A minor one was his storming into the office of the real estate agent who got him the apartment on St. Mark's Place, taking the paper spike on her desk and, holding it to her belly, demanded that she stop the garbage trucks that woke him up every morning. The second, more serious, resulted from a fight he had with his mother where he hit her and threw her radio out the window. I asked him why he hit his little, old mother and he answered, "I finally gave it to the one who deserved it," which made a kind of sense to me. The family, though, took him to court and tried to get him committed. Alfred knew enough to act quite sane that day, and was released. But he compromised and went into psychotherapy with the Gestalt therapist Lore Perls, and after a short time he seemed to be getting better.

But he didn't stay long in New York. After *The Exquisite Corpse* came out, again to unappreciative reviews, his family gave him a large sum of money, I think his share of undeclared black market cash his father had put in a safe deposit box during the war, and he left the country again, to continue his long deterioration. He had a few hours to kill before catching his plane, which he spent with Neil and me, and when he went downstairs to the waiting taxi I knew from the way he said it that his goodbye was forever.

If my bohemian generation had the romantic idea—no, the imperative—that you must destroy yourself for your art, as Hart Crane and Rimbaud did, somehow I survived this illusion, although my friend Alfred did not.

Whatever the ups and downs of their relationship during his Moroccan years, after his expulsion from Morocco he referred to Paul Bowles as his "Magic Father" who had given him Morocco and kif—he could have added, and Dris. Now his one goal was to get back into Morocco and he kept appealing to Paul to help him. After being turned away several times at the border, he succeeded in reentering the country and lived in Asilah again, with a hired boy to look after his needs. There is a touching scene, in the Millicent Dillon biography of Jane Bowles, of Alfred at a café with the now equally crazy Jane, helping her write a letter of apology to Paul for having given away all the money in his checking account while she was drunk at the Parade Bar, and promising never to do it again. This was not the first time that on her binges Jane wildly wrote out checks. Given Paul's tightness, Jane's use of money in rebelling was even more crucial than her interrupting his orderly writing habits. And she was quite aware that her uncontrollable, irrational behavior would necessitate his putting her into an asylum in Malaga, as had happened before.

Expelled once again from Morocco, for unacceptable behavior, Alfred started flying from country to country, looking for a place to settle. It is difficult to reconstruct a chronology of his erratic wanderings, especially since he wasn't writing to me anymore, although I once got a strange note, begging me to be the real Edward again, and asking if I was ready to be honest with him. I knew that he was continually tormented by voices and drums inside his head, telling him God-knows-what about me. He surfaced again in London in the late sixties where his friend Norman Glass reported that Alfred whispered to him that little green men were following him. But such a cliché about paranoiac behavior is hardly credible. Undoubtedly true is the account by his editor Diana Athill of Alfred turning up at the Andre Deutsch offices and asking her to contact the Prime Minister to get the government to stop beaming messages into his head. Athill, who, from *Jamie Is My Heart's Desire* on, edited all of his work at Andre Deutsch, is another of his remarkable women admirers. Diana is a handsome, stately woman, almost unflappable in her fascination with the more exotic, unruly segments of the population. But in all her dealings with a gallery of such unstable people—so different from the disciplined upper class gentility of her upbringing—as Alfred Chester or Hakim Jamal, Jean Seberg's Black Muslim lover, whose work she also edited and whose bed she occasionally shared, she never let them drag her over the edge with them. She remains full of sympathy and is financially generous, but is helpless to avert their drive to self-destruction, which she reports so open-eyed, but heartbreakingly, in her writings.

It was to this pillar of normality that Alfred Chester turned, lonely and alienated as he was. Though dubious, Diana Athill did what he asked and contacted her Member of Parliament, who informed her wearily that every nutter in the realm kept pestering the Prime Minister to stop the government from persecuting them. Then, having fulfilled her part of the bargain, Diana, strong, sensible and down to earth as always, gave Alfred some typing work to keep him busy, and arranged for him to get psychiatric treatment, which included a stay at the Ronald Laing clinic for schizophrenics, before he disappeared again. He continued to make erratic flights to New York, London, Paris, Capri, and Athens, as well as further futile attempts to get back into Morocco.

The literary world that had taken him up so enthusiastically forgot him fast, though a few of his stories continued to appear in *The New American Review,* thanks to editor Ted Solotaroff, who had already dealt with this thorny, difficult writer when he worked for *Commentary* magazine. It was Solotaroff who now went through the two hundred page manuscript of "The Foot," which had been sent to him by Alfred's agent, and rescued fifty of the more coherent pages for the magazine. The complete manuscript of what would have been Alfred's last novel has, unfortunately, disappeared. In his madness, I believe he destroyed much correspondence and many manuscripts himself.

After all his wanderings, Alfred, mad as a hatter, landed in Israel, where he said the tranquillizers were more effective—more likely, though unconsciously, he was going to Jerusalem to die, for though he loved the Moslem world, he never denied his Jewishness. A final essay, "Letter from a Wandering Jew," probably written in 1970–1971, described the torments of these last years, particularly his often-bizarre behavior in Israel before his death, and survives, again thanks to Ted Solotaroff who photocopied it when the agent sent it to him. If Alfred's charm has disappeared along with his sense of humor (either due to a state of mental deterioration or on his way to death), this final essay reveals a new stripped-down identity, no longer worried about who he is or whether he has an "I." To paraphrase his early mock-formulation, *il m'encule, donc je suis,* he now suffered, therefore he was. Unexpectedly for such a previously elegant, often funny, writer, he let out at the end of his life a hurt, angry bellow of rage and despair at a world he couldn't stand, almost Celine-like, not caring what anyone thought, and mixing large complaints with petty gripes—it was all the same to him by now. With a sour, don't-give-a-shit tone, he didn't try to pretty up his feelings, and snarled and snapped unreasonably at his imagined persecutors. The fact that he sent this piece to his agent meant he wanted the world to know. As a record of his last lonely years, when he rejected his friends, as well as the literary world he was part of, it is unique testimony.

He eventually rented a house in Jerusalem, one that could accommodate his dogs, another pair now, for the last two, the ones he had rescued in Greece, had died in Morocco. He was drinking heavily and popping those Israeli tranquillizers in order to silence the voices in his head, as well as the noises from outside, which grated on his nerves. The local children tormented him for being such an eccentric freak, normal behavior for children, and he was always running out and screaming at them, goading them on to torment him further, and causing an uproar in the neighborhood, just as he had done in Morocco.

He had cut himself off from all his friends by now, but somehow in Israel made contact with my old friend, the poet Robert Friend, the one person in the world he seemed able to tolerate. Besides the testimony of Alfred's final essay, it is only Robert who was able to report on this period of Alfred's life and the mysterious circumstances of his death in Jerusalem. He wrote me that he could tell how brilliant Alfred had been, though only a shadow of that remained. He and Alfred stayed in touch more by telephone than in person, so when the lease on Alfred's house was up and he was supposed to move to a new place, Robert became worried when he didn't hear from him.

Then he got the news. On the first of August, 1971, the police were called by the neighbors after they had heard the dogs barking for several days. Breaking into the house, they found Alfred's body on the floor.

If Alfred had fled reporters, he got his comeuppance now. And if he had secretly longed for his fifteen minutes of fame, he got it after death. The Israeli tabloids ran lurid headlines about perversion and drugs, suggesting that the homosexual American writer had been done in by hustlers. Pure fancy, since he never picked up anyone anymore, and kept complaining to Robert about his celibacy. Because the dogs had been locked in the closet, his death was most likely suicide, but it could have been from the combination of the drugs and drink, for if the tranquillizers in Israel were the reason he settled there, he still had to drink a lot of cognac along with them to silence the voices, and the combination was lethal. It was a miracle he had survived as long as he did.

He was forty-two years old.

Though it was announced all over Europe—his friend Norman Glass heard it on the radio in Greece—his death passed by almost unnoticed in the United States. His family sent his nephew Jeffrey Chester to bring the body home, and Alfred was buried next to his mother on Staten Island. He would have considered that the final insult, especially since, as a Jew, he had instinctively gone to Jerusalem to die.

Alfred was never a widely read or popular author in his lifetime. He belonged, rather, to a coterie of avant-garde writers that appealed to devotees of what we then called "experimental" writing. It's useless to speculate, but if he had lived, with his sanity restored, and had gone on writing, I'm pretty sure that, in light of his ambitions, he would have reached for a wider readership beyond his cult following. But his death ended that possibility, leaving behind a body of small-scale, quirky, but exacting works and the legend of a doomed, self-destructive, but larger-than-life mad genius, much in the "outlaw" genre of a Rimbaud, a Genet, or perhaps more pertinently, J. R. Ackerley. Michelle Green, in her book on the expatriate Moroccan scene, *The Dream at the End of the World*, described him in Tangier as "one of the most bizarre characters in an expatriate community where eccentricity was the norm." *Village Voice* critic Michael Feingold deepens the portrait in his estimation that "Chester carried in himself two of the great polar elements on which most 20th Century art is based: He was an intelligent homosexual—that is, a man perpetually conscious of life as a series of roles or poses to be taken on; and he was a madman—a visionary."

All who knew him agree on his captivating charm, not to mention the power and sheer fun of his writing, as well as the volatile, charismatic personality it reveals so clearly. I will let Cynthia Ozick have the last word (from a letter, April 1, 1989):

> If only I could do, right now (but it's not possible), the full-scale essay on Chester that sits in my head! Our tender baby friendship, his fury and breaking-off (and the reasons for it: definitions of *Love*), his gradual coming-round, the dispute about Thomas Mann (whom he regarded as another Somerset Maugham until he read *Death in Venice* at my behest—but until then, what scorn he poured all over me!), our competitiveness, our jealousies, his having "won" and *my* jealousy, and now *my* "having won" only because he is dead, my unending puzzlement at what brought him to Jerusalem, & on & on & on. . . . . He absolutely lives for me. He is in the first, most wound-bearing layer of my emotions.

18

Greenwich Village had always been receptive to seances and ouija board-playing, cult figures like Madame Blavatsky and Edgar Cayce, and mystical poetry of the Kahlil Gibran sort, much as the hippie world later took up astrology and Carlos Castaneda. We read about the flamboyant Gurdjieff and his thin-lipped disciple Ouspensky, for they were very much part of intellectual life in the period *entre deux guerres* that seemed so romantic to my generation. Even if fuzzy religious terminology was frowned on in modern poetry, after the war and through the fifties, as left wing politics became unfashionable and even dangerous, religion exerted a new attraction for poets. Not only major poets like W. H. Auden went religious, but young poets either converted or flirted with it. I remember Howard Griffin talking of how impressed he was, visiting a Trappist Monastery upstate New York. Robert Lowell became a wild Catholic convert for some years before switching, in a canny career move, to political radical.

But as a gay man and leftist, religion was not for me. Raised an atheist by my dogmatic father, it took me time to recognize the "spiritual" or religious dimensions and origins of my Marxist and Freudian beliefs, both of which claimed to supersede religion.

Much like Gurdjieff, I have always had an affinity for lesbians, so perhaps it was inevitable that my rigidity on spiritual matters was eventually loosened in the sixties, not only by taking peyote and smoking grass, but by meeting, in 1963, an extraordinary pair of women in the Village. At a party May Swenson and Pearl Schwartz were giving for their gay list, Neil and I spotted two voluminous, large-bottomed ladies across the room. Terminally skinny as Neil and I are, we were immediately drawn to them. May told us that she had met Alma, who was a published novelist, at the Breadloaf Summer Writers' Conference, and when she and her economist mate, Elizabeth Deran, moved to New York, they had looked May up.

Alma, the larger of the two, was a soft, undisciplined, seemingly helpless creature who allowed Betty to solve the practical problems of her life. She would turn out to be strong-minded in her own way, though. Betty, dark and snapping-eyed, was solid and sensible, but at the same time loony enough to use the ouija board to contact Maynard Keynes—not so loony, actually, since he was a world-famous economist, though dead—for solutions to economics problems at the financial research institute in Rockefeller Center where she worked, solutions that were unorthodox, but effective. After we got to know her, it became obvious that Betty's notions, no matter how far-out, had a sensible basis to them.

Neil and I visited them in their Bleecker Street apartment in the West Village and learned their story. After military service in the Navy as a WAVE during World War II, Alma was studying on the GI Bill in the Midwest, when, still without a clue that she was gay, she got married to another ex-GI. The prefab student housing they were forced to live in supplied the setting for her first novel, *A Gradual Joy*, which one of her teachers sent to a New York agent. It was published in 1953 under her real name, as opposed to her later lesbian fiction, which appeared under her pseudonym Isabel Miller. The *New York Times* review called *A Gradual Joy* "top-grade for its kind," and, ironically, for someone who was to become a militant lesbian, she said it was often cited as a manual for successful heterosexual marriage.

With royalties from the book, Alma and her husband, now a veterinarian, were able to buy a house of their own and, while having four daughters, she somehow found time to write a second novel, *Round Shape*. But this conventional life blew up when, in 1962 in a Unitarian Church, she met Elizabeth Deran, who was teaching in a nearby university. The woman who introduced them, said, "I know you two will just love each other." They did, more than that woman could have known, for Alma left her husband and children to be with Betty and they moved to Washington, D.C., where Betty found a job in a government bureau. But two women living together without boyfriends in that Cold War Era of witchhunts aroused suspicion among their colleagues, and Betty was fired from her job as a security risk.

By 1963, the couple was living in the more tolerant Greenwich Village, where they began exploring the spiritual. Both women had uncanny powers, though it was Betty who was the pioneer in their researches. Though raised in the Armenian Catholic Church in Fresno, California—she had shortened her name Deranian to Deran—Betty had gone on to become a Christian Science practitioner, which was only the first of her metaphysical studies. Besides the ouija board, the two women were involved in other occult pursuits such as palmistry, astrology, and even attempts at magic, following ancient alchemical formulae. Skeptical about such parlor games as I was—it was all very dubious, if not laughable, to me—once I let myself relax about it, I found these highly intelligent women quite astute in their contrapuntal reading of the astrological charts that Alma drew up, each adding her own insights.

Betty was a true medium, and we had many entertaining ouija board sessions, though they were more successful when it was Betty's fingers sharing the pointer with mine. With Alma and me on the board together, it only spelled out "MA-MA, MA-MA," cries from supposedly infant spirits. But Betty and I "spoke" with figures as diverse as Edgar Cayce, who advised me to use crude oil on my thinning hair, and Katherine Mansfield, who told us, paradoxically, that gay men ought to work at developing their feminine side! It was a shrewd assessment, for in the preceding dangerous decades we'd concentrated on passing as straight, and often were butcher than butch.

I also found myself getting messages from Jack London, whose books I had avidly read in my youth and then forgotten, so it was a surprise to find that he was my literary "helper." But he seemed too impatient with me in his peppery, Irish way to offer much help with my writing problems. The most electrifying session followed the assassination of John F. Kennedy, who announced to us from The Beyond that he was not at peace because, he said, his KILLER ROAMS FREE. This was the more remarkable because Betty was a Republican who believed the Warren Report on the assassination, which named Lee Harvey Oswald the lone killer. After this, she was more skeptical of officialdom.

Alma wrote late into the night in her study, and, appropriately for her mystic side, by candlelight. Their neighbor, Harry Koutoukas, the off-Broadway playwright and actor with The Ridiculous Theatre Company, said that when he came home after the gay bars closed at 4:00 a.m., he used to look up and see the candles burning in her window. Oddly, when Neil and I brought her a stone from Baden-Baden, where her forebears had come from, she was uninterested. Like her whole family, she had a typically large peasant body, inescapably Germanic, so it seemed strange to me that she was indifferent to her ancestry. But she was passionately devoted to all things American, such as hymn singing around the harmonium and painting furniture with Shaker designs. She and Betty would spend vacations driving through upstate towns, photographing Fourth of July parades. She liked repeating homespun sayings—what a little neighbor girl in rural Michigan where she grew up said to her, soberly, "There's sickness in our house." Or when she and her husband moved into their new house, him saying, "I can't wait until the dirt is our dirt."

If Betty was conservative, Alma had a radical streak. Yet, in spite of her feminism, and the gay-liberationist disapproval of "sex roles

179

and stereotypes," Alma continued to believe in the categories of "butch" and "femme." With her sexual honesty, she sensed that these stereotypes reflected a basic difference in natures, at least in women of her generation and background, a theory I adapted for a poem as "cows and bulls"—"When a bull comes into the room, the cows flock round." Observably true with straights as well as gays. Clearly Betty was the "butch" in their relationship. But even then, younger women were rejecting these roles.

Out in the country, fleshy ladies like Alma were, and still are, pretty standard. Even before feminism told women it was all right to be Junoesque, Alma enjoyed her large, soft body. She believed in the science of physical types that classified people into mesomorph (the fatties), ectomorph (skinnies), and endomorph (stocky, active types), in which she came off very well, for according to this theory, mesomorphs and ectomorphs were incapable of true sexual pleasure and only endomorphs were made for love-making, capable of endless lying around snuggling and smooching. When she was tuned into a love partner, she said, she would start vibrating in ecstasy merely coming into her lover's presence, and their nipples touching, she went into orgasm. And this could go on and on. It sounded to me like that Indian saint who sits in permanent orgasm as her disciples worship her.

I followed Betty's course of self-development with growing respect. Under her influence, after years of Freudian therapy, with its limited, if theoretically correct, blaming our messed-up lives mostly on parents and childhood traumas, it was a relief, and liberating for me, to consider other ways of looking at things. If the game of astrology was "just" fun, the character readings according to the signs seemed, in my postgroup skepticism, no more arbitrary than any other theory I had believed in. And ignoring the Christian part of it, the Christian Science idea of trusting the self-healing powers of the body began to make sense. Oddly, Betty, who led me in this direction, continued to be devoted to the medical profession, while I stopped going to doctors.

Much as James Merrill used a ouija board as a stimulus for his poetry, Alma's ouija board sessions with Betty led Alma to her next novel, the first in her new life as a gay woman. While she and Betty had been on vacation upstate New York, they discovered in a small museum in Greene County the primitive paintings of a self-taught pioneer artist Mary Ann Wilson. On the wall was a note saying that in the early nineteenth century Wilson had settled with her friend, Florence Brundage, on a farm in the area. A flashbulb went off. Two women homesteading together in early America? Was that possible? Alma and Betty drove out again to explore the ruins of the farmhouse the pioneers had lived in, and when they returned home contacted Wilson on the ouija board. Based on information from these "conversations" with her subject, Alma plotted a novel about the two women falling in love and, defying convention, daring to set out by themselves, by stagecoach and riverboat, to upstate New York, where they restored an old farmhouse.

Even in the let-it-all-hang-out sixties no publisher would touch the book, and in 1969, she and Betty published it themselves as *A Place for Us* by Isabel Miller in a small edition under the imprint of Bleecker Street Press. Though the book was only reviewed at first in the pioneer lesbian magazine, *The Ladder,* where they ran a classified ad, it quickly found an enthusiastic readership, which led McGraw Hill to publish it in 1972 under the title *Patience & Sarah.* This time it was reviewed in the *New York Times,* which compared it to the early lesbian classic, *The Well of Loneliness.* "The hope and fulfillment of *Patience & Sarah* is a more likely message for the sisterhood today. . . . Patience and Sarah remain alive long after the book is closed."

In her researches, Betty eventually came upon the teachings of the Greek-Armenian Gurdjieff, for whom, as an Armenian-American, she felt a particular affinity—suddenly, we were all reading him. She applied to the main Gurdjieff teacher in New York, a forbidding personage named Lord Pentland, for admission to one of his study groups, and quickly gained notice for her aptitude and ingenuity in "The Work." As Betty became absorbed in Gurdjieff studies, Alma turned toward the new feminism and joined a gay consciousness-raising group that included feminist pioneers Kate Millett and Sydney Abbott. But I don't think this is what finally broke Alma and Betty up. The two women were a rare, stable couple at a time when the gay world was exploding in joy over gay liberation. I had met them when, after a decidedly unsatisfying free-wheeling life of promiscuity, I was quite happy settling down with Neil. But by now both Alma as well as Neil were finding monogamy stifling. Alma had told me when she escaped married life for the lesbian world she thought lesbians had gone through so much pain to be themselves and live their lives that they must be wonderful, caring people. She gave a rueful laugh over the reality she'd discovered, that lesbians were just as cruel and selfish as everyone else, even with each other. But now she herself wanted to be out there in that cruel world. In Alma's case, actually it was her drinking as much as the constricting domestic bonds that ended the relationship with Betty. When she was drinking, the only way you could tell was that her talking became a monologue rather than a conversation. But I believe at home she was more of a problem, a very large falling-down drunk, who little Betty had to somehow get off the floor.

After separating from Betty, Alma got a job at Columbia University Press and moved into a ramshackle floor-through apartment in an old nineteenth-century house on West 19th Street that was always full of her lesbian/feminist tribe. That is where her oldest daughter Natalie came to stay with her. It's extraordinary that her four daughters, who had been abandoned when their mother, like the heroine of Ibsen's "The Doll's House," had gone out into the world to find herself, held no rancor against her. As they grew up, each sought her out in New York. Remarkably, they had come to understand her and her need to find her own way.

A few years after the Stonewall riot, and while Neil and I were out of the country, I was especially pleased to hear that Alma carried a sign during an annual Gay Pride parade that read, STAND UP, FRIEND, WITH ME, the title of my first book—she was one of those who understood it. Her tastes in poetry were broad. Besides liking the poetry of May Swenson, she also could quote reams of verse by May's *bête noir,* May Sarton, whose name and lesbianism were the only similarities between them—their poetry was very different.

Early on in her new freedom, Alma tried another live-in lover, but it didn't work. She had grown up in a big dirt-poor family in Traverse City, Michigan, with a policeman father and a mother who was a nurse and a Seventh Day Adventist, and one of Alma's complaints was that her new lover lay in the bathtub for hours with the hot water running—with her Depression-Era childhood, Alma kept worrying over the fuel being wasted to produce that hot water.

Later, she moved into Westbeth, the artists housing project in the West Village where I had also landed a studio, but she was too down-to-earth to live in such a self-consciously artsy community. Even when she moved to a building on Perry Street, which was more congenial, being full of odd Village types, she was never happy in an apartment. Her vision of life, instilled from her childhood in the Midwest, meant living in a house, folksy with rocking chairs and crocheted afghans and copies of *Yankee* in the magazine rack. So when she got a better-paying job as a copy editor at *Time Magazine,* she bought an old wooden house with a porch in Poughkeepsie and settled in with a new partner, Julie Weber, with whom she spent the rest of her life. As it turned out, her old mate, Betty Deran, now Elisabeth Deranian, also moved to Poughkeepsie, so that bond continued as strongly as ever. By this time, Alma had joined AA and given up drinking, but she still needed Betty's butchy encouragement, even discipline, to get on with her writing. This resulted in three more books, though none of them was anywhere near as successful as *Patience & Sarah,* which has remained in print ever since, as well as having been adapted as a play and an opera.

Alma had always been proud of her perfect bowel movements, and one of the joys of having a mate, she said, was to be able to call them into the bathroom and show them. But when, in 1993, Alma developed cancer of the colon and had to wear a colostomy bag, the indignity of it was unacceptable and forced her into unnatural isolation. Even when she succeeded in getting the doctor to reverse the colostomy, the victory did not last long and the cancer spread. She now refused to see anyone or submit to any further medical treatment. She spent her last days at home under hospice care, surrounded by friends and her four daughters. On her deathbed, in and out of consciousness, she was in love with all her former lovers. Elisabeth Deranian she called "the light of my life." And when another old lover flew in from San Francisco and took her hand, Alma came to and murmured, "Sweet cunt." The day before her death, the opera based on *Patience & Sarah* by Wende Persons and Paula Kimper was performed at Trinity Church in Manhattan.

Zan Knudson, the late May Swenson's partner, pronounced what I think is an appropriate epitaph. "Since May's death," she told me, "Alma is the only person to have died who May would want to be with her in heaven."

19

The Gurdjieffian idea that we are all asleep and need to awaken, though not too different from the Christian call of "Sleepers, awake!" was a strange concept, but definitely intriguing to me. Under Betty Deran's influence, I read Gurdjieff's books and all the books about him I could find, including, and especially, Boyhood with Gurdjieff *by Fritz Peters, who seemed to write more convincingly about him than any of the other followers. But unlike Betty, I was not tempted to join a Gurdjieff group or any other organization.*

Two of Fritz Peters's books, the memoir of the famous teacher and mystic, *Boyhood with Gurdjieff,* and *Finistère,* one of the first gay novels I ever read, have continued to be available in numerous editions over the years, but I had never come across anyone who knew him. As far as I could tell, Fritz had lived his life apart from the literary world, or the parts of the literary world I've been involved with.

I was naturally curious about someone who had written so brilliantly about both his spiritual master and his own sexuality. His two famous books simply didn't fit comfortably together in the mind. They appeal to different constituencies which nevertheless aren't incompatible. I should think this would make him a subject of particular interest, but Fritz himself has remained invisible, both before and since his death in 1971. This is partly due to the continuing hostility of the Gurdjieffian world toward his homosexuality. At the same time it is hard to understand the indifference of the gay world toward the author of a gay classic.

After Gurdjieff's death in 1949, the movement purporting to teach his "system," like most spiritual groups, developed a decidedly antihomosexual bias. Paradoxically, memoirs of Gurdjieff have been written by a number of his often-prominent lesbian disciples, demonstrating that there was no conflict in Gurdjieff, at least, over their sexual orientation. One can only infer that homosexuality, though not to be proclaimed, was no bar to participation in "The Work," at least for women. Gurdjieff, himself from a middle-eastern culture that wasn't hypocritical about or bothered by such things, gave top marks to young Fritz Peters's boyishly rosy behind in the community bathhouse, where the Master of Eastern Mysticism liked to line up all his naked male disciples in order to compare, with ribald comments, their bodies and particularly their sexual parts. On this last point, Gurdjieff, at least, had no reason to be shy, since he was said to have the biggest *schwantz* of all.

*I*t was after Alma Routsong broke up with Betty Deran that I first heard about Annie Lou Stavely, a teacher of the Gurdjieffian system who was living in Portland, Oregon. Although not a lesbian herself, Mrs. Stavely had been a student of one of Gurdjieff's lesbian disciples, Jane Heap, in London in the thirties and, after returning to the States at the end of the war, attracted her own circle of students in Portland, where she worked for the state university. On one of Stavely's "state" visits to the Gurdjieff center in New York, Betty, now living on her own after the breakup with Alma and in one of the Gurdjieff study groups, met her, and immediately fell in love.

In spite of the refusal of Mrs. Stavely to entertain the possibility of a love affair with a woman, Betty precipitously gave up her well-paying job in the economics think tank to follow Mrs. Stavely back to Oregon, where she hoped over time to persuade the Gurdjieff teacher that she needed a woman in her life. Meanwhile, the canny Mrs. Stavely seemed quite willing to have someone as capable as Betty around. It was after Betty had moved in with Mrs. Stavely as all-round helper that she received my letter announcing that I had met the elusive Fritz Peters. Astoundingly, I learned in her reply that Annie Lou Stavely had once had an affair with him!

Fritz was a tall, buoyant man of about sixty, with the kind of aging-boy looks of a Christopher Isherwood, or perhaps it was the similar barbershop haircut, closely clipped on the sides with a lock over the forehead, and a drinker's nose. In a free-wheeling age of longish hair and relaxed dress, Fritz persisted in wearing the conventional, slightly seedy suits I associate with alcoholics trying to look respectable—he even wore a bowtie, a dapper note left over from the fifties. And I could tell that he drank. It wasn't just the nose. Though I never saw him drunk, he had what I can only call a boozy manner.

It was not surprising to find that the author of one of the early landmarks in gay fiction, which had been published in 1951, was completely homosexual in orientation, even if, during our dinners out, he indicated that there had been a failed marriage. And later, it turned out that there were two! But that didn't surprise me either, because it wasn't unusual in that era for homosexuals to try to go straight and get married—although two attempts sounds like desperation. I certainly understood, having spent years in psychotherapy trying to change. But if Fritz had once been in conflict over his sexuality, as I had, perhaps the new open atmosphere of gay liberation had also had its beneficent effect on him, even though he expressed scorn for gay groups. It was an age of groups—recovering addicts, dykes with tykes, parents of gays—there was a group for everyone. I now saw a pugnaciousness in Fritz as he went on to attack groups in general, and I certainly agreed with him there about my therapy group. It turned out he'd had a similar negative experience, but with the Gurdjieff groups.

Fritz was living at the Arlington on East 25th Street, one of those small hotels in midtown Manhattan left over from a grander era. Once elegant, it had fallen in the world. The ornate facade was marred by graying curtains and yellowed window shades, and on the sills outside the rooms stood milk cartons and food containers. Called SROs, for Single Room Occupancy, these old hotels were occupied mostly by the elderly, often on pensions or welfare. I later saw snapshots of Fritz's room, which looked quite respectable, but at that time I imagined a sagging bedstead and stained sheets, scarred carpeting, the smell in the hallways, the old bellhop in uniform who did errands for the aging tenants, perhaps fetching a pint of booze for a desperate old soul. It had that derelict atmosphere about it.

Fritz had a job as a legal secretary, and he seemed satisfied with it, especially the irregular hours the exigencies of the firm's court cases demanded. His employers must have been delighted with such a crackerjack worker, for whatever Fritz did, he believed in doing well. But I suspected that mental troubles and possibly breakdowns, exacerbated by drink, were recurrent over the years—I hadn't yet read *The World Next Door,* his novel about a stay in a mental hospital—and by this time he had accepted the shabby level of life he could sustain. But, nevertheless, I was in awe of him as an author, and when I asked him why he wasn't writing books, his answer was that he wasn't interested in being a professional, committed to turning out one book after another. He preferred to write only when he felt he had a book in him. Later, after I read his last published novel, *The Descent,* I understood this—it was labored and boring.

I've only been able to construct a spotty chronology of Fritz Peters's life. Much is shrouded in the reluctance of survivors, both family and Gurdjieffians, to speak with me, as well as by Fritz's own reserve in writing about himself directly, though the first two novels are clearly autobiographical. The *New York Times,* in its obituary, reveals that he was born Arthur Anderson Peters in 1913 in Madison,

Wisconsin. And from the published memoirs of his lesbian aunt, the writer and editor Margaret Anderson, I learned that Fritz was a nickname derived from the infant's pugnacious resemblance to the German General Von Hindenburg. His childhood coincided with the height of pre–WWI Chicago bohemia, when Margaret Anderson founded her avant-garde literary journal *The Little Review*. Fritz's mother, Lois, as bohemian as her sister Margaret, soon dumped her unacceptably conventional husband to join, with her two little sons, Margaret's artsy entourage in a makeshift encampment on the shores of Lake Michigan. But Lois was not to stay there long before she took another fling at romance, a pattern she would often repeat, with or without the boys in tow. It was after a decade of their flapper mother's shifting household with one man or another that in 1924 the eleven-year-old Fritz and his brother, Tom, were enrolled, historically, as it turned out, in Chateau du Prieuré, Gurdjieff's "Institute for the Harmonious Development of Man" outside Paris, years so vividly recounted in Fritz's memoir *Boyhood with Gurdjieff*.

Fritz's residence at Le Prieuré, during the mid to late twenties, came about at the intervention of his aunt Margaret and her lover, Jane Heap, who had transferred *The Little Review* to France and become followers of Gurdjieff. Because Fritz's mother, Lois, was making such a mess of her life with her destructive relationships with men and absences in a mental institution, Heap and Anderson decided that living with her was unhealthy for Fritz and his brother, and persuaded the unhappy woman to relinquish the boys and allow Jane Heap to adopt them. As a passionate disciple and, later, teacher of Gurdjieff's ideas, Jane was convinced that The Institute for the Harmonious Development of Man would be an ideal place for the boys to grow up, offering them a unique opportunity to sit at the feet of the master and develop into "harmonious" men themselves. A more sensible Gertrude Stein, who was a friend of Jane and Margaret but no worshipper of Gurdjieff, didn't at all approve of the rarefied atmosphere of Le Prieuré, considering Gurdjieff's establishment an unsuitable place for American boys to grow up in. When they finally met, the strong-minded Gertrude and the mystic Gurdjieff were reported to have circled around each other warily. Jane must have agreed to some extent with Gertrude's opinion, for she asked Gertrude and her partner, Alice Toklas, to look in on the boys, give them books and see to their darning and mending, the latter Alice's province, of course. Gertrude and Alice also took the boys out on motoring excursions and celebrated American holidays with them, such as traditional Thanksgiving dinners.

These motherless, if instructive, years with Gurdjieff were indeed important to Fritz Peters's development, and perhaps living in the undeniably magnetic presence of the great man may have succeeded in rescuing him to some extent from the crippling effects of his mother's irrational behavior. He reports in *Boyhood with Gurdjieff* that he "fell in love" with Gurdjieff from the start and was something of a fanatical disciple. One of Fritz's jobs was mowing the extensive lawns at the center, and when Gurdjieff was convalescing from an automobile accident, Fritz was asked by Gurdjieff's wife to stop mowing to give the patient the quiet he needed. But just before the accident Fritz had been told by the mystic to continue mowing "no matter what happened." Therefore, Fritz thought that the mystic must have foreseen the accident and, according to his often decidedly odd but practical ideas, the mowing might have been necessary for his recovery, so the boy stubbornly refused to stop. Surprisingly, Fritz later told my friend Betty, after she got to know him, that the incident had involved not him but his brother, Tom. But he said that he didn't feel there was any requirement for an author to tell the truth. This also conformed to Gurdjieffian teaching, which allows any deception to achieve your goal.

Fritz reports in the final issue of *The Little Review,* responding to a questionnaire about his future, that he hoped to stay at Le Prieuré until the age of twenty, and always wanted to "work with Mr. G's method." But in 1929, he left willingly when his mother asked him to return to Chicago to live with her and her new husband. To get away, he had to stand up to his guardian, the formidable Jane Heap, with whom he always had a difficult relationship, and to the more formidable, but more reasonable, Gurdjieff.

It was after he returned to the United States that following his trail grows difficult. It is likely that Fritz never lost touch with Gurdjieff after returning to Chicago and accompanied him on his frequent fund-raising visits to America "to shear the sheep," as Gurdjieff outrageously put it. (Elsewhere, in the same comic, if heartless style, Gurdjieff referred to his disciples as rats he experimented on, when he wasn't assigning them animal correlatives to illustrate their faults.) Though many of his most prominent disciples were banished or became disillusioned over the master's at-times incomprehensible behavior, often calculated to shake the student from his rigid outlook, Fritz Peters and Gurdjieff seem never to have wavered in their mutual affection. It was this deep bond and intimate familiarity with Gurdjieff's teaching that led to Fritz's lifelong contempt for the presumptuous claims by the followers to teach "The Work."

Whatever Fritz was doing with his life after Le Prieuré, he was not exhibiting any direction or purpose. According to him, because of the spotty education he had received at Le Prieuré, he found it impossible to graduate from high school or qualify for college. This is unconvincing, for, surely, someone as intelligent as he could have caught up with the educational requirements, if he wanted to. In 1934, he was in New York, studying typing and shorthand at a business school. But he returned to Chicago from time to time, probably because of his mother. It was from Chicago, in the late thirties, that he commented on the problems the black novelist Jean Toomer was having in setting up a Gurdjieff study group there, especially with the newspapers, supporting the prejudices of the era, hounding Toomer for marrying a white woman.

Wherever Fritz spent the late thirties, or how, he was definitely in Europe during World War II. By 1942, he was an enlisted man serving in the 29th Infantry Division. And it was in London, waiting for D-Day that Fritz had the affair with Betty's beloved Annie Lou Stavely, who was in one of Jane Heap's study groups there. After Le Prieuré closed down for good and was sold in 1933, Heap had started conducting her own Gurdjieff groups, first in Paris, then in London. Mrs. Stavely was reportedly married to a gay man, and in a letter to

Fritz, she reveals her feelings about the marriage by calling the period of her affair with him "an oasis in the desert." The poetry that Fritz gave her (and which she gave to me after his death) was ghastly, but reveals his already charming, sophisticated, if cynical self. This heterosexual affair must have continued during Fritz's various leaves and furloughs from the American army during combat duty in the later stages of the war.

During the Battle of the Bulge, all clerical staff, including Fritz, were rushed into the battle zone to stem the German breakthrough and the slaughter around him was a horrifying experience. When the pressure let up, Fritz managed to secure leave from the front and visit Gurdjieff in Paris. He was clearly in a state of battle fatigue, if not shell shock, and Gurdjieff, using esoteric healing powers, had a restorative effect, if only a temporary one, on the young soldier's nerves. In retrospect, thinking of how crazy I, myself, was after the war from my own harrowing experiences, it had to have been his period of combat that left its mark, and along with the underlying instability from childhood dislocation, led to the postwar collapse and hospitalization reported in fictional terms in his first novel *The World Next Door*, which was published in 1949.

It seems to have been a brief postwar marriage to Mary Louise Aswell, the distinguished literary editor of *Harper's Bazaar*, that got Fritz writing at last. The protagonist in *The World Next Door* is clearly that of Fritz, with the characteristic arrogance and the feisty, almost quarrelsome nature I remember so well. The novel confirms, not surprisingly, that his mother too had spent considerable time in mental institutions, though by then she has settled down in a fairly stable marriage. Committed after a breakdown to a Veterans Administration mental ward, the hero is subjected to brutal procedures, including shock treatment. Not only must that have been startling at the time, but he also talks about homosexuality in an open way. Perhaps Fritz got away with this because his character was in a nut house. Likewise for the descriptions of the patients masturbating in the wards, and sadistic guards forcing inmates to give them blowjobs—raw stuff for 1949. The patient admits to a resident doctor that he has had a homosexual experience, and even admits that he was in love with the man, but denies that he is a homosexual because the sex "just wasn't any good." Besides, "it didn't last. . . . It wasn't right, somehow." But then it turns out that on his military record is still another homosexual experience involving a general, which the army tried to hush up. He even admits that "in the beginning, I was willing to be a fairy . . . but it didn't turn out that way." The implication is that he had decided not to be gay. I took that as a description of Fritz's own early attitudes on his homosexuality, shaped by the era's benighted attitudes toward it.

Unlike the psychoanalytic novels that were coming into vogue, *The World Next Door* never explores the deeper causes of the protagonist's breakdown, beyond vague mentions of serving in the recent war and conflict with his mother. Fritz, like most Gurdjieffians, was anti-Freudian. But the novel brilliantly analyzes the politics of hospitalization, and is unsparing in describing the outer manifestations of insanity, plus the strategies the hero uses to gain his release. For this, it was warmly received, which encouraged Fritz to take the next step and write *Finistère,* a further confrontation of his homosexuality. Whatever the situation of their marriage, Mary Louise Aswell was celebrated for introducing a number of homosexual writers into the pages of *Harper's Bazaar,* notably Truman Capote and Tennessee Williams, and she would certainly not have exhibited the normal homophobia of the era.

Finistère, published in 1951, is for me the quintessential homosexual novel of the postwar decade and ends typically, as the period demanded, with the suicide of the young protagonist. In Fritz Peters's obituary in the *New York Times* in 1979, the subject of the novel was described as "a destructive homosexual relationship," although the book was clearly about the destruction of a youth by his family after they discover his love affair with his tutor, a very different cup of tea indeed, but in keeping with the *Times*'s homophobic editorial policy of that era.

All the major media had the same bias. I remember, when *Finistère* appeared, discussing it with my friend from Paris, Harry Goldgar, who, in hopes of becoming a reviewer for *Time Magazine,* was assigned by the book editor to write a sample review of the novel. A professional reporter, Harry asked the editor whether to take a viewpoint that would conform to *Time*'s homophobia of the period, or to review it honestly. The editor demanded honesty, but then failed to hire my friend when he treated the book sympathetically.

The traumatic events recounted in *Finistère* are most likely to have occurred during or shortly after Fritz's four satisfying years at Le Prieuré, during a stay with his mother and her current husband. Although there are fictional elements in the novel, such as the boy's suicide, I don't for a minute believe that the basic plot was just made up. An adolescent American boy joins his mother, who is spending a period in the French provinces with her new husband. She hires a French tutor for her son, and the master–pupil relationship blossoms into a love affair, which gives the boy a tremendous boost in self-confidence and independence. But when this is discovered and broken up, his stepfather compounds the boy's shock and grief by making a pass at him. In the context of the era's negative attitudes toward homosexual behavior, and the humiliation the boy suffers, it is quite believable that he becomes suicidal, though his walking into the sea follows the requisite literary formula of that time—if you're homosexual, the only thing you can do is kill yourself. But the novel is beautifully written and has authenticity and intelligence.

Looking back, I continue to be puzzled at myself for not asking Fritz, on our dinners out in the Village, anything at all about *Finistère*'s genesis and how much of it was autobiographical, much less about the story of his life. But he had something wounded in him and I respected the depths of pain, the scars of humiliation that his cynical manner denied. I would never have brought up his past unless he brought it up first. At that time, I was tussling with my own lifelong feelings of worthlessness and sensed a fellow sufferer in him. But I will never stop kicking myself that when I had the chance to quiz him, I let it pass. Whatever the truth in this story, about the same period in his adolescence there is also evidence of a sex episode with his brother, Tom, which he dealt with in a later unpublished novel. Clearly, homosexuality was already problematical for Fritz.

Shortly after *Finistère*, which got respectable reviews, appeared his third novel, *The Descent*, in 1952. This one had a Santa Fe setting, where Fritz was living during a second marriage, after the divorce from Aswell. It disappeared with barely a ripple, and depressing as that must have been for him, along with the conflict between married life and his homosexual needs, his writing seems to have lost its momentum, and he was not to have another success with a book until the mid-sixties, when the circumstances of his life were very different. This would be *Boyhood with Gurdjieff*, published in 1964, with its description of Fritz's teenage years spent at Le Prieuré.

No matter what he did with his life, Fritz could never escape his identification with Gurdjieff, as if he had inherited part of the mantle, along with the awe, and considerable resentment, of the followers, and was uncomfortable with it, especially with the cult that developed after Gurdjieff's death. Writing *Boyhood with Gurdjieff* must have been an attempt to deal with this burden, but since the book instantly became a classic in the enormous and growing Gurdjieffian library, it put the unfortunate Fritz back into the center of the maelstrom. Still, even while shying away from it, he had to be struggling on a deeper level to lay claim to his Gurdjieffian inheritance, for by writing the book, he established himself as one of the unimpeachable authorities on the subject.

But he didn't seem at all interested, either, in exploiting his reputation in the Gurdjieff world. It was astonishing to me that this man, who, from the evidence of *Boyhood with Gurdjieff*, was as much an authority on Gurdjieff as anyone alive, considered all established groups teaching the so-called Work inauthentic and denied that this teaching had anything to do with what Gurdjieff taught. If they were interested in discovering the real Gurdjieff they should have been paying attention to him. But this didn't seem to be the case.

In the postwar period up to Gurdjieff's death in 1949, Fritz managed to attend some of his famous dinner parties in Paris, which the master used as an opportunity for various teaching exercises, often involving humiliating his stuffier guests, supposedly for their own good. But Gurdjieff's technique of getting his disciples drunk, again for their own good, could not have been a positive influence on the young veteran, for whom drinking would remain a lifelong problem. Moreover, Gurdjieff's axiom, "Whatever you do, do a lot of it," though good advice for his cautious followers, would have been dangerous justification for an incipient alcoholic, especially one who would spend most of his life trying to drown his guilt and live straight.

It was in this postwar period that Fritz's problems with the Gurdjieff groups began. While I doubt that Gurdjieff himself had the least problem with Fritz's homosexuality, the movement somehow became dominated by the famous rock-jawed puritanical disciple of Gurdjieff, Ouspensky, who was adamantly opposed to homosexuality, considering it to be a wrong use of energy. The attitude of the "higher ups" in the movement, as one follower described it to me, was that Fritz was just another "homosexual living in Greenwich Village, as if his place was 'under the rug.'" Even without other reason to, was it any wonder that Fritz drank? And it was these same "higher ups" who derided him for taking seriously what they considered a comic turn on the part of the master, in which Gurdjieff anointed Fritz as his heir.

This happened at one of Gurdjieff's postwar dinner parties in Paris, when someone had asked the great teacher who was his true heir. With his great, luminous eyes, Gurdjieff looked around the table at the disciples, many renowned, who had come from far and wide, all of whose hearts were probably beating like Cinderella's sisters in hopes of being chosen by the prince, when suddenly, pointing to the astonished young man, Gurdjieff announced, "Fritz! Fritz is my heir."

Gurdjieff's followers never forgave Fritz for that, or recognized him.

$\mathcal{E}$ver since Fritz's death, I've persisted in trying to find out more about him, sending out letters on the slimmest chance of acquaintance. Close-mouthed like all the surviving Gurdjieffians, Annie Lou Stavely answered my queries by first saying that Fritz was better forgotten. Later relenting, she sent me a folder full of photos he had left in her care, family snapshots with his children in Albuquerque, and others he appears to have taken to show his children his room at the Arlington Hotel, the law office where he worked, and one of his lawyer bosses, a good-looking young family man named MacCarthy, for whom he obviously had a special fondness, and with whom he socialized during his irregular hours on the job. Also among the pictures were pages of an older family album with snapshots of the infant Fritz and his brother, Tom, a girlish Fritz of nineteen, Fritz, the guide at the Chicago World's Fair of 1933, and Fritz, the GI.

With my attempts to contact his family leading nowhere and Mrs. Stavely and even his publishers stonewalling me, it was in the gay world that I struck gold. My complaints about my frustrations to a correspondent, the writer Samuel Steward, produced a remarkable account of him having sex with Fritz, and shortly after, the painter Paul Cadmus found in his diary notations of dinner parties with Fritz in the sixties. So for a brief time, at least, he had mixed in gay and artistic circles! It was through them that I located his papers at Boston University, where his daughter Katherine had deposited them, and which revealed more details of his life and work, though she has, up to now, refused to answer my queries.

Samuel Steward, best known under his pseudonym Phil Andros as a writer of gay porn, and an adviser to the famous Dr. Kinsey on homosexuality, wrote me before his death in 1994 that he had kept notes on all his sex partners, his Stud File, as he called it, and could give me details of an escapade with Fritz, whom he had pursued in Chicago in 1952 because of his admiration for *Finistère*. According to Steward's notes, Fritz was living in Rogers Park then, "the place (Chicago), size of dingdong (average, parlor), and what happened (I blew him). . . . I remember him as being blond and really drunk." Even so, "Fritz was reluctant when I finally did get him in bed because his underwear wasn't the cleanest. . . . He burst into tears about five minutes after he shot his wad, and began to drink even more . . . ranting about how he really wasn't gay."

This not only explains Fritz's marriage, as well as its breakup, but makes the writing and publication of *Finistère,* so daring for its time, so sympathetic to the boy's homosexuality, a mystery. One can only wonder at the complexities of the human heart, and Fritz's was one of the more complicated. Steward's letter concludes, "I'm sorry, but he seemed so difficult to know, so withdrawn and afraid of being near or around someone gay or being afraid of being thought gay himself that I just couldn't spend the time with him that I should have."

The painter, Paul Cadmus, told me that in 1963 Fritz was living in New York with Lloyd Lozes Goff, one of Cadmus's models from the thirties and a painter by then in his own right. Cadmus had gone to their Manhattan apartment for dinner parties. "Yes, indeed, Lloyd and Fritz were 'lovers,'" Cadmus noted in his diary. "I seem to remember it was to be 'forever' but . . . I gather Fritz was quite 'unstable.'"

Lloyd Goff was a decade older than the fifty-year-old Fritz Peters, and must have offered security to a man who had fled his feelings for so long. If so, it is to Goff that we owe that marvelous book, *Boyhood with Gurdjieff,* written during their time together. Significantly, the author's photo on the book jacket was taken by Goff. In a burst of energy, Fritz turned out two more novels, *Night Flight,* published in England, though mysteriously not in the United States, and another as-yet-unpublished novel, the manuscript dedicated to Lloyd Goff, attesting to the seriousness of the affair and his gratitude to the man who helped him accept himself at last.

This unpublished novel, in manuscript form among his papers, has several chapters about Fritz's relationship with his brother, focusing on their sexual experience during adolescence, which was significant for Fritz though not for his brother, who turned out to be straight.

Lloyd and Fritz were still together four years later, by the evidence of Cadmus's social calendar of 1967. But the creative streak along with the love affair eventually ended, and Fritz, probably following his Gurdjieffian-inspired unruly temperament, was soon on the loose. Working irregular hours as a legal secretary and living at the Arlington Hotel, he again retreated from a literary life, though he did manage to complete a somewhat sketchy further memoir, *Gurdjieff Remembered,* published in 1971 by Samuel Weiser, founder of the leading bookstore for spiritual literature in New York City. Before his death, years later in Albuquerque, Fritz began another novel, and put together a third book on Gurdjieff, *A Balanced Man.* Although Samuel Weiser was unwilling to publish it, probably because it was a sweeping together of fragments left out of the two other Gurdjieff books, the manuscript circulated surreptitiously among Gurdjieffians in "The Work." Currently, the rights to Fritz's books are in such a tangle that a recent compilation of his three Gurdjieff books in one volume by Bardic Press, for which I supplied the photo of Fritz, has been blocked by a lawsuit.

I was in Portland, Oregon, in 1973, giving poetry readings around the Northwest and staying in the house of Nina Lowry who got me a gig at Portland State University, the same university Annie Lou Stavely worked for, when I spoke to Nina about the Gurdjieffian guru. Nina recognized the name at once, exclaiming, "You don't mean little old Mrs. Stavely, secretary of the Theatre Arts Department? She can hardly answer the phone properly!" This, in a tone that dismissed Mrs. Stavely as anyone ever to be taken seriously. I trusted Nina's opinion, but Gurdjieffians are supposed to blend in with the population, I thought to myself, and reserved judgment.

On another tour in the Northwest, I visited Betty Deran in the old-fashioned wooden house where she was then living with Mrs. Stavely, still not as the lover she would have wished to be, but as assistant and companion. Betty had quickly become invaluable, taking over many of the tasks of everyday life, and especially, helping with Mrs. Stavely's ever-growing number of followers. I gave Mrs. Stavely high marks for being smart enough to recognize Betty as one of the rare problem-solvers on the planet.

Mrs. Stavely, who was probably used to lesbians coming on to her from her Jane Heap days, was unfortunately still adamant against trying it out for herself. But if Betty never succeeded in winning her over, Mrs. Stavely managed to make Betty try heterosexuality, which she acceded to, briefly, in hopes of getting Mrs. Stavely to loosen up in turn. Cunning Annie Lou, though, did not have a yielding nature and never reciprocated the experiment. Although her affair with Fritz during and after the war had probably broken up Mrs. Stavely's already-foundering marriage, it must have been this affair that had given the sexually uncertain Fritz the confidence to get married to Mary Louise Aswell. Turning gay men straight is a curious ambition of some heterosexual women. In the case of Fritz it temporarily succeeded, much as Mrs. Stavely's attempt to convert Betty was only briefly successful.

When Mrs. Stavely retired from her job at the university in Portland, she bought a farm nearby in the countryside, where Betty and her other disciples followed her. As Gurdjieff had done, she kept them all busy building new wings and porches onto the house, changing the entranceway, and launching into various erratic projects with murky educational motives. Visiting them there, and seeing Mrs. Stavely living in a torn-up house amid the construction and feeling sorry for her, I asked her when it would be finished. "Never, if I can help it," she replied firmly. On consideration, I said to myself that this was one smart lady to have set herself up so well for old age. I could see that she would be taken care of devotedly until her death by her "students"—which turned out to be the case. And the harder she made it for them, the more devoted they were.

In 1975, Fritz and I were having dinner at the Gran Ticino restaurant, one of his habitual hangouts in Greenwich Village, also patronized by the then mayor, the sexually ambiguous Ed Koch, who was there that evening with a young "assistant," when Fritz announced to me that he and Annie Lou Stavely had made contact with each other again, almost certainly through the sly intervention of Betty, who was not above such things, and Mrs. Stavely had invited Fritz to visit her farm. Curiously, after this initial foray to Oregon Fritz came back highly elated, announcing to me that Mrs. Stavely had proposed to him that he move to the farm and teach the Gurdjieff system. He described for me his bouts of drinking with her male disciples, who were wowed by meeting someone so close to the legendary master, and, under the influence of alcohol, the steamy embraces they had shared in the rural darkness. And he clearly reveled in being treated as an important personage, the heir of Gurdjieff. Perhaps, too, he saw the Oregon colony as a good place to slip into a peaceful old age, surrounded and looked after by adoring young people, as Mrs. Stavely was, in comparison to which a third-rate New York hotel room offered very little.

Scandals and defections are nothing unusual in the history of Gurdjieffian groups, which from the beginning were rent with betrayals, suspicions, accusations, and frequent disillusionment and departures, even expulsions. Mrs. Stavely might have initially seen Fritz as a useful agent in "awakening" her followers in Oregon, radiating the Gurdjieffian spirit he had imbibed directly from the master, or even, with his outspoken, abrasive manner, as a necessary irritant toward that awakening. Though she couldn't have foreseen the extent of his drinking and open homosexual behavior, which was more shocking against the conservative backdrop of Oregon, his great prestige as the author of *Boyhood with Gurdjieff* could not be denied. And he was, presumably, an old friend, whatever the stormy events of the past had been. Perhaps he was ready to settle down and be a suitable companion for her, someone in her own age group, who shared her past associations. She might even have had a remote hope of reawakening their sex life!

In *The World Next Door,* Fritz talked about his Christ Complex. Now his emotional instability was only increased by the near-worship he got from Mrs. Stavely's followers, and he was clearly in a manic phase when he returned from the initial visit and regaled me at the Gran Ticino with his adventures. After he had wound up his affairs in New York and was ready to fly out to Oregon to settle on the farm, he announced grandly to me, "You may accompany me to the airport," as if he were God's anointed. This meant that I was being honored by being chosen to drive The Great Man to Kennedy Airport in my battered VW bus. It was not quite the vehicle he merited, but he was oblivious. At last he was being enthroned as Gurdjieff's heir. I got the distinct impression that he was going to be the farm's Resident Guru, with Mrs. Stavely his unlikely Handmaiden.

But the iron-willed Annie Lou Stavely was not about to accept second billing. It was no time at all, perhaps a week or two after Fritz left, before I got a telephone call from him, not in Oregon but, astonishingly, New Mexico, informing me that the whole thing had blown up. And from Betty I learned that from the minute he arrived, he really had started giving orders and turning the place upside down, trying to run it as Gurdjieff would have, besides drinking everything in sight. Betty had enjoyed having a gay man on the place with whom she could speak frankly. But his behavior had been so impossible, so disruptive to the orderly routine of classes and "teaching" projects, that Annie Lou had him shipped out on a plane for Albuquerque, where, he told me on the phone, he had moved in with an old friend of eighty-three, who lived in a big adobe house, and needed someone to cook and deal with household matters that were getting to be too much for her.

It was after Fritz's death, when I informed Mrs. Stavely that I wished to write a memoir of him, that she relented and sent me the sheaf of photographs that he must have inadvertently left behind when she reasserted her authority and hustled him off to the plane, and the drinking and revelry on the farm had ceased and order was restored.

Soon after this, Betty herself caused a rumpus on Mrs. Stavely's farm, where by now, with her problem-solving nature, she had made herself indispensable as Mrs. Stavely's "right hand man." Gurdjieffian philosophy was not against sexuality, and Gurdjieff himself had had a well-known, even scandalous, neo-pagan love life among his numerous female disciples, spreading his biological progeny far and wide. But under the aegis of Mrs. Stavely, "The Work" took on the more puritan cast of the London-based Ouspensky school, and when Betty fell in love with the wife of one of the farm's young aspirants toward harmonious development, Gurdjieff-style, and it was reciprocated, this was considered disruptive by the strait-laced Mrs. Stavely, and my friend and her new lover were expelled.

Betty was unabashed, and without a backward look, she and her friend went off to India to join the entourage of Bhagwan Shri Rajneesh, the latest guru on the scene, and one who was, unlike Mrs. Stavely, a great promoter of free love in all forms. This new devotion to Bhagwan may even have been set up and encouraged by Mrs. Stavely as a way of getting rid of the disobedient, troublesome couple. As a Gurdjieffian, such manipulative behavior would be entirely acceptable.

I heard from Fritz in Albuquerque from time to time, long rambling phone calls that often interrupted Neil and me at the typewriter, and only ended when I told him I had to go back to work, which he always respected. This was while Neil and I were working on *Village*. He also sent letters occasionally. He was eighty pages into a new novel of his own, he told me, he played the piano for recreation, and I learned for the first time about his children. His son, also called Fritz, but nicknamed Peto, was at the University of Arizona and his daughter, Katherine, was a teacher at a school for the deaf in Santa Fe, though it didn't sound like he saw them much. It would be perfectly understandable if they were leery of this unconventional parent, who had caused so much disruption earlier in their lives.

For his part, Fritz was avoiding what I suspect were many old acquaintances in the area. There had been a drift of Gurdjieffians to the Southwest over the years, attracted by the spiritual centers of Taos and Frank Lloyd Wright's Taliesin West, which may have been what drew Fritz to the place himself after the war. But in his letters to me in the seventies, Fritz expressed contempt for these people who were so eager to worship him, something he felt was unearned.

There were to be no more manic phases, his brief fling at wearing the crown that he had inherited from Gurdjieff was over, and he was back to cynical normal. But if Fritz had landed on his feet again after the expulsion from Oregon and become *The Balanced Man* of the title of his last book, it was not to last. His elderly house-mate

Julia was rapidly going senile. He told me that one day when the roof was being repaired, she went out on the lawn naked, and shouted up to the workmen, "Which one of you is going to come down and fuck me?"

Shortly after, Julia no longer recognized Fritz, asked him what he was doing there, and ordered him to get the hell out of her house. Her family took over, and seeing Fritz as a moocher trying to get his hands on the estate, got a court order and evicted him. His lawyer told him he had no choice but to comply, and he found an apartment in downtown Albuquerque that he shared with an immigrant from India, not a lover but someone whom he said he found tolerable. He was thinking of returning to New York, perhaps for the publication of the new Gurdjieff book. Another publisher was interested in reprinting *Finistère* and his other books as well. There was a brief, hurried letter describing ailments—blood pressure, heart, dentures, and medical treatments. Then I got a call from him in the hospital. He promised to write fully.

He died, according to the brief *New York Times* obituary, on December 19, 1979, in Los Cruces, New Mexico.

Perhaps his was an author's ideal fate, the man forgotten, and the works remembered. Nevertheless, I believe that his was a life that also deserves to be rescued from oblivion. I see his two classics as representing two sides of a nature that could never quite be reconciled, resulting in a strangely unfocused and, despite the considerable achievement of these books, unachieved life.

Out west on one of my reading tours in the seventies, the period when so many different spiritual fads and disciplines were in the air, I was sitting around with a group of students and mentioned Gurdjieff. A young woman in a granny dress and lank hair broke in with "Oh, he's peaked," which seemed to imply that she and her friends had absorbed Gurdjieff's teachings, reached that level of wisdom, and gone on to the next wave, perhaps Carlos Castaneda, Maharishi Mahesh Yogi, and beyond. The young grasp things more by instinct, and don't have the time for lengthy studies. But perhaps she was also saying that the excitement of discovery was over.

I, too, these days, have lost the thrill of discovering new possibilities that once lurked in the books of Gurdjieff and other teachers, and the hope that my life would be suddenly transformed. Poetry has remained my "path," and along with daily yoga exercises, I've accepted that I have to look after myself, whatever the perils of life. Yet my thinking was changed by those years of my friendship with Betty and Alma, and then Fritz, and I live differently today because of them.

20

After *Stand Up, Friend, With Me* came out in 1963, I'd had exactly the kind of career I wanted. It was a small but satisfying one, where I could handle everything by myself, with a classy publisher, good reception around the country on my reading tours, reviews, fan mail—all the attention I needed. I had finally appeared on the stage of the Kaufman Auditorium of the YMHA Poetry Center, where I'd seen great poets like Robert Frost, W. H. Auden, and Dylan Thomas read their work. I even earned my living as a poet—barely enough to live on, maybe, but enough.

When Betty and Alma cast my horoscope, it forecast, correctly, "trouble with publishers," and in the early seventies, I found myself without a publisher when, after real-estate losses by the owner Barney Rosset, Grove Press was sold. Luckily, my old friend Stanley Moss, wealthy from his spectacular dealing in Old Masters, was starting a publishing house of his own, Sheep Meadow Press, which brought out my next book, *A Full Heart*. The book went too far for critic M. L. Rosenthal. A lot of the poems dealt with spiritual intuitions and experiences I was having under the influence of Betty

Deran, and he savaged the book in the *New York Times*. And with my switch from a major publisher to a small press, my charmed decade ended.

More than that, Neil becoming blind changed my life forever.

In 1972, an operation for a brain tumor took away most of Neil's sight, and taking care of him became my primary responsibility, more important than my career. It seemed that a cycle had finished. I had lost the illusion that my poetry would change the world, but now I could really feel useful, if only to one person, and not wanting to leave him alone for long and with my dislike of the visiting-poet routine at colleges, I cut way down on giving readings.

I still had to support myself, though. By the time Neil had recovered from the operation and went off to a Veterans Administration blind training school, I was dead broke. But luckily I got invited to be poet-in-residence for a term at Eckerd College in St. Petersburg, Florida, and I headed south in my VW van. I had taught poetry workshops in colleges before, but Eckerd was my first and only experience living on a college campus and confirmed for me that it was not the life I wanted to lead. Where publishers once supported poetry as a prestige builder, universities were now doing it and the majority of poets ended up teaching. But for me, poetry didn't belong to academia.

After his training, Neil was able to walk around New York City bravely with his white cane and could manage much of the business of life on his own, but he wasn't much good in the kitchen and there were many other things a pair of eyes was indispensable for, as well as my useful hands that could replace lamp sockets, sweep up broken glass, and untangle his tape player. But eyes or no eyes, he was an expert typist. When he was sighted, he had published half a dozen soft-porn novels, and though he could still write a first draft on the typewriter, he could no longer read back what he wrote and quickly grew discouraged, which led to my working with him on his fiction. It was my introduction to the complexities of prose.

I was planning on going to Yaddo again, only a month this time, so, before leaving, I discussed the plot of a novel with him, based on a story he had written in one go—he called them "quick writes"—and helped him outline it chapter by chapter so that he could do "quick writes" of the chapters during my absence. By the time I got back, he had finished a first draft of the novel, and I helped him revise it. The result was *The Potency Clinic,* a comic coming-out novel, by Bruce Elliot, one of his pseudonyms from his soft-porn days. But though I sent it on the rounds of publishers, none of them was ready for its sassy humor, so in 1978 we published it ourselves in a small edition under the imprint of Alma and Betty's Bleecker Street Press. I found the experience of being a publisher great fun—from locating a printer, getting quotes for publicity from other writers, sending out review copies and announcements to publications and bookstores, to filling orders, being reviewed, and hearing from readers. The novel even got picked up by a trio of young Germans who were setting up a gay publishing house in Berlin, Albino Verlag, and wanted the German-language rights to *Potency Clinic* for their first season's list, which included Jean Cocteau and James Purdy. They were attracted to the novel, they said, especially because it was satirical, a rare quality in gay novels at that time.

Neil had always lived for his trips to Europe, which were oxygen to him, but after becoming blind he saw little point in traveling anymore. A year after his operation, however, when director Joseph Chaikin took his Open Theatre to London for a run at the Roundhouse Theatre, with his sister Shami in the cast—both Joe and Shami, whom I knew from my acting days, had befriended Neil in the hospital—we followed them, renting a bed-sit for the month. Neil quickly discovered that, even with his diminished sight, foreign travel was still vastly rewarding. And I found I could cope with the extra burdens of leading him around and handling all the arrangements, though I continue to this day to have nightmares about missing trains and planes and, worst of all, losing him in foreign cities.

After *Potency Clinic,* wherever we were or whatever we were doing, Neil and I kept inventing plots for novels. We had so many ideas we talked of going into the plots business. So we were more than ready for another project, when, out of the blue, Bob Wyatt, an editor at Avon Books, which published original paperback novels, gave us the chance to write a big, popular "generations" novel about Greenwich Village. *Village* by Bruce Elliot, a pseudonym of Neil's that now became ours, follows four generations of a Greenwich Village family starting in 1845, when the Village was a rural backwater of Manhattan to the 1970s when gentrification forced young artists and gays, whom the Village had nurtured, to move to low rent neighborhoods elsewhere. We researched Village and New York history, which I found fascinating and would have thrown it all in for its own sake, as James Michener did in his blockbusters, but Neil was the novelist, not I, and he was adamant that everything we used had to be integral to the plot. There was still a lot of history anyway, because much of the story grew out of historical events. We had a lot of fun with plotting, some of it borrowed from our favorite movies and books, but much of it original, incorporating issues of race and religion that are significant in American life.

Collaboration is a strenuous method of writing. The strain on a relationship is such that it's a miracle you don't kill each other. Or rather, I think it can only succeed if there is no possibility of your ever breaking up, as was our case. Every bit of the novel was written together, Neil at the typewriter with me sitting next to him scrawling revisions on the manuscript. We only settled on a sentence after many, often fierce, struggles and rewrites. Miraculously, all was forgiven when a chapter was done.

Perhaps it was due to our necessarily laborious method, but we worked far harder and for longer hours than I ever had at poetry. Writing prose is a more "literary" exercise than poetry. I try to make the language in my poetry invisible, but in prose that can be monotonous and elaborate words are often more effective.

One chunk of the novel was written that summer in a schoolhouse on playwright Jean-Claude Van Itallie's farm in the green, rolling countryside of northern Massachusetts. Jean-Claude had already won a Pulitzer Prize for writing "America, Hurrah!" for Joseph Chaikin's Open Theater. Shami Chaikin and her actress girlfriend Karen Ludwig were also staying on the farm, and when Neil and I had a cookout and invited them over to our schoolhouse for grilled hamburgers, we were uncertain whether to ask our host Jean-Claude over too, because he was a raw foodie—fruit for lunch and vegetables for dinner, on the dubious principle that, consumed together, they didn't digest well. Jean-Claude also did fruit fasts, where he would eat nothing but blueberries, or watermelon, or whatever was in season, for several days. All the devotees of the raw diet become gaunt, Jean-Claude no exception, but it was considered to be a good thing, because, according to their doomsday theory, in the event of a catastrophe where the population was starving you would be safe from criminals since they'd look at you and figure you had nothing to rob. He was quite unfazed by our hamburger pig-out, and brought little containers of his own food, the grated vegetables he ate in the evening.

Another section of the book was written in my brother-in-law Ack Van Rooyen's house in The Hague, that he had inherited after the death of his parents. Ack and my sister Barbara were still living in Germany, and though most of the house was rented out, they kept the attic apartment for their occasional visits, until they could move back to Holland permanently. That winter, violent North Sea squalls beat on the tiled roof over our attic, but a little gas stove kept us perfectly warm. After a morning's work on the novel, we would often take the antique Number 11 tram to Scheveningen, The Hague's beach front, with its old-fashioned boardwalk and windbreaks to shelter behind. On the way home we often stopped at the fish market in the nearby port to eat raw herrings, dipping them in chopped onions and holding them up by the tail to nibble at from the bottom end. After the shopkeepers on the high street got to know me they urged me to speak Dutch, though I could only struggle with the language and its impossible gutterals. This was the first of numerous stays in Holland and the beginning of our love affair with the Dutch. In fact, we felt Holland was our second home, until we switched to London.

We turned out *Village* in eighteen months, on schedule, and for the first time I experienced the full treatment from a publisher—after conferences, our editor even walked us to the elevator! What a difference from Grove Press where the editor left me standing like a schoolboy before his desk! No expense was spared to give the book popular appeal. An artist was commissioned to paint original scenes from the book for the end papers, fairly cheesy, but impressive for an original paperback, and there were three different-colored covers for the bookstore racks. *Village* made the B. Dalton book chain's best-seller list, and there was a window devoted to it at the store's Village branch, as well as placards in the subways and full-page ads in women's magazines. It was astounding how much money we earned. With 220,000 copies sold, it was exhilarating to get those large royalty checks after the chickenfeed from poetry. Neil and I felt quite giddy for awhile, and saw ourselves making a living writing novels from then on.

And indeed, our editor got us a contract for another novel, this one set in a Manhattan midtown office. Unfortunately, though we threw in drug dealing, suicide, wife beating, a sexy rat of a boss who leads our heroine typist on a merry chase for years, *The Office* by Bruce Elliott (another "t" was added to our pseudonym, perhaps a bad omen) did not sell. Suddenly, we were box office poison, which ended Bruce Elliot(t)'s brief, high-flying career. No matter how many book proposals we've submitted since, and we've sketched out a lot of them, none was ever accepted. Besides novel plots, we keep plugging away at screenplays, one based on the life of Alfred Chester, and even have a libretto for an opera set in Nazi Germany—all for the drawer. And now that old manuscripts can be scanned into the computer to be worked on, we've revised *Village*, which has had a second life as *The Villagers*, this time published under our own names.

Although I went to Yaddo during Neil's early years of blindness, I now tried not to be away from home too long and limited my reading tours to a few days. I scheduled one where I had several gigs back-to-back in the Long Beach–Los Angeles area in a three day period, and found it exhilarating zipping around the freeways in a rented car. During an interview, I was asked why my poetry was especially popular there. The interviewer said she thought that this was somewhat strange since I'm very much a New York poet, and the west coast doesn't usually think much of New York, where poetry is determinedly literary. I do have a special connection with Long Beach, which is something of a bohemian outpost, not to mention a lively poetry scene. This began when poet Gerald Locklin and his fellow poet Charles Stetler, both on the faculty of the English Department of Long Beach State College, wrote an article about me in *The Minnesota Review* called "Stand Up Poet"—not only from the title of my first book, *Stand Up, Friend, With Me,* but also as in "stand-up comic," referring to the way my poems, unlike the usual poetry reading, could entertain an audience, and which set the standard for a new generation. After my second book, *Variety Photoplays,* with its "old movie" poems, was published, a lot of the poets in the Los Angeles area, among them Stetler and Locklin along with the remarkable Ron Koertge, started writing their own movie poems. Long Beach poetry, as Gerry Locklin has written, represents "the movement towards the spoken idiom," and, according to Locklin, I'm even considered, along with Charles Bukowski, one of the "fathers" of Long Beach poetry.

Since I felt more appreciated on the west coast, in the early nineties I switched to the California-based Black Sparrow Press, which published a large, handsome collection of my poetry, *Counting Myself Lucky, Selected Poems 1963–1992.* It made me feel back on track, and even won a Lambda award.

I'd always tried to avoid doing anything but poetry, but after the experience of writing fiction with Neil, I was loosening up. On my reading tours, which covered most of the country except a few states in the deep South, I was impressed with the number of poets I met who were completely unknown to me. In fact, the countryside was crawling with them, and most resented the dominance of the Northeast, which gave me the idea for an anthology that would show what poets were doing in each region. I pitched it to Ted Solotaroff, who was then an editor at Bantam Books, he liked it, and got me a contract for *A Geography of Poets.* Neil and I went to live in San Francisco for several months, so I could escape the usual New York–centered view of what was going on "out there" in the country and present a balanced selection of poets for once.

But that turned out to be just the trouble. The editor of the *New York Times* book review section told me my anthology was anti–New York, which perhaps explained why they didn't review it. Nevertheless, it remained in print for several years and had its effect—I keep running into people, especially on the west coast, who studied it in their literature classes and got their ideas of poetry from it.

One inescapable fact about putting together an anthology is that you have to read a lot of poetry. I always advise young poets that you can't write poetry unless you read it, and read it closely, but I myself am not what could be called an omnivorous reader of poetry. I never went through a phase of devouring Byron and Shelley and Keats, like many poets I know, and have never even read Dante. I find certain poems thrilling, like the 23rd Psalm, but a lot seems irrelevant and boring, of interest only to scholars, and I don't see being a poet a scholarly occupation. After *Geography* I lost track again of what was going on in poetry, so when Gerry Locklin and Chuck Stetler suggested that we do a sequel I was grateful for being forced to do all the necessary reading and catch up on what had been going on in the poetry world since the last poetry-reading binge. The result was *A New Geography of Poets* published in 1992 by the University of Arkansas Press.

If Gerald Locklin is generally unknown in America, perhaps it is simply that no one knows what to make of his poetry, since he's both a scholar and a populist, and poetry critics don't like populism. I can only hope American poetry is going in his direction. In world poetry he is easier to place, with his droll ironies, his easy (though it's not as easy as it looks), quirky, intelligent responses to the events in his life. There are poets, the Rilke- and Eliot-types, who wait for the Big Idea, and then again those others, the Brechts, who write out of everything that happens to them, almost as a diary—the way Picasso said he painted. Gerry is one of those others—and the only poet I know who writes about everything, which has resulted in dozens of books published by obscure presses. Reading him, I keep thinking of Gertrude Stein's nun-like admonition to Ernest Hemingway, "Remarks, Ernest, are not Literature." I wish Hemingway had answered, as Gerry would, "Why the hell not, I'd like to know?" He doesn't have to keep announcing in every poem that *This is poetry*. In fact, he says in one of his poems, that the people he writes for do not read poetry. Unfortunately, the wall of silence around poets has kept those very people ignorant of him.

He's been published in Germany, and actually has an underground reputation in Britain. Once when he was there on an exchange teaching deal and Neil and I were in London, Gerry gave the most unusual reading I've ever gone to. It was only witnessed by a handful of people and, in retrospect, continues to amaze me. It was part of a series that took place in the upstairs room of a Holborn pub. But it wasn't very well publicized and only a small group of earnest poetry lovers showed up, most of whom sat across the aisle from me and the group of friends I had persuaded to come, hoping it would tune them in to the phenomenon of Long Beach poetry.

The series organizer, a pale, almost inarticulate youth, shyly said a few words about Gerry, giving the audience little idea of his background and achievements, which, at that time, included fifty-three books, making him one of the most extensively published poets in the United States, yet is, as Bukowski called him, "one of the great undiscovered talents of our time." After the young presenter retired to a nearby chair, and Gerry announced his first poem with the words, "When I perform this piece, I don't know why, but something always happens," and began reading, the sound of retching was heard. The young series organizer was bent over in his chair, a hand trying to staunch the flow from his mouth, all the beer he had gulped down for courage, that ran through his fingers and puddled on the floor. Gerry stopped reading and stood there, looking on unjudging, simply observing the human condition in his bemused Olympian way, a condition that he understood, sympathized with, and allowed to run its course.

Staggering down the aisle, his mouth still dribbling down his sweater, the poetry presenter stopped to puke once more, splattering the audience—fortunately for us, he hadn't been eating curry and it was only beer. Again by the door he let loose a farewell flood and fled. On the podium, Gerry grinned and, before continuing his reading, commemorated the moment by announcing in an awed voice that he'd had some pretty strange reactions to his poetry before, but this was the most unusual one he'd ever got.

I've searched Gerry's work for ideology, but have found only this: A defense of the male spirit. Educated by strict nuns in Rochester, as he was, and surviving it, this is perhaps understandable. If men in this country have been turned into toads, in every toad, to paraphrase Cyril Connolly, there is a man screaming to get out, or as in the fairytale, a prince. The toad metaphor is Gerry's, and has been explored in his book *The Toad Poems*. The male spirit in him remains honest, bighearted, sentimental, generous, gentle, vulnerable, but sassy in the face of adversity—qualities that could be applied to as few American poets as to presidents. I think of him as the wonderful, protective big brother every sensitive little boy needs.

21

After her Perdue fellowship was over in 1967, May Swenson returned to New York with her new partner, blonde, zoftig, yet athletic Zan Knudson—Stanley Moss told me with a grin that was the kind of woman he went for. They didn't settle in the Village, but bought a house in Sea Cliff, on the North Shore of Long Island, where both pursued a disciplined writing schedule. Zan started turning out a string of young adult novels, and collaborated with May on several sports poems anthologies. The house was situated on a bluff overlooking the Long Island Sound, and was ideal for the kind of natural observations May made her poems out of. Unfortunately, it was really a summerhouse and so drafty that May developed asthma, forcing them to spend winters in places like California and Florida. It also had an enormous stairway to climb up from the road, which must have been hard to manage with asthma.

When I briefly had a car in the seventies, Neil and I would drive out occasionally with the poet Arthur Gregor, who, with his Viennese formality, was a great favorite of Zan's—she saw the comic in all of us over-dedicated poets. I always enjoyed Zan with her gruff, no-bullshit manner. She would cook large delicious meals for us, and then retire upstairs to watch football games on television, for athletics was one of her passions and the subject of her fiction. But I believe she retreated more from shyness than unfriendliness. She also spent much time, when she had to finish a novel, sequestered in a house she built in Delaware.

It was at this time, for a year or two in the transition to suburban life, and adjusting to the fragile state of her health, that May had trouble writing. She missed New York, especially the Village, and when I went to Europe one summer, she took over my studio, where she wrote a poem, "Staying in Ed's Place," that appeared in the *New Yorker*. She continued to despair over the state of the poetry world, and said to me once that when poets started getting money, watch out, which I then thought meant the world was in a spiritually perilous condition. But now I think she meant that it would set off fierce competition for the high rewards that were possible, and it wouldn't necessarily be the most talented poets who won. In the years since, her gloom certainly seems to be justified.

Zan was sometimes overly direct, if not brutal, in getting rid of friends, especially the literary old-timers May knew whom she considered bores. Once, when May, with Zan as always driving, came into New York, we went to lunch at Pennyfeathers, a popular coffee shop on Sheridan Square, and the novelist Marguerite Young, already ancient and half-senile, shambled in swathed in her gypsy skirts and shawls. The minute Marguerite approached our table and started talking to me in a grotesque, flirtatious manner, Zan let out a blast at her for butting in. "Get the hell away from here, you old bag," she yelled. And discombobulated, poor Marguerite fled, her colorful rags flapping.

Marguerite Young, author of *Miss MacIntosh, My Darling*, lived on Bleecker Street in a top floor apartment that she filled with angel dolls. I visited her there once and met Anaïs Nin, whose face, painted like a porcelain doll, was artfully swathed in a chiffon veil, a presentation that denied the ravages of age and illness—for she was shortly to die. I often ran into Marguerite in her shmattas sashaying

217

down the street, and she would stop to talk of her two books-in-the-works about the socialist Eugene Debs and James Whitcomb Riley, both of whom were from Indiana, where Marguerite herself came from. Marguerite had roomed with Jean Garrigue in college, and was always quick to deny that they had been lovers, claiming irrelevantly that at the time she'd been having an affair with one of her professors. After Howard Griffin died in Europe where he'd been living for years, Marguerite complained to me that he had promised her a screen covered with a collage of angels that she had seen in his house in England, but that Nell Blaine, his heir, would not have it shipped over to her. I discussed it with Nell, who told me it was a matter of twenty-five dollars for shipping costs, so I just quietly gave it to her and Marguerite got her screen.

But if Zan alienated a number of May's old friends, I was one of the lucky ones who survived. It was May's influence at the Academy of Arts and Letters, where she was a member, that got me the Prix de Rome in 1981. With *Village* about to be published, Neil and I left for the American Academy in Rome for a year, feeling that from then on, mistakenly, as it turned out, we would be able to make a living writing popular novels and could spend long periods of time abroad. Unfortunately, our experience at the Academy was not a happy one. I had a marvelous studio in the garden to work in—a stone cottage up a flight of steps, built against an ancient wall, with lush vegetation around—it was magical. But the living arrangements were another matter. The Academy was okay about Neil coming with me, but living there was uncomfortable for Neil. Unlike married couples who got private apartments off campus, they put us into a dorm room in the main building, with the communal bathroom down the hall and with the graduate student mateyness between the fellows. Unable to see who's around you makes socializing difficult, and in the dining room he was faced with sitting among strangers at long shared tables. And the food was abysmal. So we decided to rent our own apartment nearby. But when I informed the office of our plan, it caused a crisis. "This is an educational institution with rules," I was told severely by the director, and if I moved out, I would relinquish my fellowship. I reminded her that the American Academy in Rome had been forced to give up control over the literary fellowship after the scandal in the fifties when they refused to accept the novelist John Williams because he was black. I threatened to write the American Academy of Arts and Letters that had awarded me the fellowship, and would also write the *New York Review of Books* detailing this new outrage.

The director backed down, and Neil and I escaped the confines of the American Academy to an apartment nearby. This was a much better living arrangement and I continued to work in my studio in the academy garden. But Rome, beautiful as it was, was not a success, and I never felt at home there as I do in so many other European cities. Leaving in the spring of 1982 was a relief, and we headed for Berlin where Neil's novel, *Die Potenz Klinik* by Bruce Elliot, translated into German by one of our publishers, Gerhard Hoffmann, was being launched.

It was a blissful June, and for our entire week in Berlin blackbirds sang thrillingly outside the window of our room in a pension. One of the publishing team of Albino Verlag, Peter Schmittinger, who has since died of AIDS, showed us around West Berlin in his car, and there was a book signing in Prinz Eisenherz, the gay bookstore, where I blithely signed Neil's name, Bruce Elliot.

We were back in New York, when May Swenson told me that she and Zan wanted to sell the Sea Cliff house and buy a co-op apartment in the Village. They were able to consider the move only because May had won a MacArthur Award, and I kept on the lookout for one that seemed possible, but by that time the real estate market had collapsed and the Sea Cliff house would have brought a much lower price. So, with her MacArthur money, May bought a share in Zan's Delaware house, which was well-insulated and heated, and started to spend a lot of time there. It was in Delaware, in December 1989, that the asthma attack occurred that carried her off.

Though she left the Village many years before her death," I said, speaking in the auditorium of the New York Historical Society in 1991 as part of a memorial celebration of her life and work, "May

219

Swenson will always be a Villager for me, for she was part of the old Village that has disappeared. Her moving away coincided with the end of Greenwich Village as The Village, the Village we knew, when it became a high-rent neighborhood that the young and unconventional could no longer afford, and creative and radical life shifted to the so-called East Village, that for us Villagers will always be the Lower East Side."

The audience, that evening, was composed of the three major aspects of May's life, none of which significantly overlapped. Besides representatives of the poetry world, it included a large contingent of family members from Utah, whom she had remained close to, even while rejecting their Mormon faith, plus the third group, an impressive number of lesbians, both old friends and young admirers, including her two long-term lovers, Pearl and Zan, who sat, significantly, on opposite sides of the hall. There was an atmosphere of devotion, even awe, in the assembly, that testified to the fact that May Swenson, though she had lived a modest, retiring life, had emerged after death to become, for many, a cult figure.

In tribute, I read May's poem, "Snow in New York," in which she describes so memorably coming in out of the cold to perch on a stool of Riker's Coffee Shop, on 8th Street, the Village's Main Street, while the conveyor belt, with its "bleeding triangles of pie," moves from kitchen to counter, and looking out at the snow over the steam of her coffee, she meditates on the magical process of making a poem. Several others on the platform with me—fellow poets, a family member, and an old Utah friend—also read her poems, most of which I myself would have chosen. What was remarkable about hearing them recited in public was that, since her death, they had increased in power and become iconic.

"Even if May had moved back to the Village," my tribute at her memorial concluded, "she would have found it very different. I would have loved having her and Zan nearby, but I'm sure she would have been disappointed, for hardly anyone she knew is left, and in its essence the Village has changed. Even the lunch counter at Bigelow's is gone, as well as the Riker's on 8th Street that she wrote about so unforgettably, and other poems that still evoke an era in Greenwich Village history and my own youth, of which I remember her, more than any other Village resident, as the presiding spirit."

22

*A*fter my stay in Paris in the late forties, I hadn't returned for thirteen years, not until 1963 when I went with Neil, but Ralph Pomeroy, in a restless search for success and romance, couldn't be fixed in one place and was always going to Europe, shuttling among San Francisco, London, New York, or anywhere he had a chance at the Big Breakthrough. His talents and energies were the kind that were easily stifled by settling anywhere for long. I always told him he should live a bicoastal life, or, even better, between London and New York. He had an array of talents that he was always quick to exploit if the opportunity arose. But success kept eluding him. Freddie Kuh's analysis was that Ralph was cursed with being multitalented. Several times he managed a stay of a year or two in London, supporting himself by freelancing. He edited for a London publisher a couple of slight but charming coffee table books on ice cream and breakfast. Then, the immigration authorities caught up with him and he had to leave. But he was an ideal roving correspondent for London and New York art magazines, reporting on art shows wherever he happened to be.

Ralph still kept up with the power couple, Monroe Wheeler and Glenway Wescott, visiting them at their country house near Princeton, and after Wescott's death, his wealthy sister-in-law, Barbara Wescott, took Ralph on art jaunts to the continent. He also went with her to galleries and advised her on what to buy. In this, with his essential innocence, he didn't think of his own advantage—once after she had bought, on his recommendation, a painting in a gallery, outside on the sidewalk she told him to go back in and claim his finder's fee. Usually, this was five percent of the sale price. Ralph had never done this before, but under her stern tutelage returned and got his commission, which the gallery owner expected to pay.

With the restaurant booming, Freddie resurrected old literary ambitions and treated Ralph to a stay in Barcelona, where they collaborated on a novel—a nostalgic evocation of the summer of 1948, that golden time of our youth on the Left Bank when we had all met—called, appropriately, *That Summer in Paris*. It never found a publisher, and soon Ralph became aware that he wasn't going to make it big as a poet either and concentrated on art. The nail in the coffin of his poetry career had resulted from the publication of a book, *In the Financial District*, which was inspired by living in the shadow of Wall Street, and contained some of his best poems. This was another dead end. Even though it was published by a prestigious publisher, Macmillan, it didn't get a single review, and Arthur Gregor, then Macmillan's poetry editor, said it was the only time that happened to any of his poets.

It was to the art world that Ralph in his later phase devoted himself. He published a glossy art book on Theodoros Stamos, and had shows of his own in galleries—paintings, constructions, shaped canvases, collages, whatever seemed to be the latest thing. But after each event, puzzlingly, things never developed further. Alice Toklas was dead right about his painting. He had a true artist's sensibility, but his work, aiming at what was hot in the art world, followed the fashion rather than led it, and by the time he had a show, it was no longer quite the talk of the town. Perhaps the trouble was that every time it looked like things were developing for him, Ralph would shoot off to London or San Francisco or wherever some opportunity, or lover, beckoned. Following the truism that New York doesn't forgive you, or remember you, if you leave it, he was offered a visiting curatorship at the University Museum in Halifax, Nova Scotia, but by the time he came back to New York two years later, things had already changed, as they do in the art world, and he found himself on the outside of the scene, and had to take a lowly gallery job again.

Neil and I would sometimes meet up with him when we were in San Francisco, or in London where he once introduced us to his current boyfriend, a charming hippie-style youth from San Francisco. Ralph always tried to shove Europe and its wonders down the throats of his lovers, in order to show them all his favorite places and ignite their interest in great art—a hopeless task since most of them had no interest in any of it. We'd also see him in the intermittent periods he lived in New York—at various times, he had a Madison Avenue apartment, a SoHo loft, and even a warehousey space in the Wall Street area among the skyscrapers. But he was often glimpsed fleetingly, for he lived faster than we did. Typically, I caught sight of him on the back of a motorcycle in full leather, roaring through the Village.

Ralph's graduation into S & M was somewhat of a mystery to me, a sneakers-type guy, and it got him into trouble. A too-vigorous session left his wrist fractured and in a splint. Another time, he was in the hospital with a collapsed lung from an early hours stabbing after leaving The Eagle's Nest, a leather hangout. Leather seemed inappropriate on someone his age, with such a puny body and no buns, but when he went to the MacDowell Colony on a fellowship, David del Tredici, who was there at the time, told me that Ralph arrived with a footlocker of leather and chains, perhaps the only fellow at that sedate arts colony to have ever done such a thing. A boyfriend would roar in on a Harley-Davidson for "sessions" in Ralph's studio, safely off in the woods. David was invited to sit in on one, and reported that it was a tame affair, more a matter of dressing up ritually in leather drag, but with little evidence of arousal.

As he got older, it became harder to scramble for a living and Ralph tried to parlay his art gallery experience into getting a museum curatorship. He came within a hairsbreadth of making it. It looked as if he would finally land a real job, the job of his dreams, when he mounted, as guest curator, a show of "soft art" at the Newark Museum—it just looked like rag dolls and pillows to me, but it was cutting edge stuff and the directors were impressed. They offered him a permanent curatorship. It was in the bag. All he had to do was fill in the application "just as a formality" . . .

—In every life there are moments when your fate hangs in the balance.—

. . . and where the employment form asked about his education, which admittedly was spotty, but, after all, with his on-the-job experience . . . and he had been assured they wanted him, the job was his . . . so, assuming it wouldn't make any difference, he blithely put in "no college" . . .

. . . eliciting a horrified "Oh, we're *so* sorry! Our hands are tied" from the director—for by state rules that lack of a degree disqualified him from the job.

But during one of his San Francisco periods he committed his worst gaffe, one that further determined his future. Freddie had set him up in a nice little apartment in a building he owned in North Beach, around the corner from the Spaghetti Factory, where Ralph was working as a waiter. Freddie was a relaxed boss, and his dozen or so employees were free to deposit the diners' money in the cash register themselves. To his horror, he discovered that his waiters, including his best and oldest friend Ralph, were pocketing not just their tips but also skimming off the proceeds. Fred realized that all the handsome new furnishings of Ralph's apartment had been paid for by money stolen from him, as well as those gifts of flowers and candy that Ralph was always so generous with.

Their relationship was never the same again. Ralph's lame explanation to me was that all the waiters did it.

From then on some of the fun of the Factory was gone. It was run like a business and Freddie strictly monitored the receipts. When I visited on reading tours, I saw that he no longer held his big lunches for friends and hangers-on where he would push tables together and bring opulent platters of food from the kitchen and an armload of bottles of wine, presiding over the company like a king.

In Ralph's final period in New York, he was sharing an apartment on the upper west side with his lover, Tom, whom he'd met at The Eagle's Nest. Tom, he said, was his top man, though I'd never have known it from looking at him—Tom even worked in childrens' theatre, which didn't seem macho in the least. But perhaps he was more studly than I knew, because he lived for his motorcycle, and Ralph, aging but valiant, would sit behind Tom and hold on for dear life as the leather clad duo roared through the countryside to motorcycle conventions. But if this relationship gave Ralph personal fulfillment and stability, it also grounded him in a way that wasn't stimulating to his free-wheeling talents. Nor was his sales job at the Forum Gallery on Madison Avenue where, under the hardboiled director, Bella Fishko, he found little scope for his curatorial talents. So when he was offered a job lecturing at a San Francisco arts college, he made the painful decision to relocate again, leaving Tom behind.

The first chance he got, Tom rode out to San Francisco on his motorcycle to visit Ralph, but while driving home across the monotonous Utah desert he fell asleep, swerved off the road and crashed into a ditch. Tom left no will and his family seized all his possessions. All that poor Ralph inherited was their joint debts and his only solution was to declare bankruptcy. Ralph had always been a drinker, but now he became a lush. On his visits to New York, he was always three sheets to the wind. When he came over he was often furious, cursing the subways for taking him to the wrong part of town. I invited him to dinner with Alice Morris, the editor who had published him in *Harper's Bazaar* in his faraway youth and who lived in my building. Alice's speech, of another era, invoked Miss Porter's finishing school, and the subtle swing to her short, fair hair was a tribute to the artistry of a haircutter at the Plaza. She didn't betray the least surprise when in the middle of dinner Ralph's head dropped over onto his plate of food. We all ignored him and bravely kept the conversation going, until he woke up and resumed eating as if nothing had happened.

I thought Ralph still looked pretty good—he had a full head of hair, even if it was white—but he complained to me that he was finding it hard, even wearing full leather, to make out in the bars. I said it might be his hair, bought a kit in the drugstore and dyed his hair blond, which seemed, briefly, to improve his love life.

Then the San Francisco teaching job ended, and, with no pension and no savings, Ralph was trying to live on his Social Security of five hundred dollars a month. In the past, when he was broke, he'd always sold off whatever he could. The book he'd collaborated on with Andy Warhol was long gone—a pity, since it would now bring in a fortune. And he'd pretty much sold his correspondence with the famous figures he knew, plus paintings given him by many of the artists he'd written about, and even antique Native American rugs he'd collected. He found a fellow lush in the neighborhood bar he patronized to move in and share the rent, but the man's income as a tour guide was unreliable, and the bills piled up. Even with his volatile nature, which could always reinvent itself, Ralph's problem now was his utter despair. He was on the outside of the world of the arts, which goes by very fast, and it's not easy to get back in without the card of youth to play, especially when there is always a whole new generation of high energy young artists scrambling for the rewards.

He had made up with Freddie Kuh by this time, but his big disappointment was that his lifelong friend refused to invite him to live with him in his Sonoma Valley house, where Fred had retired after selling the Spaghetti Factory—though after the stealing episode Ralph shouldn't have been surprised. Freddie told me he didn't want a resident drunk drinking up all his liquor, but of course it was more than that.

When Freddie died, leaving Ralph thirty thousand dollars, it was too little and too late. His health ruined by heavy drinking, Ralph only survived him by a year.

I have no doubt that it is as a poet that he will be remembered. After I failed to interest any publishers, even in his home state of Illinois, to bring out his posthumous *Selected Poems*, astonishingly, or perhaps inevitably, he was discovered by Camille Paglia, the provocative art historian and cultural commentator, who chose his poem "Corner" for her anthology of great poems, *Break, Blow, Burn.* This bodes well for the survival of his poetry. "Corner" is a nervy poem in which a street corner hustler and a motorcycle cop eye each other appraisingly. I'm sure that with their mutual Catholic background and appreciation of leather and Tom O'Finland drawings Paglia and Ralph would have adored each other.

23

I'm still not entirely comfortable with talk of "spirituality" and "the spiritual," which you get a big dose of on the west coast. Throughout the years, I've seen a lot of poets bucking for sainthood, most often going in for one version or another of Oriental religions. Frankly, I always preferred Allen Ginsberg in his political activist mode, rather than as a chanting Buddhist. But James Broughton, even in his pose of an illuminati, was a poet of seductive charm and good sense. Another "spiritual poet," Arthur Gregor, is such an old friend, and a good poet, besides, that I accept his religious side as part of his decidedly romantic character, which includes a good dollop of nuttiness. Along with Dunstan Thompson, Broughton and Gregor represent three different ways gay poets have managed to incorporate religion into their lives.

Of course, some people merely stick to, or go back to, the religion they were raised in. To me, they were brainwashed from the beginning but I don't necessarily dismiss them as misguided. The novelist Joseph Caldwell, a darling little man of bubbling *energy with intense, button eyes, as cute as ever as an old party with his frosted bush of hair, eyebrows and mustache, has never wavered in his Catholicism, which works for him, though he's happily found a priest who will hear his Confessions. Dunstan Thompson, also raised a Roman Catholic, was more conflicted and I don't think he ever really resolved the issue of his sexuality and religion, or indeed, his poetry and religion.*

I'd never lost my admiration for Dunstan Thompson's poetry, after I discovered it during the war, and had long harbored the idea of perhaps editing a new edition of his poems. For a start, I wrote a brief appreciation, including a sampler of his poems, for *Poetry Pilot,* the newsletter of the Academy of American Poets, which came to the attention of Philip Trower, his surviving partner—I had never heard of Trower before he wrote me. All I knew about Dunstan was that, after his marvelous, well-received books in the forties, he had left the United States to live in England, gotten religion, and unaccountably disappeared from view in the early fifties. So, during a stay in London, I finally seized the opportunity to explore the mystery of his later life.

Neil and I had settled into a rented studio flat there, when I contacted Philip Trower who was living in a remote village on the North Sea, and he came down to London to meet us. A kindly man who worked as a Vatican reporter for Roman Catholic publications, Trower immediately demystified Dunstan's disappearance, and told me it was "simply" that, after his youthful hell raising, Dunstan had returned to the Catholic Church. Devout and repentant, he had retired with Trower, who converted to Catholicism himself, to the seaside village of Cley-Next-The-Sea in Norfolk near the shrine of Our Lady of Walsingham, where he lived until his death in 1974, and where Trower has stayed on.

I spoke to him of my mystification at never seeing any poems of Dunstan's in print after those early books, except for one poem in the *New Yorker* in the fifties, but Trower assured me that Dunstan had never stopped writing poetry, and in fact, at the time we met,

Trower was in the process of putting together a volume of the later poetry. When I finally read the sizeable, posthumous collection, *Poems 1950–1974*, it was evident that if religion had transformed Dunstan from brilliant bad boy to repentant sinner, it had also transformed his poetry. The formal structure was still there, but gone was the sinful glitter of the language, the outrageously gay love poems to soldiers and sailors and airmen in World War II. Now there was weeping and breast-beating as he reviewed his life, wallowing in his guilt.

Whatever Trower's "simple" version of Dunstan's transformation—not "conversion to Catholicism" he corrected me, but "return"—I decided that the only believable explanation for him to have changed so radically, so suddenly, was that he had to have had a nervous breakdown. Or, I theorized, he may have been arrested, as so many gays in England were, back in the fifties before the Wolfenden Amendment decriminalized consensual gay sex between adults, and the humiliation drove him into the arms of the church again. But when I dared to suggest such a thing, Trower, a very reserved man, told me that was not the case, that it was simply the effect of Dunstan's turning devout. Taking into account the enormous change in his poetry from the early work to the later, I'm still not sure I believe that there wasn't a traumatic experience. Unless his return to religion was like a conversion, which can certainly produce extraordinary changes in a person. Or perhaps it was falling in love with Trower that opened the floodgates of remorse. No way to bring that up with such a conservative man. I felt like a wild barbarian to harbor such thoughts.

With the return to the church, Trower assured me, Dunstan had also renounced worldly activities, including his budding poetry career, and as the new poems accumulated, unpublished, he'd let the memory of his first books, and his growing reputation, fade. In fact, he made it quite explicit to Trower—and this was the bombshell that sunk my idea to rescue his poetry from oblivion—that he did not want those early poems reprinted even after his death, and Trower, his literary executor, was following his instructions by limiting the new volume to poetry from 1950–1974, the devout years. I'm afraid I had already violated this wish when I published the appreciation in *Poetry Pilot*. Copies of the early books are, in any case, easily available on the Internet.

It's quite extraordinary that Dunstan Thompson, who sacrificed his own ambitions as a poet to strive for holiness, condemned the equally devout Christian T. S. Eliot for his success in positioning himself as King of Poetry, and at the same time supported a contender for the crown, Conrad Aiken, who believed that he should have been the Anointed One. Aiken published many well-received books of poetry in his lifetime, and is now pretty much dismissed. But Aiken is memorable as one of a handful of poets whose lives were scarred by the violent death of a relative—Lucille Clifton, who found her mother murdered in her Baltimore project apartment; Thom Gunn who came home from school to find his mother had hung herself in a closet; and Aiken, whose mother shot his father, leading to a messy murder trial during his adolescence.

Dunstan seemed to despise Eliot for his success—as if even Eliot's religion had its political uses, putting him above the fray. It's reassuring to me to know that, religious though he was, devoted to the higher aesthetics, Eliot enjoyed shit jokes, according to W. H. Auden, who would send them on to him when he heard any. But most poets, no matter how high-minded, fight tooth and claw for publication, awards, recognition, though they often do it in underhanded ways through friends and connections, so they can preserve an image of being above it all. Poets like Robert Lowell, for example, were ruthless career builders—in his case, perhaps because of his lineage, he believed he deserved to be number one.

Dunstan actually came from a privileged world that encompassed wealthy relatives in Newport, Rhode Island, and High Church officials in Maryland, the state that began as the center of Catholicism among the thirteen colonies. He accompanied his devout mother on visits to these Princes of the Church, and got quite an indoctrination into the religion. On the other hand, once he went away to Harvard he cut loose, and the riotous atmosphere of the war years abroad gave him a thorough introduction to the Pleasures of Satan 101. It was at Harvard that he got to know aspiring writers like Harry Brown who, like him, landed a cushy job in wartime London, where my ground officer friend, Coman Leavenworth, went around with them and reported the juicy details to me when he came back to our airbase.

When Dunstan left the United States for good in 1948, he flew to the Middle East to write a travel book, published in England as *The Phoenix in the Desert*. The opening sequence describing an early transatlantic flight is a classic. Also notable is its portrait of the luxurious life of the British Colonial class in Cairo, soon to be wiped away with Nasser's revolution. It was in Egypt that Dunstan met Philip Trower, who was posted there with the British Forces. Were they lovers? I assumed that, but Trower is of the old school and I couldn't ask. After they settled down together in England after the war, according to Trower, Dunstan's religious upbringing reasserted itself, gradually transforming the poetry as well, and the wild child was chained.

Yet gay scholar and poet David Bergman told me that Dunstan Thompson had to be the gayest poet of World War II, and indeed most of his poems of that era had the word "gay" in them, well before it gained wide currency. Trower, however, made it clear to me that Dunstan would not have wanted to be included in any anthology of gay poets, like May Swenson or any of the gay and lesbian poets of my generation, who saw themselves part of modern poetry. The gay movement, with supremely confident "out" poets like Adrienne Rich, Felice Picano, and Marilyn Hacker, would bristle at that, but I think the literary establishment still would agree that it's diminishing for a serious poet to be called anything but, simply, a poet.

However, Dunstan Thompson in his later phase, when many of the poems were on religious themes, could perhaps have another incarnation, for poet and director of the National Endowment of the Arts Dana Gioia, a Catholic himself, considers him the leading Catholic poet of the period as well. But, like Gerard Manley Hopkins, being Catholic and gay are hardly incompatible. It's just that the Church doesn't seem to understand that yet.

Although Modern Poetry started out as a rebellion against Victorian and Edwardian rhetorical usages and sentimentality, moderns also sought language that rose above the commonplace, the dreary clichés of the newspapers, the blind patriotism, the ordinary man's conventional thinking. On the other hand, Ezra Pound's "no ideas but in things," one of Modern Poetry's early battle cries, also seemed limiting. In no time at all, Modern Poetry drifted into chamber music mode, and there seemed to be no escape from high-minded abstract thought and language or high philosophical subject matter. Dunstan's later poetry, religious though it is, avoids that trap. There are certainly different ways to be spiritual, and to be gay.

The east coast has a natural affinity for Freud, who though fanciful in his theories seems more practical and down to earth—getting into the nitty-gritty of sex, as he does—as compared to the west coast, which prefers the more mystical Jung, with his Collective Unconscious, his Racial Memory. In this, Jung allied himself to religious traditions, which suits the Pacific Rim where poets succumb to the lure of Zen practice, Indian or home-grown gurus, Native American peyote rites, and such. Even there, where once poets claimed to be the standard bearers of Joy, that ambition has been upped to Ecstasy, if not Enlightenment. Holier than thou, there's even competition as to who is closer to achieving this ultimate state—saintly old fools devoting their poetry to the subject of bliss, which doesn't prevent them from falling into periods of depression. But they don't write about that.

Even arriving at quasi-sainthood, American poets who climb on the Soul Train are unable, as Dunstan Thompson did, to relinquish the struggle for attention, ambition for worldly glory. But then, they're not Christian ascetics, like Dunstan tried to be. At any rate, no matter how high-minded an act they put on, they are constantly maneuvering for advantage in the poetry world. Irrationally, they seem to expect their holiness to give them some kind of priority in the fame racket. Lay monk Brother Antoninus, his lecture agent told me, even instructed the agent to lay on the purple in his brochure to get him reading gigs. Catholicism aside, Brother Antoninus, when I caught one of his readings in San Luis Obispo, claimed, like Native Americans, to be in tune with animals which somehow justified him wearing his hippie fringed deerskin shirt.

James Broughton with his elfin look and illuminated eyes was perhaps the best of the "holy man" poets in the Bay Area. Broughton, who was a noted avant-garde filmmaker in the forties and fifties, the era of Maya Deren, became a devotee of Jung. Acceding to the homophobia of the period, he allowed himself to be steered by his Jungian friends into a heterosexual marriage. This left him thoroughly miserable, until at the age of sixty-two he was rescued by an extraordinary Canadian youth thirty-five years younger named Joel Singer, who reawakened his sexuality and for whom he wrote a superb sequence of love poems. Broughton's open celebration of his homosexuality from then on is quite unusual among the Enlightened Ones of the spiritual world, though the great Sufi poet Rumi exclusively addressed God through his male lovers. A quite amusing film made by Joel of a Faerie countryside encampment shows the ancient James Broughton buck naked in the California sunshine, embracing other withered old timers with mutual glee in their Faerie brotherhood.

Broughton, who used to come with Joel to New York for tributes to his films, asked me to write a preface to one of his books, the diary of a winter alone in the wilds where he supposedly achieved his Enlightenment. Knowing his dissatisfactions with his career, in my essay I couldn't suppress a trace of mockery masking my skepticism, which he instantly spotted, and rewrote my preface in a more suitably adulatory tone, even publishing his version under my name! But beyond his holy man pretensions, his poems are clever, lively, and charming, and though they proclaim Joy to the World—what he calls the Big Joy—reveal, and revel in, a characteristic playfulness that is irresistible. Joel's devoted care rose to the heights of heroism when Broughton, in his eighties, deteriorated with age and Joel remained with him to ensure that he reached a peaceful end.

*A*nother considerable poet of spirituality, very different from James Broughton and Dunstan Thompson, is Arthur Gregor, whom I met in Paris in 1948, well before he went on his Pilgrimage to India and a guru, a trek that many poets would be making over the years. Actually, for a decade after Arthur and I met, I didn't really get to know him, for he mixed in a well-heeled New York arts milieu that I was uncomfortable with. And his Old World, buttoned-up formality, as well as his spiritual concerns, were alien to me then, when I was determinedly an outsider and an underdog.

In announcements of readings and literary events I kept seeing his name coupled with the poet Jean Garrigue, for they were bosom buddies and soul mates, if never lovers. Even when he lived in the Village Arthur wasn't a bohemian, whereas Jean, who moved there straight from college in Indiana, was a true Edna St. Vincent Millay–style bohemian, an independent woman both professionally and sexually, with many lovers of both sexes, though she was basically a lesbian. In his poetry, Arthur shares with Jean a kind of "exaltation" of expression that modern poetry had long been suspicious of, but is easy for poets to fall into. I don't mean they indulged simply in self-expression, which is the hallmark of the amateur. Their romantic cries were shaped by controlled language and form that only skillful poets are capable of.

Jean Garrigue was a beauty, trim and boyish, and both men and women were drawn to her—she was Stanley Kunitz's great love in the fifties. I came to adore her myself, and regretted the awkwardness between us that developed when her violinist niece eloped with Alfred Chester's pianist boyfriend, and she made the unfortunate remark to the furious Alfred to "let the lovers go," ending their decade-long friendship. Unfortunately, she saw me as being in the Alfred camp. But in the early seventies, when Jean was terminally ill with cancer, I met her on the street and simply took her in my arms. She died shortly after, in 1972.

It was after Alfred left for Morocco in 1963 that my friendship with Arthur Gregor really developed, and we were thrown into even closer contact when we were both published by Stanley Moss's Sheep

Meadow Press, which Stanley had started as soon as he became a millionaire. Arthur had known Stanley even longer than I had, and the three of us were often together. Stanley, who had matured into a Renaissance prince of a man, was by now living in an enormous apartment in a luxury tower on New York's upscale Central Park West—it was his view of the park's Sheep Meadow that supplied the name of his publishing house. From Central Park West, he was soon to graduate to an art-filled mansion in Riverdale, on the bluff overlooking the Hudson where Toscanini had had his own palazzo.

Arthur, Stanley, and I, though we come from very different backgrounds and are very different poets, share the same poetic tradition, the world of modern poetry that by the late forties had settled into a tight, exclusive little cult, ruled—grimly, I would say, benevolently, according to Arthur—by its mandarins: T. S. Eliot, the undisputed supremo, with high virgin priestess Marianne Moore and stuffed-shirt arch-priest Wallace Stevens. Besides these and the problematic Ezra Pound, never of much interest to me as a poet and despicable in his anti-Semitism and fascism, were the other more independent, though no less respected, masters of modern poetry such as Robert Frost, W. H. Auden, e. e. cummings, William Carlos Williams, and, especially, Hart Crane, who though dead, was more alive for me than any of the others, for his gay sensibility shone through his cryptic poetry. Deciphering Crane's syntax and textural complexities is good training for the poetic ear, and in addition he offers boldly romantic daydreams: "In all the argosy of your bright hair. . . ." Ah, that made up for all the era's prejudice against homosexuality, which was reflected as well in the literary establishment.

While it took me until I was nearly forty to get a book published, Arthur Gregor was being published when he was still a youth—on one of his later book covers there's a charming portrait of him by painter Hyde Solomon as a blissfully romantic young poet. By the late 1940s, when Arthur made his debut with *Octavian Shooting Targets,* the radicalism that started modern poetry on its dizzying course had long since fossilized into the eccentricities and opacities of the aging Masters, each with the distinctive voice and unassailable

237

technique, if nothing new to say—it was only Robert Frost who spoke out against Senator Joseph McCarthy and the witchhunt. It wasn't until the Beatnik Bad Boys of the fifties "forced open the gates to let in the rabble," as Arthur indignantly described it to me, that it seemed to me that poetry could breathe again. Of course, it would never be the same, either, without the high standards of an elite, but we were also freed to speak the real language and celebrate different ideals. What a relief now to write about my life and concerns— being gay and Jewish and even poor! And use the everyday words, even the familiar, forbidden dirty words!

Unlike me, Arthur was comfortable in the Manhattan literary world with its strictures of politesse, and with his affluent, cultivated friends who gave dress up dinner parties. If I was a child of humble, unworldly immigrants, Arthur Gregor was born into a solid bourgeois background, a world of tradition and formality symbolized by the noble edifices of end-of-empire Vienna, a world that was to be shattered by the lightning bolt of Nazism, a world whose past he would evoke so hauntingly in his poetry.

If radical thinking once condemned spirituality as superstition, to Arthur, raised in a city built of the rubble of still earlier civilizations, historic stones that seemed to speak to him of mysteries, spirituality was a serious matter. In his poems, he returns again and again to the Vienna of his childhood, which becomes for him more than a garden of nostalgia, the key to his memories, but an entrée into a spiritual domain that, after he made the "Journey to the East" in the fifties, has been the subject of his poetry, and through which he interprets his life experience.

But on the other hand, Arthur cannot escape the harsh realities of his life and times. His memoir *A Longing in the Land* is a hair-raising account of his family's escape from his beloved Vienna after Hitler's Anschluss, when the Nazis incorporated Austria into the Third Reich, as well as the story of his adaptation to, and disillusionment with, American life, which finally led him to France, where he lives today. And in the poems, too, are fragments of memories of that traumatic departure, still vivid, still raw:

238

As the train pulls out of the station,
as we look back and see the huge suspended clock,
as we look back at what we have left,
at what we have had to leave . . .

This betrayal by his native land, for Hitler was greeted with joy by his fellow Austrians, underlined what must have been evident all along—that Austria was already a deeply anti-Semitic country. It was made even worse for Arthur, imbued as he was with Viennese culture and the German language—a language he now despises. Unlike me in anti-Semitic America, Arthur grew up unashamed of his Jewishness, and even went to a Jewish *gymnasium*. It was a point of pride to him that his mother came from a famous Hassidic family in Poland and was never reconciled to worldly Viennese mores. But along with Judaism, its traditions passed on to him through his family, he has also been (crucially, can one say?) formed by Christianity, inescapable in Vienna as capitol of the Catholic Holy Roman Empire—a religion that he sees as having produced the highest European achievement, as attested to in its sacred architecture and especially by the music of Bach. The later connection with Indian mysticism would complete a triad, the triple roots of his spirituality.

My Eastern European parents, who came to the United States as children in the influx of immigrants at the turn of the twentieth century, managed to escape the slums of the Lower East Side, but they never rose much in the world and essentially remained simple shtetl Jews. Arthur's family also arrived in America with nothing but the clothes on their back, but they quickly regained the privileged level they were accustomed to—such is the difference between immigrants and émigrés. But even for the Goldenbergs—Arthur later changed his name—there was a rocky period at the beginning of their American sojourn. Stranded in dreary Newark, Arthur once told me with a laugh, his mother took to her bed, it was so unacceptable to be there. Fifteen-year-old Arthur, the only English speaker in the family, even had to go out and work to support them, delivering groceries on a bicycle—it was as if Proust had to get a job—for Arthur was always the dandy, raised as a little prince, and his Viennese class consciousness reasserted itself as soon as it could. He still carries himself with an almost military erectness, and the slight accent he has never lost gives him an air of authority that is foreign, but with a debonair quality—think Billy Wilder holding a cigarette. His poetry, too, has always had a lilt. One of the roots of its distinctiveness is the *mittel*-European literary tradition, with its particular worship of high art—think Rilke—that looks down on the baser instincts, the "rabble," fully aware of its superiority—a paradox, considering the humanitarian strain in Middle-European intellectual thought, which Arthur also represents.

It was only a few years before Arthur's family, on their feet again thanks to his father's business acumen, escaped Newark to the refugee enclave in upper Manhattan called "Little Berlin," and not much longer for Arthur himself to be welcomed into the ranks of modern poetry by having poems accepted by *Poetry* (Chicago), which in that postwar poetry world was the equivalent of being knighted! After *Octavian Shooting Targets,* his books followed at regular intervals, and he became poetry editor at a prestigious publisher. In New York that puts you at the center of the action!

But at the same time, his worldliness was in conflict with his spiritual development. Returning from India ". . . where I'd heard pronounced / the secret of earth as heaven," he gives us tantalizing glimpses of his guru

> . . . in whose stone-like pose
> all sorrows and all joys dissolved. . . .

He has never wavered since, and all his poetry weaves variations on this theme, whatever the fashions in poetry dictate.

But the more spiritually developed Arthur became, the more he suffered from his lack of a sense of belonging in America, an America increasingly corrupted by its postwar wealth and power, and it was this that led him back to Europe with its ancient landscape, with its evidences of connection to the past, his own past:

240

. . . from terraces high above sloping flowery fields,
from classical hillsides
possibilities for a union with
the great good gained
long before the streets,
the dark and narrow, broad
and tree-lined streets
where I had been at home
were gone.

In this experience, the immigrant of my background and the émi-gré of his are the same—his memory of what was lost in the Middle Passage to "exile" may be more concrete, since he remembers exactly what was relinquished, but mine, even with second-generation, sec-ondhand memory of it, is just as poignant—it's in my blood. It's part of what makes returning to Europe such a reward, for some-thing in me, too, belongs there.

Music, especially, provides Arthur sacred moments that remind the soul of its higher purpose, its quest for an eternal home, the re-turn to the river whence it sprang, the river that flows on, but re-mains. These mysteries are also sensed in the surge of feelings released by the sight of male beauty, feelings that he would claim are not nec-essarily erotic, but hint at a splendid world of the spirit that homosex-uality seems to promise entrée into. What I would simply call sexual attraction he sees as a longing for a return to *wholeness, belonging*—which, however, is not possible in this world, or perhaps only in our beginnings when we were "connected," before worldliness robbed us of the instinctive blessings we're born with. So in life we are yearning back, always back, to the oneness of our beginnings. Already in his first book, *Octavian Shooting Targets,* Arthur was mourning that loss.

Most uniquely, where for most of us gays, sex is a matter of sweaty bodies, cocks, mouths, and assholes—for him it is a spiritual experience,

. . . characteristic of only the spirits
attributed to gods.

It is especially in chance encounters, perhaps in no more than a fleeting glance, a passing exchange of looks with another man that, for him, the divine recognition often manifests itself:

> . . . That we had seen each other in
> each other's faces without disguise . . .

or again:

> . . . when the figure
> having stepped forth from out of the dark,
> looked at in daylight would always fade back; —
> for it will not be trapped
> what had infused itself in eyes
> . . . as when a legendary bird
> on having achieved a god's desire, rose up
> and disappeared back into the clouds.

Here is reflected his notion that homosexuality is so special as perhaps to be reserved for the Gods. And connects with Constantine Cavafy's celebration of the god-like beauty of the young men of Alexandria, who, consistent with ancient Greek myths, may actually be gods visiting earth in disguise.

Cavafy is the modern master of homoeroticism and nostalgia, and Arthur pays tribute to the Alexandrian Greek, especially in a Cavafian poem sequence called "The Park." As Cavafy invested Hellenic history with a homoerotic significance, Arthur does the same with the formal gardens of Vienna's parks, the Prater and the Augarten, where as a boy he already sensed the hanky-panky going on in the bushes—what they meant to the ten year old before he had intimations of his own sexuality, and what they have meant to him throughout his life. In his first book, Arthur treated gayness as decadence, but delicious decadence. Now, like Cavafy, he has come to appreciate its role in human fulfillment, and recalls, steamily, "darkened rooms" where other men "left their world behind" and "have sought refuge and release."

> "for what but for closeness to
> that innermost core outwardly expressed

242

have I ransacked figures, forms,
out-of-the-way rooms for yield of it—
what but for the love it holds,
what but for the love it gives!"

That is a stirring affirmation! But like Dunstan Thompson and May Swenson, Arthur Gregor would never identify himself as a gay poet, refusing to be fit into any niches.

In his eighties, living in France, his newly adopted country filled with the echoes of the past, with the slow, deep growth of a civilization that Arthur feels himself a product of, he is still writing his characteristic poems, the syntax somewhat formal, reflecting his foreign origins, and his vocabulary remaining, unapologetically, within the bounds of good taste. The themes front and center in all his books are presented more explicitly in his late, lovely poems. One still can't always quite pin his meaning down, since he deals in a mysterious, space between the concrete world and the unseen, or the unseen realms that certain landscapes and buildings and figures evoke, a way that leads to the world of the spirit promised in great art. Completely secular person as I am, this doesn't interfere with my enjoyment of his graceful, haunting, and elusive poetry. In a way, my poor grasp of his meanings is not inappropriate because this is a poetry of something more sensed than known, and is put together from hints, intuitions, by a sense akin to the olfactory, like the half-remembered state between sleep and waking. It's all of a piece with my unlikely friendship with this odd duck of a man, so different from anyone of my background.

When Neil and I visit him in his apartment in Paris's 7th Arrondissement or in his country house in the Loire Valley, it seems as if, after the major upheavals of our age as well as the petty poetry wars, he was flung up on a far shore, where he survives intact, while our world here in America is collapsing into disarray and noisy confusion.

24

*I*n the early eighties, ten years after Alfred Chester's death, with his work out of print and only a few old friends remembering his brilliance and his wit, I decided that it was a disgrace that someone so talented and so symbolic of his period (the end of bohemianism pretty much coinciding with his and Jane Bowles's death), should be forgotten, and I began my Alfred Chester Project to revive his reputation and get his work back into print. If, during Alfred's writing life, it was still economically possible for major publishers to issue work like his with its limited audience, I quickly learned that not only were publishers reluctant to invest in someone who could hardly be expected to sell more than a few hundred copies, but editors also kept telling me that they couldn't publish Alfred Chester because he was forgotten—which, I replied, was exactly why he should be reissued! It took several years, but I finally connected with Kent Carroll of Carroll & Graf, who had worked for Grove Press and had the guts to reissue, in 1986, Alfred's bizarre novel *The Exquisite Corpse* with an introduction by Diana Athill. A few years later, Black Sparrow Press published *Head of a Sad Angel, Stories 1953–1966* with an appendix of memoirs by old friends, and *Looking for Genet,* his collected essays and reviews. I transferred my archive of Alfred's books, correspondence, and other materials to the University of Delaware library where they're available to researchers, and every once in a while I send to a select mailing list an issue of the Alfred Chester Society Newsletter, announcing current publication and/or reprints of his work, reviews, and other information of interest to his fans. I finally feel that the Alfred Chester Revival is underway.

As a postscript to the story, when Neil and I rented an apartment in Tangier in 1989, I took the opportunity of visiting Paul Bowles, whom I hadn't seen since our unexpected arrival at his house in Asilah in 1963, thinking that I'd be able to talk about Alfred with him. But first, we went to pay a memorial visit to Alfred's apartment house, where he had given us the cocktail party that featured martinis and kif.

Tangier is built over a lot of hills, valleys, and gulleys, making it hard to keep track of directions. Sidi Bujari 28, where Alfred lived from the autumn of 1963 to the winter of 1965, lies well beyond the downtown, and Neil and I had a little trouble finding it, since the tourist map of Tangier ends short of that residential neighborhood, but it is roughly between the Marshan, the European quarter, and the Mountain where the foreign swells live. From our visit to Alfred and Dris there, we have photos of the four of us on his terrace, but Sidi Bujari looked quite different now, surprisingly modern, in fact, though even here, as if left over from an earlier time, there was a little shack of a teashop across from a neat, triangular park with benches where mothers were watching their children play, and men were talking quietly over glasses of mint tea.

In 1964 Alfred's building had been a handsome, rambling old mansion divided into flats. I remember that the terrace of Alfred's apartment on the middle floor had a wonderful view over the hills. Almost derelict a quarter century later, the dilapidated building stood out like a Gothic eyesore on the street of well-kept, middle-class, Mediterranean villas. Roots of overgrown eucalyptus trees in the unkempt front yard had cracked through the cement walk, and the steps up to the front door were crumbling away. Small windows under the roof were broken, and you would think no one lived there anymore, except for a motorbike parked to one side, and a crudely painted 28 on a rusty, chicken wire fence around the property. A listing mail box and a crudely painted arrow to a side entrance indicated a current inhabitant. Even the weather here seemed gloomier than the rest of the block, as if the pretty villas bloomed in the sun with tropical flowers and geraniums around them, while over this house where Alfred had lived dark clouds hung morbidly.

The disreputable look of the place seemed a fitting memorial to Alfred, as if his combative spirit had returned to haunt it, keeping it as freakish in the respectable neighborhood as he had felt in his life. Even as a ghost, he would fight on not to be evicted, as he had so often done in his lifetime—I would hate to have been Alfred's landlord.

I had mailed a note to Paul Bowles a few days before, asking if I could see him, and it seemed that in no time Neil and I came home to our rented apartment from the covered market at the Socco Grande, loaded with shopping bags, to find a friendly reply under our door inviting me to tea. On this occasion Neil didn't go with me, so I faced the dragon alone. I took a taxi, since I was unacquainted with Paul's neighborhood.

The driver knew the Villa Itesa where Paul lived, and drove me there, even though I gave him the wrong address—Paul was that well known in Tangier. The Itesa was an undistinguished apartment bloc standing alone in a quiet middle-class residential area of Tangier, well beyond the bustle of the center of town, with its raffish mix of classes from rich to poor, where Neil and I were living for the several weeks we planned to spend there and where we hardly saw a foreigner, much less an American. You really knew you were in Morocco. Across the road from Paul's is the walled compound of The Voice of America and the American Consulate, with gun-toting soldiers patrolling the sidewalk around it. How can he live here? I thought. It's like an armed camp. But of course, if you knew him this is where he'd live. It's safe.

The driver dropped me off at the rear of the building, and passing a watchful concierge, I took the elevator to the top floor. Though drab and utilitarian, the building was in much better condition than our rundown belle-époque apartment house, whose elevator had broken down long ago. Paul and Jane Bowles had lived in the Itesa since 1957. Jane's flat was now owned by the painter Buffie Johnson, who with the novelist Gordon Sager I'd been so judgmental about when I met them in Paris in 1949. If it was a mystery to me how such people got the money to drift around the world, Paul, like them, had been able to live without an obvious source of income—though the millionaire friends that Alfred had spoken of and inspired his blackmail attempt might have explained it. By the time of my visit, there was no doubt anymore where the money was coming from, with all his works in print, a movie of his novel, *The Sheltering Sky*, and a major Paul Bowles revival. When Neil and I walked past the bookshop on Tangier's Boulevard Pasteur, his books in English, Spanish, and French translation filled the window.

As I rang his doorbell, I was cursing myself for not bringing a gift, or at least some pastry. A dark, saturnine Moroccan let me in, barely mumbling a word. I couldn't tell if he was servant or friend, and if I should shake his hand. This I learned later was Mohammed Mrabet, Paul's current companion, helper, and bodyguard, who was considered dangerous, in what way I wasn't told, though from those brooding eyes I could well believe it. And in the manner of one of those scary servants in a horror movie, he didn't welcome me in any way, simply held aside a heavy drape over a doorway for me to enter the living room, without following me in himself.

It was stiflingly hot inside. Paul, reclining on cushions on the floor, seemed to be holding an audience for several other visitors. He half rose to greet me, looking surprised, as if I was the last person in the world he was expecting to see. This was unsettling, but Paul liked to throw people off balance, and I was reassured by the undeniable fact that he did have his chauffeur drive him into town to deliver the note under my door. Paul was considerably aged from twenty-five years before, at the time of Alfred's arrival at his house in

247

Asilah with Neil and me unexpectedly in tow. His face now was that of a superannuated boy scout with a false upper plate and a fixed, pert expression, and his shrunken body seemed to be of one piece, without chest and hips or waist between, as if it had consolidated. A life of no exercise is disastrous for the body, especially by old age. But he did have all his hair.

One of the guests was a darkly handsome young Central American writer, Rodrigo Rey Rosa, whom I had met in New York's SoHo with former Tangier expatriate, the poet Ira Cohen. Rey Rosa had been a student of Paul's, and Paul thought well enough of him to translate his stories into English. Also there was journalist Walter Clemons, who had flown in from New York specially to interview Paul for a biography of Gore Vidal.

Despite Paul's act of surprise at seeing me as if I had arrived uninvited, I couldn't help suspecting that he had asked me over to prevent Clemons from quizzing him about Vidal. This is not so farfetched, because Paul was always nervous about anything personal coming out. He also had a way of setting up a paranoid atmosphere that made you suspicious of everything he did. Or perhaps it is something in me that was susceptible to him in that way.

Faced with an awkward situation, I tend to start blabbing out of self-consciousness and say all kinds of outrageous things. I can't stop myself, and there, at Paul's, I found myself bad-mouthing a mutual friend in New York, at which Paul turned to his protégé to protest, "Oh, but we like him, he's a friend of ours!" I was irritated because of course I also liked him, and felt it was Paul who made me say those terrible things.

Paul's power was so controlling and he was so reserved that I tried to lessen the awkwardness paralyzing the room. Saying the first thing that came into my head, I dropped the alarming news of a mutual friend being HIV-positive, hoping to get some kind of response. Nothing. Then, going further, I brought up an old friend of Paul's, Maurice Grosser, the painter, who had still been sexually active well into his eighties and had recently died, perhaps the oldest AIDS death in the United States (or maybe that record was set by Virgil

248

Thomson, who shared sexual favors with Grosser's HIV positive boy-friend and died in his nineties). This evoked Paul's stern comment, closing the door firmly on that issue, that anyone discovered to have AIDS in Morocco was quietly put to death by the authorities.

That should have shut me up, I suppose, but trying another tack, I told him how much I enjoyed reading the recently published biography of him by Christopher Sawyer-Lauçanno. Another mistake. He dismissed the book as being mostly gossip supplied by Virgil Thomson and full of errors. I argued that for a biography to be interesting didn't necessarily have anything to do with being factually correct. I said no interview with me had ever been accurate, which might offend me but readers couldn't care less as long as it made a good story. Walter Clemons, who wrote for *Newsweek*, joined in to agree with me. I was beginning to sympathize with Clemons in his task of worming anything out of Paul. Paul claimed not to have cooperated with Sawyer-Lauçanno on the biography, though Sawyer-Lauçanno had insisted to me that Paul talked with him extensively and openly about his life during numerous visits to him in Tangier. The bone of contention was clearly that the book was not submitted to Paul before publication for vetting, as was a more recent French biography by Robert Briatte, acceptable because it didn't violate Paul's fanatic discretion about personal matters.

In the stifling atmosphere, I kept bringing up people that Paul and I had in common, and mentioned Michelle Green, another author who had spent a lot of time in Tangier the year before, doing research for her entertaining book on the expatriate colony since the war, *The Dream at the End of the World.* Paul dismissed her by saying that all she was interested in was who had slept with whom and such-like, and with a triumphant expression on his face claimed that none of the old residents on the Mountain whom she had interviewed told her anything, maintaining a clubby solidarity. I knew from my talks with Michelle Green that this was absolutely untrue and that those wealthy expatriates, many of them colorful eccentrics, had all blabbed plenty. Jane Bowles used to socialize with this set, for whom the Moroccans were merely picturesque natives, servants, and purchasable sex partners. Jane's ladies, as Alfred used to call them, met for tea at an elegant patisserie named Porte's, and I could imagine her entertaining her friends in the devastatingly witty manner I remembered from her holding forth on Paul's terrace in Asilah in 1963 as her butch girlfriend Sharifa sat brooding. With evident enjoyment, Paul now launched into a shamelessly gossipy account of the shady affairs during the war of the patisserie's collaborationist proprietress, Mme. Porte, with the Nazis in the feverish International Zone of Tangier.

Paul himself had adopted the upper class manner, dry and reserved, of a retired British colonial. All he lacked was the accent. In the tone of the rich complaining about the servants, he lambasted the Moroccan post office for holding back some of his mail, Salman Rushdie's *Satanic Verses*, for example, or even tapes of his own songs. I had noticed in my occasional correspondence with him that he was always dubious about the Moroccan post office, although everything I'd sent him got through. As if mocking the "natives," he went on to tell about a building in Tangier that collapsed just as it was completed, proving their incompetence to do anything right. I could imagine his friends on The Mountain laughing at just such a story.

I seemed to have started off all wrong, so what did I have to lose? I brought up the subject of drugs—back in the sixties when I had last seen him, Paul was always smoking kif, nothing secret about that—by asking if I could still go into one of the native tea shops and buy a "branch" of kif as I used to do (kif in the unprocessed state). Alarmed, he said it was much better to get a Moroccan to buy it for you. That seemed to be how he lived in Morocco now, for it was his servants who dealt with Morocco for him, for safety perhaps, as the location of the building he lived in, in the shadow of the American consulate, seemed to indicate. It was this self-protectiveness that had enabled him to survive, where Jane and Alfred did not. At any rate, I gathered that drugs was a subject he, as a foreign resident, didn't care to discuss, or, perhaps, as a supposed expert he was questioned about it so often he was bored with it.

Here, Mohammed Mrabet came into the room and sat silent, morose and vaguely threatening, before walking out. Maybe he was just checking to see that Paul was all right, or was he aware somehow that a "dangerous" subject had been raised? Paranoia again. The ominous mood was broken when a pretty, young maidservant came through laughing, and laughter was heard from another room, at which Paul gave a dessicated boyish grin of pleasure and said how lively the servants were together and how much he enjoyed them. I sensed that they were his Morocco now.

For the West, Paul Bowles was *the* landmark in Tangier, and for some years taught a writing workshop that attracted students from all over, one of them the young Central American in the room. Paul told us, with malicious glee, that Salman Rushdie's wife, Marianne Wiggins, had also been one of his students, but after he refused to confirm her own high opinion of her talent, she quit in a huff early in the course. He was almost bragging, I was surprised to see, as he talked of how much interest there was in him in Europe (at the same time dismissing America, where unacceptable books about him were being published), even getting in a mention of Bertolucci and the film project.

He reminded me here of aged Kimon Friar in Athens. In the forties, Kimon was codirector, with John Malcolm Brinnin, of the YMHA-Poetry Center in New York, but I hadn't met him until 1949, when I spent several months in Greece. In New York, Kimon had been the poetry teacher and lover of the young James Merrill, but when Merrill's mother, a grande dame of society, heard about it, she paid Kimon to get out of the country to end the unsuitable liaison. Kimon's family was ethnic Greek from Turkey, and when Kimon was a boy, in the terrible upheavals and slaughters after the collapse of the Ottoman Empire, they had had to flee from Asia Minor. So it was natural that, "expelled" from New York, he would settle in Greece, where he lived the rest of his life, largely doing translations from important Greek poets like Kazantzakis. When I was in Greece in 1949, he was living on the isle of Poros where he had built a house for his handsome sailor boyfriend and his new wife.

Breaking up her son's love affair with Kimon was a useless, even foolhardy, thing for Mrs. Merrill to do, since Jimmy would eventually follow Kimon to Greece and progress to other Greek lovers himself. Again in Greece in the 1980s, I visited Kimon in his cluttered top floor apartment in a pleasant neighborhood of central Athens. An old man by then and worried about his heart, he kept insisting on his uniqueness as a translator of Greek authors, which had attracted the notice of various Kennedys who sought him out when they visited Greece—he brought out scrapbooks and proudly showed me photos of himself with the Kennedys and other celebrities. Over the hill myself, I am starting to understand this syndrome: It is just the fear and loneliness of old age, where the absence of everything youth meant has to be filled with something, and fame is one of the possible consolations.

Another old-timer trait of Paul's was his reiteration that we couldn't possibly experience the real Morocco like he had, and kept saying grimly that everything had gotten worse. His touchstone, of course, was the free-for-all International Zone of Tangier, before it was tamed in the reunification with Morocco. But I felt comfortable in the city as it was—in fact with my Semitic looks I was often taken for Moroccan—and I protested that I found Tangier quite livable now, with the city visibly more prosperous. My God, I was even able to rent a typewriter, like in the real world! ·

Of course, it always was a comfortable city, partly because of the French colonial inheritance—sidewalk cafés, apartments with balconies, French bread, wine—mitigating some of the harshness of the sun, the landscape, and the poverty. The avenues now had splendid, even glittering cafés and teashops full of middle-class Moroccan men (though still no women), where once there would mostly have been foreigners, and the only Moroccans the boyfriends, assorted hustlers and beggars, and shoeshine boys. But Paul saw this as Morocco becoming Europeanized, less Moroccan. It is true that the kif-culture had receded, with its irrationality, magic, paranoia, and acceptance of poverty. I didn't see people smoking kif on the street as before, but did spot them indoors with their pipes. Paul said that bars even tolerated Moroccans coming in to drink, if they were wearing a shirt and tie. This was still illegal and the bars were occasionally raided, but middleclass Moroccans shrugged off the mild penalties.

People of all classes continued to wear the native robe, the djellaba, even over western suits, and many women were veiled, though the veil often slipped beneath the nose, as if the mouth alone had to be covered or, as this made it seem, bound. The national costume gave the city, with its date palms and whitewashed houses, a biblical look. And things were hardly too modern to complain about, as far as I could see. The tourists in the big hotels on the beach who came for package holidays of sea, sun, sand, and local color, might get more than they bargained for, though. Walking along the beach on the sweep of harbor, past the pale, happy northerners in their bathing suits, the water seemed idyllically blue and clean, but a hundred yards further along, just beyond the beach where the local people were swimming, the sewers of Tangier emptied their sludge in a foul black stream that spread out into the blue waters of the almost enclosed harbor. The stench there was almost unbearable. So perhaps except for the surface, not much had changed.

The contrasts in the Moslem world—the smells, the colors—were sharper than ours, not only between rich and poor, but between ancient and modern. On the road back from the beach Neil and I passed a tiny man in djellaba and turban, astride an appropriately tiny donkey coming into town, with his produce in two huge baskets slung across the animal's back. As we in our western garb passed him, his eyes looking at us with equal wonder, Neil said it was like the meeting of two thousand years. We speculated about his traditional life in a rural village, bereft of modern conveniences, and without getting romantic over it, maybe preferable to the way the poor live in our slums, even with VCRs and cars.

At Paul's, Walter Clemons assumed that I was a longtime resident of Morocco. Though we'd made half a dozen trips to Morocco and traveled around the country, this was, in fact, the first time Neil and I had spent any stretch of time there or rented a flat. I had been told by a genuine old Moroccan hand that renting a furnished apartment in Tangier was impossible, and anyway it would be too noisy to bear, because of the large families living around you. But Neil and I had already rented apartments in several other cities abroad, and rather than go on living in a hotel, comfortable and cheap as ours was, and having to eat in restaurants, we decided to try and find one here.

When we were first in Tangier in the sixties, everybody spoke Spanish as the second language, but nowadays, by government fiat, they had switched to French. Fortunately, my French, though barely adequate in Paris, is perfectly serviceable in the Arab world and in fact gets better because there isn't such a high standard to live up to. Still, the real estate agent we approached spoke nothing but Arabic and his assistant had to translate for us. From past experience in the Moslem world, I've learned you can trust business people much more than in the West. The agent, a short, dark-complexioned man, younger than his serious demeanor and mustache made him seem, was not at all discouraging about finding us a place to live. After showing us a vast, gloomy apartment, wrecked by years of temporary tenants, he led us rapidly through the warren of streets of the neighborhood into an old apartment house, once bourgeois-respectable for the French occupiers, but since their expulsion run down. Leading us up an unlit stairway—the elevator was permanently out of order—and leaving us in the gloom of the hallway, he went into an apartment and talked voluminously in Moghrebi with the occupants, before returning shortly to announce that the family would move out and let us rent it.

Inside, we found an attractive, high-ceilinged living room, perfectly French in proportion, but furnished Arab-style with low couches around the walls. Mid-morning though it was, we had disturbed the family at breakfast, for the low table held a coffee pot, cups, and bread. A child's toys were scattered about the floor, but no wife or child was visible. The husband, a pleasant man in his thirties, spoke excellent French, and I told him that I felt uncomfortable about displacing the family at a moment's notice. But he reassured me, saying that many people he knew took advantage of the opportunity to rent their apartments to tourists and make some money. Besides, he had been unemployed since the police had raided his brother's bar where he worked, and it would be no hardship to move in with his wife's family in Fez.

We examined the rest of the flat—entrance hall, bathroom with a big old-fashioned tub, and bedroom with a king-sized bed, upholstered whorishly in zebra plush, and a poster of a provocative naked woman on the wall. After seeing this, I was surprised that when I asked to see the kitchen the husband told me with a sheepish grin that his wife and child were there. Modern as he appeared, he wouldn't let strangers look at his wife.

Neil and I decided to take a chance and rent the apartment, and though the kitchen sink turned out to have no hot water, and the plush-upholstered bed felt buggy, we got used to the place. It was an adventure being the only foreigners in the building, and indeed the neighborhood. The French doors on the balcony gave the living room its light, and opened out over a fenced-in courtyard below with a collection of hovels. I never got tired of watching the activities of this mini-community where chickens pecked at the dirt and children played. The people were poor but respectable, women forever bending over and wiping with rags the stony earth around their shacks. There was much washing of clothes in tubs filled by hand with buckets of water brought from a single water tap that serviced the whole court. In the morning, a schoolboy, spic and span in shirt and slacks, emerged with his books and set out for school. I watched two "armies" of children, with garbage pail lids for shields and wooden swords made from crates, shrieking as they battled each other like little warriors of Saladin. The girls, though they threw themselves into the fray too, were pushed aside by the greater ferocity of the boys. Finally, they all collapsed, children again, breaking their swords into pieces and tossing them around in a frenzy.

I quickly located the neighborhood bakery, where I went out every morning for a baguette, passing on a street corner a crazy boy who was as filthy as the heap of rags he lived on and never strayed from. In spite of his abysmal state, he was handsome, with shaggy black hair and beard, and neighbors brought him food and water. I had the impression that he had simply given up the struggle. Astonishing was the fact that people didn't get up early in this neighborhood, and at eight in the morning, I always seemed to be the only customer at the bakery. Equally surprising, though gratifying, and a refutation of the dire prediction of noisy families, was the fact that television sets were turned off early as people went to bed, and by eight o'clock the nights were almost silent, except for the crowing of cocks at all hours and the barking of dogs, which one hears everywhere in the Moslem world, either guarding the property, like the two curs in the courtyard of our apartment house, or roaming the streets in packs, devouring garbage. I can't imagine anyone being disturbed by the calling of the muezzin as it rang out over the rooftops just before dawn. I always woke to listen.

One could live better in Tangier on a modest amount of money than anywhere else I knew, even as a tourist. There were small but comfortable hotels and the restaurants had improved tremendously since our last visit. If you cooked for yourself, food in the markets was unbelievably cheap. Paul Bowles, famous as he was, still lived simply, but even with three servants, it didn't take a fortune. In his modest flat he chose to be without a television set or telephone (while Jane was alive, she had the phone in her apartment, and screened his calls). I did see a radio in his living room, the kind with shortwave bands—for listening to the BBC World Service, I imagined, similar to the one Neil and I always carry with us on our travels. You can also get BBC programs from Gibraltar and Spanish radio stations from just across the Straits. (It was amusing on Radio Dos, the Spanish classical music station, to hear Mozart referred to as *un hombre,* and Bach called Juan Sebastian Bach.) In our rented flat there was an old television set that brought in only one Moroccan station, a state channel. This showed mostly speeches, dubbed movies, Arabic music concerts, news, in both French and Moghrebi. We watched two remarkable programs. One was a cooking show, where the chef described how the dishes were prepared, but instead of demonstrating this himself he had a silent female drudge doing all the work. Perhaps this was considered more suitable for a culture where women still wore veils and men didn't cook.

The second was an Arab world conference in Casablanca, showing the leaders, as each got off the plane, being greeted in an identical ceremony by the Moroccan king of the time, Hassan II, that included the ritual eating of a date and sipping camels milk. The conference mostly consisted of long speeches, during which some of the Heads of State dozed off, caught by the camera panning around the room. The Moroccan king was also visibly bored to death. His eyelids, droopy anyway, drooped further, and he hid his nodding head behind papers he was supposedly studying, much like the bums in the Automat I remember from the 1930s, holding a newspaper in front of them. Yasser Arafat, I'm sorry to say, produced the most snores, and the more he ranted and waved his arms about, the less attention anyone paid. On the other hand, after the session, the cameras showed a cuddly, lovable Arafat in private conversation with other leaders.

After a week of this kind of programming, grateful as I was for the opportunity to see the faces of these exotic rulers, I called in a local repairman to see if the set couldn't be adjusted to bring in Spanish and Gibraltarian TV, but it turned out that a special aerial on the roof was required, and it wasn't worth the investment for only a few weeks.

Even if the Moroccan quality of life has been diluted, as Paul claimed, there's nothing to make you feel more like you're in a Moslem country than arriving in the middle of Ramadan, as Neil and I did. It is the month in the Moslem calendar when everything is turned topsy turvy—no eating at all from sunup to sundown, so the locals gorged all night, and there was very little allowance for the fact that foreigners might not want to follow this schedule. In Casablanca, where our plane from New York landed, we found a restaurant open for dinner, but weren't so lucky for breakfast. With our hotel dining room closed for the month, the manager shrugged and pointed vaguely down the street, implying there would be someplace in that direction that could serve us. Not so. We ended up eating in a glitzy luxury hotel where for what seemed like a fortune an elaborate but stale breakfast was served in a vast, empty dining room, with waiters and waitresses in folkloric costume standing around idle.

Then, leaving for Tangier on the bus, nothing to eat was available at the various stops along the way, which were usually teeming with vendors selling nuts, fruit, pizza-like breads, and kabobs—all banished for Ramadan. In Larache, half-way up the coast to Tangier where Jean Genet was buried, the best restaurant in town had closed for the month, and we were told that the owners had escaped to Europe for the duration. After sundown, when eating was permitted, it was not much better. The starving crowds rushed into the restaurants and devoured all the harira soup, traditional to break the fast with, before we got there.

In Tangier, though, a resort town, enough restaurants were open for tourists and the foreign colony to make eating no problem. Still we were uncomfortable with passersby staring in through the open doors of the hotel dining room in disapproval of foreigners violating Ramadan. Even here at sundown the streets became deserted as the populace raced home for meals, except for three small picture-book boys, sitting on the curb with big wooden bowls of harira soup on their knees, large spoons poised in the air, waiting for the muezzin call that would allow them to break their daylong fast. Grinning, they waved us over wildly, making room for us to sit down with them and share their harira soup. Everywhere, people were delighted when we ordered the soup of Ramadan.

Paul, continuing his argument about how much the "new" Morocco had changed, and for the worse, brought up the rash of muggings. A friend of his staying in Jane's old apartment was followed home by a couple of thugs after eating out in a restaurant. They seized him in front of the Itesa but he was able to wriggle out of his jacket and run across to the protection of the guards patrolling around the Voice of America. Even Bertolucci, he said, when the Italian film director was shooting *The Sheltering Sky*, was mugged right outside the Minzah, the most elegant hotel in Tangier, situated on a busy thoroughfare.

258

Mugging, in the context of Morocco, seemed to me as a hardened New Yorker one device the desperately poor had to improve their status. Hustling the tourists was another. Neil and I were bedeviled by a beggar youth we couldn't get rid of. One day, coming toward us on Boulevard Pasteur, he greeted us with open arms as if we had met before, and since it may have been so, and he seemed pleasant enough, even handsome, and spoke such excellent English, we stopped. We quickly realized our mistake. It was a hustle. He launched into a story that he had studied at the American School, which explained his fluent English at least, but that since his mother had died his luck had run out. Now he lived with his father in a nearby village, and somehow managed to get into Tangier every day.

A European would have dealt with him properly—class difference would have protected him. Even if he took the youth home for sex and paid him off, there would be no further involvement. Americans, though, are open to everyone, curious about their lives, getting trapped. From then on, whenever we walked on the boulevard, sat at a café, or went to the post office, there was no avoiding him. As if he was plotting our movements, there he was with his desperate smile, waiting for us at key spots. His suit seemed shabbier by the day, and he looked as if he was going downhill fast. I would ask him in a paternal fashion if he had eaten anything, and give him a little money for something to eat, just to get rid of him. I don't think he spent it on food, but for coffee at a sidewalk café, where he could sit for hours and meet people. His dream, clearly, was to be part of the glamorous world of the Boulevard Pasteur with its middle-class people, both foreigners and Moroccans. And he was begging us to include him in our lives, invite him to sit with us at cafés, come to our apartment, teach us Moghrebi, with the ultimate hope that we would take him with us when we left. But even though we felt sorry for him, there was no way we could rescue him.

To avoid him, we started using the back streets, which resulted in us adopting a quite interesting café called The Atlantic, somewhat off the main drag, where a collection of old English queens, long-time residents of Tangier—I'm trying not to think what they thought about us—usually gathered around a table in a corner of the terrasse. Here we could sit in peace with a glass of real orange juice under the trees that shaded the busy rue de Fez, free from our pest. Unfortunately, he seemed to have become dependent on our hand-outs, and though we succeeded in keeping him from discovering where we lived, he dogged our trail for the rest of our stay, some-times cursing us loudly when he spotted us fleeing him.

I had actually hoped to talk with Paul about Alfred. But their relationship had been mysterious and complex enough that Paul seemed skittish about going into it. I raised the subject with him by saying I had just been to look at the building Alfred had lived in, whereupon Paul, sticking to the safest aspect of the subject, launched into a little history of the building, the changes of owner-ship, and how notorious its reputation had become after Alfred left—drug-dealing residents, knife fights and a murder, and more re-cently a fire.

He looked bemused when I said how important he had been in Alfred's life, as if he couldn't imagine this, or anyone thinking he had any connection to such a dubious character. In fact, Paul made it sound as if, really, Alfred Chester had been Jane's friend, as the "acceptable" biography by the Frenchman Robert Briatte claims, though, as I well knew, it had been Paul who was so taken with Al-fred in New York in the winter of 1962–1963 that he kept urging him to come to Morocco.

To defuse a dangerous subject, or so it appeared, Paul began talk-ing in an amusing way about Alfred as one more eccentric member of the Tangier scene. He told the story of Alfred inviting him and Jane to lunch, after Alfred's wig had burned up. Paul claimed he hadn't noticed the wig, anyway, and so said nothing about its disap-pearance. But it turned out that Alfred had invited them specially to display his bald head for the first time, and was disappointed by the lack of response. "But then," Paul said, "I never look at people."

He gave his own version of the notorious letter in which he threat-ened to have Alfred "rubbed out." By exaggerating the language of the letter in his account, Paul made it seem inconceivable that anyone could have taken it seriously. Paul's role in the sad fate of both his wife Jane and Alfred Chester, the two of them charming, eccentric, hyper, and doomed, is still to be explored—both insane and exiled from Morocco, they died about a year apart, Jane in an asylum in Spain, Alfred, the better Jew, in Jerusalem. Perhaps, like the relationship of Ted Hughes to Sylvia Plath's suicide, Paul's role will always remain open to question.

The similarities between Jane and Alfred were startling: Both fell under Paul's spell, and it was Paul, the Pied Piper, who led them to Morocco, where they plunged into Moroccan life in a way Paul never risked doing himself. Unlike Paul, neither Alfred nor Jane were in the least self-protective, believed in going to the limit, and never hesitated to swallow pills of any kind. Though, unlike Alfred, who was a confirmed bohemian, Jane was torn between being a lady like the aristocrats on the Mountain and, like the heroine of *The Sheltering Sky*, letting herself be blotted out by the native world. Perhaps, simply, or not so simply, with their weaknesses and strengths, Jane and Alfred were Paul's natural victims. They had the human qualities, the "juice," he lacked, and like the spider, Paul sat in his web where they were trapped, and fed off them. Jane even signed some of her letters "The Spider's Wife."

I thought the saddest thing about the relationship between Jane and Paul was that she felt so guilty over taking any money from him, or living off him, and then when crazy, giving his money away. She was obviously making a long-withheld protest not only against his stinginess but also against a prime condition for being his wife, that she had no right to his support and was expected to provide for herself. Jane always had to go berserk to disturb Paul's aplomb, or his writing schedule (like all great artists, he was monumentally selfish about this), but she (also an artist, and equally selfish) did succeed. He must have suffered horribly throughout the years of her uncontrollable disintegration.

Alfred's behavior also caused Paul a certain amount of trouble. He was always threatening to "expose" them. Yet, in spite of it being no secret anymore that the Bowleses were both gay and the whole Tangier colony, like Bloomsbury, was rife with homosexuality, Paul ingenuously asked me in a letter, "Expose what?" and Jane kept cautioning Alfred that it "wasn't done" to let the outside world know about their private lives (as in the case of the "rub out" letter). However, to be fair, Paul might also have been observing the custom of the country, since homosexuality in the Arab world, though traditional, is not something you need to proclaim—gay activities are part of the culture, whatever the law might say. Paul's circumspection on this matter suited Morocco. And presenting a respectable front—he was a WASP, after all—was important to him.

As we talked of Alfred's era in Morocco, Paul seemed to be shying away from any mention, much less discussion of this subject, which was perhaps the reason, I again thought to myself, that he was not giving Walter Clemons the least chance to get onto the possibly racy subject of Gore Vidal, for which he had come so far.

Paul always presented himself, and had been seen, as reserved, imperturbable, and controlled, but when John Martin, the publisher of Black Sparrow Press, was considering a book of Alfred's Moroccan letters that I collected, in which Alfred reported, among other revelations, Paul throwing tantrums and smashing things, Paul denounced this as a lie, and refused to give his okay to the book. He also pooh-poohed Alfred's belief that he spoke in subtext. He emphasized to me and John Martin that he did not want Alfred's versions of events of the period to be published, when they were untrue, since once in print they would gain credibility.

Whether Paul had any role in having Alfred expelled from Morocco, I didn't manage to get out of him. But apparently Paul couldn't, or didn't do anything to prevent it. He only told me at our non-"tea" that Alfred's landlord, a Dutchman, who lived across the hall from Paul in the Villa Itesa, announced triumphantly one day that he had finally managed to get Alfred deported, and Paul did not protest. This was understandable, for if Alfred had heard of the apartment through Paul in the first place, as is probable, Paul would have felt guilty toward his landlord neighbor for foisting on him such a difficult tenant. Still, Alfred in exile always saw Paul as powerful enough to give him back Morocco if he chose, and pleaded with him in letter after letter to help him return. This was clearly a fantasy, but it had some truth at its core, for Paul was the presiding spirit over Alfred Chester's Moroccan period.

In any case, it was not Paul but Susan Sontag who precipitated the final breakdown from which Alfred never recovered. But to be fair to Paul, I finally couldn't have been more pleased when for a moment he dropped his defensive mask and said about Alfred with a grin, "Oh, but he was wonderfully entertaining to talk to."

I was feeling uncomfortable and out of place in that company. Paul and I were too much at odds, and I didn't want to keep arguing with him, especially in front of the others. I wasn't sure how long I should stay on—no tea was, or seemed likely to be, served—so I stood up. Paul, too, got to his feet, and when I stammered something about seeing him again, he looked blankly at me. (I remember that Jane also had the same quality of making me feel like a boob.) I foolishly blundered on, and knowing that he used to go to the Café de Paris on the Place de France, suggested that perhaps we could meet there. This evoked a denial that he ever went to cafés. I was ready to protest that he did have his chauffeur drive him into the city, and it was not such a preposterous suggestion, but I was somehow violating his code of behavior—perhaps by trying to pin him down—and felt a wall erected between us. So I finally had the sense to shut up and get out of there.

After this "audience" (that seemed the only word for it), I walked back to our rented, slummy flat with a mixture of admiration and envy for the way Paul Bowles had set himself up for old age. It took an iron will to do it, as those around him destroyed themselves. I was reminded of Annie Lou Stavely, the Gurdjieffian guru in Portland, surrounded by a community of disciples who would obey her for as long as she could give orders, and would look after her to the end. Like her, Paul had managed his life very well. If, by that time, most of his old friends were dead, he had plenty of new ones, and in his last years would not be alone. Already, it was *de rigueur* to visit him

263

on a trip to Tangier. Like so many others in that benign climate, he looked like he'd live on and on, a living monument. And he was certainly enjoying his new-found celebrity, where documentaries of him were constantly being made and biographies, acceptable and unacceptable, published, part of a Paul Bowles industry of world scope.

Though Paul didn't like to leave Tangier anymore, with the promise of medical attention he'd flown to Paris for one night to appear on the literary interview program *Apostrophe*—and reported the city as beautiful as he remembered it, but had no desire to stay. And several years later there was a visit to Atlanta in a quest for treatment for his painful, crippled legs. But he was obviously prepared to die in his adopted country, and be buried, I could have sworn, in Tangier's English Cemetery, attached to St. Andrew's Church, above the sea. Neil and I went there, the day after my visit to him, and walked under shady trees by the graves of members of the foreign colony, largely British colonials, but also with more dubious residents mixed in. Ella St. John, 1889–1975, was buried with Dora Thompson, 1883–1975, ancient ones, perhaps lovers, who were lucky enough to die almost together. Another headstone read, "Walter Burton Harris, Born August 29th, 1866. He came to Tangier in 1886 and was associated with the Times as correspondent in Morocco and elsewhere from 1887 till his death, April 4th, 1933. He loved the Moorish people and was their friend." So Harris came to Morocco at age twenty and managed to live his whole life away from the puritanism of Victorian England. Almost like Paul Bowles. Then, we came upon: "In loving memory of Jay Haselwood, 1914–1966." A close friend of Paul's, who ran the Parade Bar, the most popular bar for foreigners in Tangier. Like Genet's grave in Larache, forty miles away, I was sure that Paul's would become a place of pilgrimage for the restless, rebellious young.

Since I never received another invitation to "tea," I didn't go back and, because Paul didn't have a phone, there was no way to call and say goodbye when I left Tangier. But when I got back to New York, I received another note from him, saying he was sorry he hadn't seen me again, and to drop in the next time I was in Morocco. The message was so friendly that it gave me the odd feeling that I must have dreamed the awkward visit to him, and nothing real had taken place at all.

Incredibly, Paul was not buried in his beloved Tangier, but his ashes were transported reverently by his disciples and buried next to his parents in upstate New York. Surely, he would have hated that. Or did he enjoy the posthumous irony?

25

After the explosion of the Stonewall riots in 1969, which ushered in the new era of gay freedom and openness, it seemed as if the police, as of old, were encouraging gay life to move out to the edges of the city, out of sight, in particular to the industrial West Village, where freight companies still parked their fleets of trucks on the streets along the Hudson River waterfront, and the great pier sheds, which had once resounded with stevedores unloading ships, stood dark, empty and rotting. There, the sexual energy and the creativity released by gay liberation took over the parked trucks and the derelict piers. This was always somewhat of a sex scene, with stevedores looking for blowjobs after work, but now the West Village waterfront was an orgiastic display unlike any seen before.

It was in the midst of this lawless but fast-changing neighborhood, in the commercial wasteland along the Hudson River, that Westbeth, a subsidized artists' housing project, was opened up in 1970, where Old Bohemia would make its last stand in the Village.

$\mathcal{D}$uring the seventies and eighties, as Village rents soared, it's no wonder that most of the younger artists bypassed the gentrified Village and gravitated to what used to be called the Lower East Side, by then renamed the classier-sounding East Village, and beyond that to enclaves in Brooklyn and Queens. But Neil and I managed to hang on by getting a loft studio in Westbeth, where many Village artists and writers found a refuge.

A square-block cluster of buildings, Westbeth was formerly the Bell Telephone Labs where the Talkies and Hi Fi were pioneered. Less known is the fact that during WWII it was also part of the Manhattan Project where the Norden bombsight was designed with which my B-17 Flying Fortress and thousands of others bombed Nazi Germany. Somewhere in the maze of the basement is said to be a huge electromagnet that couldn't be removed, and perhaps accounts for the prevalence of twins being born to the younger residents and employees.

On one side of the building is still a gash, an open corridor two floors high, where the tracks of the Hudson Elevated Railroad once went through, and it was on land left from the removal of the elevated tracks to the south of Westbeth that the neighboring Jane Jacobs houses were built, which, with the decline of shipping at the nearby piers, began the revival of this waterfront district for residential use. The conversion of the building to living quarters, designed by the architect Richard Meier, preserved the unusual wavy ceilings, which poet Tom Schmidt's clever daughter Alyssa, visiting Neil and me from the West Coast, said was like living inside a scallop shell. Giving the thirteen-story building a distinctive outline is a red-tiled Florentine palazzo perched on top, which is used by the Merce Cunningham dance company, so that our elevators are always full of healthy young dancers coming and going. The ravaged and arthritic, but still elegant, Maestro himself is also frequently to be seen hobbling through the lobby.

If Yaddo was a good place to get to know artists, Westbeth turned out to be full of artists I'd known over the years, including my favorite painter Herman Rose and his actress wife Elia Braca who has often shared programs with me reading my poetry. Elia and I collaborated most recently in a celebration of Westbeth and Greenwich Village, which featured the work of two poets related by their pure bohemian spirit—Jean Garrigue, who had moved to Westbeth before she died in 1972, and a similarly passionate figure of a generation before, Edna St. Vincent Millay. Elia Braca is a darkly exotic woman with large Middle-Eastern eyes and a tumble of black hair—her mother was Turkish and her father an Egyptian fortune teller, the Professor Cairo of the Oscar Wilde circle. She's an unusual contrast to her artist husband Herman, a schlemiel of a Brooklyn Jew who hardly knows what day it is, but in his letters reveals his original, probing, and deeply thoughtful mind. Herman can work on his paintings for years with meticulous brush strokes, so I was lucky he only took a year for his first portrait of me with guitar, when I bicycled in from Long Island. I later posed for his "Orpheus in Central Park," now in the Hirschhorn Collection in Washington D.C., in which I, as Orpheus the Troubadour, sat naked on a stool (in lieu of a Central Park boulder) as if strumming a lyre that Herman fashioned out of twigs, much as year after year he constructed funny little wheeled carts out of discarded baby strollers to hold his canvases and paints for working out of doors. While I sat there in the buff, Elia tiptoed around the room, her eyes twinkling with delight. Unfortunately, this wasn't conducive to relaxing, and I'm afraid the painting is no advertisement for my endowment.

In the years since I met Tobias Schneebaum at Yaddo in 1955, when the Flits so dramatically overwhelmed the Rocks, I had only occasionally seen him when he was in New York in between his hairraising explorations of the exotic parts of the world, and showing his paintings of jungles and jaguars at a Madison Avenue Gallery. He landed in Westbeth, too, and lives on the floor above me, so we pick up each others' mail when we're off on our various trips. With his warm eyes and big friendly nose, he has a face that the actress Joan Fontaine, who sat next to him at a dinner party once, described as "Pakistani." "I like your Pakistani friend," she told the host, and when, at the host's request, Tobias walked her home, she stopped outside her door and turned to him. "I bet you'd like to seduce me," she said, looking up at him with those eyes so memorable from *Re-becca* and *Jane Eyre*. He got out of it, he says with a sheepish grin, but doesn't remember how.

Even if your looks aren't the all-American-boy kind, you don't have to go to the ends of the earth to find sex. And Tobias wasn't all that inhibited—as a desperate teenager, he'd shared his bed with a young uncle, who introduced him to the pleasures of male bonding. Eventually, though, making out with his jungle dwellers proved, for Tobias, to be the most rewarding. Much like Robert Friend, he has a quality that ethnics immediately cotton to. He could go into the jungle in shorts and sneakers and in no time be living with New Guinea tribesmen, or the naked Amazonians, who turned out to be just a bunch of sexy, polymorphous perverse guys, but with just one little quirk difficult to swallow, so to speak—cannibalism. He actually took one bite of human flesh, just to go along with the gang. That was it, but it's been hard to escape. He was a cannibal on *What's My Line,* and the film that featured him, *Keep the River on Your Right,* was subtitled *A Modern Cannibal's Tale.*

The lofts of Westbeth are all sizes and shapes, some with vast views of the harbor you could die for. Our third floor studio looks out on a courtyard with trees out the window—when Neil and I moved here from the fifth floor, tenants in the building, incredulous, said, "You're moving *down*?" But it's a large space, with a sleeping platform where Neil perches, listening to his talking books, while I work at my computer underneath. He still clambers up and down the ladder with admirable agility. I have a corner workshop with my tools, and am always fixing and building things. Once, an elegant young man who was visiting expressed puzzlement over our un-adorned bathroom, saying, "You guys aren't gay!" Then on the way out he spotted my tool board, and exclaimed, "I know what you are, you're dykes!" After that, Neil and I made a great effort to decorate the bathroom, but I'm afraid our place is still pretty basic, except for the glorious rugs brought back from exotic lands.

Tobias looks over the majestic Hudson River, Herman and Elia have windows, eight of them in a row, but David Del Tredici, a composer I met at Yaddo in the seventies, has, suitably, a cave of a studio on the street level where his banging on the piano doesn't disturb anyone. It even has its own door to the street for discreet comings and goings, but isn't an undiluted advantage since the steps are convenient for strangers in the night to make out noisily on. David, a bright-eyed man of high, almost manic energy, has set one of my poems to music, and I've incorporated quite a few of his irresistible remarks into my poems. Starting out as a concert pianist on the West Coast, he switched to composing when he couldn't see performing the great warhorses for the rest of his life. Still, he's a brilliant sight reader, and once when I was feverish and tossing I kept hearing his almost satanic playing in my head.

At the time we met at Yaddo, David was being pursued by a Miss Woods of the housekeeping staff, who had adopted the persona of a middle-aged English governess, cockney accent and all. She slipped passionate notes about her desperation for him under his door, and being firm with her was no use. But David was not the only one she had a passion for. Miss Woods told me herself that when Philip Roth was in residence, she would sit outside his door all night because he couldn't sleep. Someone who had made a million dollars from his writing, she said with motherly concern, would naturally have sleeping problems from the anxiety of living up to his reputation with his next book, and she wanted to be there in case he needed her. But I always suspected that she did her mash notes routine with him too.

A newer arrival in the building has been a young artist, David Alexander, who is the boyfriend of an old, old poet friend, Richard Howard. David and Richard met at a reading I gave where Richard, introducing me, said that there were two types of Jews, prophet and schlemiel, of which I was schlemiel, roughly translatable as a loser, or maybe just a fuck up. I'd already been spotted as a schlemiel at a reading I gave in Santa Cruz where the students told me afterwards that I was like the ultimate schlemiel, Woody Allen, which was kind of flattering, if only to be compared to a movie star.

Richard Howard invented the acronym HD—Homosexual Dread—which perfectly describes the reaction you sometimes get from some uptight straight men. Meeting the Israeli poet Yehuda Amichai, for example, I was astonished that he displayed advanced symptoms of HD, when he shrank from me as if I was trying to make out with him! Or maybe he was afraid it was catching! Neil and I have adapted HD to HB, Horror of the Blind, and AB, Adoration of the Blind, representing the two extreme reactions of sighted people to the blind, something Neil has become an expert on.

When I met him in the sixties, Richard, just one of the eager young poets on the New York scene, was living with the novelist Sanford Friedman, author of the early gay novel *Totempole*. A stocky man with a shaved bullet head and clear gray eyes that reflect his limited tolerance for mere sociable chat by going from amusement to indifference in a flash, Richard is inexplicably scholarly for a poet. Or perhaps it seems to me that way, with my limited education. In his early years at a publishing house job, Richard had the inconceivable task of editing the dictionary—going through it and improving the definitions of all the words of our language—which he did three times! This is reflected in the sometimes-arcane words he uses in his writing, much like W. H. Auden, a poet we both admire. Richard is literary to the core, and when driving with him through the glorious hill towns of Italy, Sandy Friedman told me, Richard kept his nose in an old Baedeker open in his lap, reading aloud from it to Sandy at the wheel, who was drinking in the landscape. Richard was always a tremendously hard worker and deserves all his honors. The bookshelf of his translations from the French includes the memoirs of de Gaulle, for which he was made a *Chevalier d'Honneur* by the French government. A masterful book of poetry criticism, *Alone with America,* should have won him a Pulitzer Prize, but instead, he got it for his next book of poems, *Untitled Subjects.*

The demands of his own poetry with its elaborate structure and language are relieved by his use of narrative and his dramatic sense, somewhat in the High Victorian, Robert Browning mode, who wrote similarly long narratives. If I might have dismissed Richard's early poems as little more than clever technical exercises, in each successive book he's proved that discipline and practice pay off. The poems have not only gotten better but are entertaining performance material, which he reads dramatically with an avuncular playfulness that evokes Beerbohm's drawing of Tennyson reading to Queen Victoria.

I'm particularly fond of Richard's poem about American expatriate Morton Fullerton, the son of a Vermont minister who certainly lived up to the reputation of clergymen's sons and daughters. It was said that, in the gay nineties, Fullerton slept with all the guys in the Oscar Wilde and Henry James circles in London, then went straight and devoted his dick to the ladies, chief among them the regal New York socialite novelist Edith Wharton, who, her sexuality finally liberated by this experienced lover, crawled across the floor like the Victorian woman she was to hug his knees, imploring him to make love to her! Richard's sly poem, which takes place after Fullerton's death, has a former male lover of Fullerton's being sent to Paris by Henry James, who was also mad about Fullerton, to accompany Edith Wharton in the carriage to the cemetery with Fullerton's ashes, leading to Wharton's awakening to the fact that she was not Fullerton's only "widow"—it's a delicious invention and peeks behind the veils history draws over gay lives.

Richard is a Villager but not really a bohemian. He lives in the grander environs of Washington Square in an apartment around the corner from Henry James's boyhood home, where, at least on my last visit, only the ceiling and the floor were not covered with books. Like *New Yorker* poetry editor Howard Moss, he chose the Village not only as a gay haven, but for its literary associations, especially Henry James. I'm pretty sure that Richard Howard, like Howard Moss, would choose Marcel Proust as his other guardian angel.

Once, Richard and I both taught a poetry workshop at Sarah Lawrence College, in which each of us had a segment of the course. Since mine followed his, I sat in on his initial class to see what he'd have his students doing, and was astonished, even awed, when he spoke extempore about poetry for the whole two hours. His first assignment to the students was staggering—to write a poem of two stanzas, the first using one hand on the typewriter keyboard with words only made up of the letters of those keys, and the second stanza with the other hand, using only the letters of its keys. It would certainly jolt anyone out of her preconceived ideas of poetry, and no one could submit a dumb appreciation of the sunset! A month later, when I started my stint with the same students and announced I expected them to write a poem a week, they nearly fainted. Half of them were so intimidated by the demands Richard had made on them that they didn't show up for my next class! But he's right—writing poetry is not easy and you've got to take it seriously or get lost. I approve of his rigorousness.

I hadn't had anything to do with Susan Sontag since Alfred Chester's death. We had little in common, not enough to keep it going. Richard Howard's lifelong friendship with her, however, survived the stresses of their flourishing careers. It began in their early days when they haunted literary gatherings together on their way up the ladder to success, continuing through her struggles with cancer, and latterly the ups and downs of her relationship with photographer Annie Leibovitz, and the split-up after Leibovitz had a baby at the age of fifty—the father of the baby has been undisclosed, but rumor has it that the sperm was donated by Susan's son, journalist David Rieff, which, if true, would make Susan its grandmother! Not a very loving grandmother, it appears, since reportedly she broke up with Leibovitz over her presumed grandchild—Leibovitz gave more attention to the baby than to Susan.

Richard is extremely generous, and has reputedly given away a lot of his money—I heard that he once distributed a fortune he inherited to needy artists. Though he can be forbidding in public, he can also drop it and be perfectly natural—when Neil and I went to dinner with him and David, I was struck by how kindly, tenderly, simply this complicated man spoke to his lover. It is another mark in his favor that he is a dog person. Like Stanley Moss, he has always had marvelous dogs, my favorite being Max, a large, enthusiastic bulldog who could leap vertically five feet into the air and lick your face. There was even a certain resemblance between Richard and Max.

David Alexander is a charming person in his own right, extraordinarily good-natured and laid back—he'd have to be, to accompany such a famous man to so many literary events, fancy dinners, and gigs around the country, where he must be practically invisible, as Neil once was with me. With the new tolerance of gays, David is perfectly acceptable anywhere now as Richard Howard's partner. When Richard taught at the University of Houston, David says they were the pet gay couple of the oil millionaire arts patrons who invited them out. It was only with the high-and-mighty Sontag, Richard's great buddy, that David didn't cut the mustard. He reports with a sigh—and these are his words—that she generally seemed to act as if he were profoundly uninformed. About anything.

*A*fternoons, when Neil and I go out for walks, we pass through a Greenwich Village that we know intimately from living here for half a century, but one whose history we also researched and wrote about in our novel *The Villagers*. "The Village is not what it was"—a theme repeated by each generation throughout the novel's 145-year span—is our complaint too. Visually, the most dramatic alteration is Seventh Avenue, which, at the time of the First World War was slashed right through the heart of the Village, with many buildings demolished or cut in half to put in the subway as well as the avenue—it's still pretty raw in places. One improvement to the landscape, though, was the tearing down, more recently, of the derelict West Side elevated highway along the waterfront, opening up the streets to a view of the Hudson River and the far shore of New Jersey. The sex scene along the waterfront is also gone—the deserted pier sheds, the scene of historic orgies, have burned down or were blown away in hurricanes, the truck fleets dispersed, and a pretty park built along the river. As the transvestite whores displaying their wares have become a thing of the past, so too are the johns in curb-crawling cars, some of them Hasidic Jews in long earlocks and religious garb, cruising round and round for an anonymous quickie, before returning to family values and religious constraints in Brooklyn or New Jersey—who could blame them! Among the factories, warehouses and the Federal Prison, all converted to high-rental condos, stands a gleaming centerpiece of three crystal-glass Richard Meier towers where celebrities live. This stretch of the Village along the Hudson River certainly deserves its new name, The Gold Coast.

As we walk through the handsome, tree-lined streets of federal houses with memories for us of the literary and bohemian past, we still remember the sounds of typewriters of hopeful young writers working on their novels, and trilling scales of singers or musicians with ambitions of concert and showbiz careers. Buildings where friends used to live, stores that were once something else—everything that used to be is still there for us, ghostly behind the new façades. Perhaps we too are ghosts! We even run into the ghosts of old friends—on Bleecker Street, where luxury clothing boutiques are pushing out the antique shops that formerly pushed out the Italian mom-and-pop stores, Marguerite Young still in shawls and shmattas, stops us to discuss her book on Debs, and further down we pass below the windows of the apartment where Alma Routsong did the ouija board with Betty Deran to get the plot for *Patience & Sarah*. On Greenwich Avenue is a lush garden where the women's prison used to stand—Grace Paley was incarcerated there for a night after an antiwar demonstration. When it was demolished, the garden refused to grow for years, as if the tears of the women behind the barred windows and their families on the sidewalk calling up to them had left the ground salt and barren. May Swenson's house on Perry Street, where she held parties on her terrace overlooking the St. John's Church gardens. After her death, I tried to get a memorial plaque put up to honor her, but the church wouldn't allow it. Although not as often nowadays, we still come across piles of possessions thrown out after old Villagers die or move away—dusty books, canvases and sculptures, manuscripts, and the quaint furnishings typical of bohemian apartments—the seashell ashtrays, the brick and board shelves, Mexican ponchos, and other folk artifacts Villagers loved.

So many of the Village artists who found refuge in my building are also dying off—director Joseph Chaikin, who used to read to Neil; photographer Diane Arbus, the most prominent of a dozen suicides in the building; jazz great Gil Evans; and poets Jean Garrigue and Muriel Rukeyser, are just a few of them. And most recently, even Tobias Schneebaum. There's only a dwindling band of old timers left from a bohemian era that did not survive the twentieth century and can hardly be comprehended by this one.

In the spring of 2005, when Neil and I were in Paris, we visited Susan Sontag's grave at the Cimetière Montparnasse. It was still without a headstone, but a simple plaque identified it. I stood there feeling empty, the old battles between her and Alfred Chester now just good stories to tell, just history. But walking away it hit me what a remarkable woman she was and how special it was to have known her.

Susan had shown tremendous courage in her battles against three bouts of cancer, the first of which produced her best book, Illness as Metaphor, and the third of which she lost when she opted for risky bone-marrow replacement therapy. Her ex-lover, the celebrated photographer Annie Leibovitz, flew her home from the hospital in Seattle in a private plane to New York's Sloan-Kettering. Her death was notable enough to compete with the tsunami on the front page of the New York Times.

Oddly, Susan requested that she not be cremated, and I must confess that when I heard this my old Susan-bashing instincts, which I'd vowed to relinquish after her cancer recurred, popped up again, unable to resist the notion that she wanted her grave site to serve as a shrine for her admirers to worship at. But it seems she forecast that correctly. Her son David brought her body to Paris for burial—an old girlfriend of Susan's, the French actress Nicole Stephane (notably, in Cocteau's Les Enfants Terribles), was able to wangle a plot in the overcrowded Montparnasse cemetery where notables such as Alfred Dreyfus are buried—and about a hundred people from all over the world came for the burial. The cemetery guide who led us to the gravesite told us there was indeed a stream of young people already visiting it.

It used to be such fun to badmouth Susan Sontag for her intellectual pretensions, for her sense of entitlement, for her ambitions—for instance, saying bitchily that she wouldn't come out as gay because she was bucking for the Nobel Prize in Literature. But even before her death in early 2005 I began to admire her when, after 9/11, she spoke out so courageously, writing in the New Yorker that we should try to understand what our enemies were about, and got attacked for it, as if understanding were the same as condoning. She went on to become a rare voice opposing the folly of the Iraq war and the Bush administration's antagonism to the civilizing traditions of European culture.

The gossip of her private life aside, her disappearance from the arena of discourse has made it clear what a gap her death has left, what an extraordinary figure she was in American life, not only as a literary celebrity but the rare public intellectual. Her son might have inherited her estate, but it is the United States, a country that needs to wake up to the damage it is doing to the world, that has inherited, and must struggle with, her legacy.

$Index$

279

280

LIVING OUT
Gay and Lesbian Autobiographies

Joan Larkin and David Bergman
SERIES EDITORS

Raphael Kadushin
SERIES ACQUISITION EDITOR